Perception and Design in Tennyson's
Idylls of the King

PERCEPTION AND DESIGN
IN TENNYSON'S
IDYLLS OF THE KING

John R. Reed

Ohio University Press Athens, Ohio

To George H. Ford

CONTENTS

Perception and Design in Tennyson's
Idylls of the King

PREFACE

My CONCEPT OF the moral design in Tennyson's poetry resembles the pattern of conversion described by Professor J. H. Buckley in *The Victorian Temper*. Drawing upon the nineteenth-century commentator R. H. Hutton's remarks, Buckley describes conversion as coming

> not to the careless profligate, but rather to the troubled soul beset
> with a liberating 'despair,' a genuine weariness of the ego, and 'a
> passionate desire to find some new centre of life' which might 'renovate the springs and purify the aims of the soiled and exhausted
> nature.[1]

This moral design is evident in earlier literature; for example in Saint Augustine's *Confessions*, if not the parables of Christ.[2] Augustine provided the image of an intelligent, but proud and sensuous, spirit given to doubt and self-indulgence, who, after a prolonged internal conflict, humbles himself, accepting baptism and going on to devote himself actively in a cause that he considers selfless and just. I am not hereby suggesting that Tennyson derived his moral views from Augustine, but merely that the design governing Tennyson's religious imagination was one of

3

long standing in the Christian tradition.[3] Most simply stated, this design involves the contention of the supreme sin, pride, with the supreme virtue, love. Pride hardens the heart by shutting the individual off from sources of self-knowledge and grace. When vanity is permitted to usurp the imagination, the phenomenal world becomes a mere extension of the self and is transformed by the viewing eye. Love, too, transforms the world according to its vision. It renders service to the world through faith, and by so doing becomes a partner in creation and growth. Pride, on the other hand, forever fails in its endeavor to reduce the world to a personal vassalage, and, accordingly, begets discontent, which, coupled with self-indulgence, occasions moods which appropriate the mind's control and uncoop self-destructive passions. Pride creates moods of doubt. If the self cannot understand God, immortality, or other ontological and teleological mysteries, then certainly such answers are not available. Stymied by the inevitable frustration that the Unknowable cannot be known, the vain heart renounces belief, and with it the resolution that, if it cannot solve, may console and inspirit.

Prideful doubt is barren for Tennyson and usually prefigures self-destruction through inanition or self-injury. Redemption comes—again as Augustine would suggest—as a form of grace. Tennyson, however, secularizes the grace that is, for Augustine, a supernatural intervention. For Tennyson, it resembles a chemical alteration, often immediate, frequently rearranging at once the mind's molecular fabric. Renewal occurs in a change of mood, in a sensation, an intuition. No logic could persuade the mind. Something outside the self might provide the necessary intuitional spark, but no item in the circumstantial world can persuade. Once this grace finds admission, the heart is melted, humility replaces pride, and love rekindles, making possible once more disciplined action and belief. This is, roughly, the pattern with which I am concerned. It is the design that I see operating as a cohesive force for much of Tennyson's poetry.

An overarching, if vague, design is not remarkable, however interesting it may be in itself. But to witness the details of the faith of which that design is a product consistently articulated in the very substance of the composition expressing that faith, is to acknowledge an astonishing mastery of the poetic craft. It is, perhaps, the more amazing to modern readers insofar as the nature of the faith in question is at once so general and so privately specific.

W. Stacy Johnson, in the first chapter of *The Voices Of Matthew Arnold*, felt it necessary to stipulate a marked quality of Victorian poets, which, to some extent, defines them. Listing, as his examples, Tennyson, Browning, Swinburne, Hopkins, Morris, Patmore, and the Rossettis (he might have added the unreligious, but moral, Meredith), he explains that "for all of them the questions of a man's proper relation with other men, and with God or the Universe, are peculiarly serious."[4] I consider this emphasis an important one, since it might otherwise be easy to overlook the highly moral ambience in which these writers composed their works. My view is that this ambience affected not only the ideas, but the substance of at least Tennyson's poetry. And I would add that, ordinarily, the peculiar seriousness of Victorian poets demonstrated itself in a curiously secular form.

My special concern is with Tennyson's *Idylls of the King*, which seems, more than any of his major works, to have been underrated in terms of its moral import.[5] *In Memoriam* would be a superb example for me to use in describing the moral design of Tennyson's work, but I have decided against it. I consider available examinations of that work quite satisfactory already, and at least two interpretations of the design of the poem resemble my own.[6] Furthermore, it is in the *Idylls of the King* that the very texture of poetic technique elaborates and supports the broader testimony of faith.

Tennyson, I feel, was conscious of the design and themes that I shall describe. Both are apparent in more poems than I deal with, for I have chosen to examine in detail only some few in which they are suitably evident. Although there is no simple progression in Tennyson's use of moral design from expositional to parabolic, I have chosen to illustrate the design in that order, beginning with the more expositional "The Two Voices," proceeding to *Maud*, and concluding with the most elaborate of parables, the *Idylls of the King*. Tennyson composed a sufficient number of directly expository moral poems, but his best works are those which follow some fabular scheme, for he was himself aware of the inadequacy of simple naming.[7] It may have been true that in mythologies and old religions the names of deities and graces were essential to their supernatural qualities, that denomination, in fact, served as the consecration of theurgic forces; but, as Tennyson was well aware, there could be no persuading through mere signification and categorization. His religion was intuitional, and, feeling that what the soul experienced within itself, not what it observed abstractly, was what moved it, he preferred to *re-enact* the pattern of redemption rather than *define* it, and so he said in *In Memoriam*.

> Though truths in manhood darkly join,
> Deep-seated in our mystic frame,
> We yield all blessing to the name
> Of Him that made them current coin;
>
> For Wisdom dealt with mortal powers,
> Where truth in closest words shall fail,
> When truth embodied in a tale
> Shall enter in at lowly doors. (xxxvi, p. 984)[8]

Buckley has demonstrated some philosophical resemblances between the thought of Tennyson and of Kierkegaard. It may easily be objected that Kierkegaard makes the complexity and profundity of his thought readily apparent to a modern reader, whereas Tennyson's thought seems simplistic. The obvious response to such an objection is that Tennyson had no intention of explaining his religious beliefs in his poetry. Nor is it necessary to defend him as a species of intellectual cripple. His purpose was not to explain belief or to defend it, but to describe and celebrate the moral values he held. "A poem," Basil Willey remarks, writing of Tennyson, "like a piece of ritual, *enacts* what a credal statement merely *propounds*."[9] Feeling words in rhetorical uniform less effective for delivering a truth than words freely approximating events, Tennyson, for the most part, hoped not to persuade, but to evoke emotions through a parabolic method. Nonetheless, certain implications of his thought suggest that Tennyson was not far removed from traditional philosophers, and that he revealed sympathies with some more adventurous thinkers of his time. Tennyson read eagerly in philosophy and could speak intelligently with his learned friends on various philosophical subjects, though, it is true, he was as much given to pronouncement, especially in the later years, as he was to discussion.[10] Of Giordano Bruno, Tennyson said:

"His view of God is in some ways mine. Bruno was a poet, holding his mind ever open to new truths, and believing in an infinite universe as the necessary effect of the infinite divine Power."[11]

And Tennyson might have gone on to agree, "in some ways," with a contemporary poet's view of God. Matthew Arnold, having explained that no one would claim that there was a verifiable first cause that we denominate God, continues:

But that all things seem to us to have what we call a law of their being, and to tend to fulfil it, is certain and admitted; though whether we call this *God* or not, is a matter of choice. Suppose, however, we call it *God*, we then give the name of God to a certain and admitted reality.

Arnold goes on to conclude that "There is, then, a real power which makes for righteousness; and it is the greatest of realities for us"—a sentiment similar to Tennyson's.[12] Surely Tennyson's poems display the coming of grace as a function of self-fulfilment, yet he would seldom attempt to nominalize his belief when he could manifest it. Accordingly, his best poems are not about man and God, but about God-in-man.

It is likely that Tennyson would have found much to agree with in such philosophers as Friedrich Schleiermacher, who expressed the belief that each individual recapitulates the universal in his own specific manner; or who determined the dependency of the material world upon the infinite as the focus of religious belief; or who, while not dismissing the power of intellect and designating feelings as the basis of human nature, could also project an image of ethical growth through nature and man in terms of will and control.[18] It is not unlikely that Tennyson might have found some points of agreement with Ludwig Feuerbach, though he would not have dismissed the concept of personal immortality as Feuerbach did. But Feuerbach conceived of God as the ultimate projection of man's own infinite nature. In his view, man's longings for the ideal are informed in the imputed lineaments of a deity. Man's moods design his God. Tennyson may never have gone so far as Feuerbach, but he certainly saw the extent to which man's vanity and his moods transformed the values of the world he perceived. Far more than nature wore the colors of the spirit according to Tennyson.

> What find I in the highest place,
>   But mine own phantom chanting hymns?
> And on the depths of death there swims
>   The reflex of a human face. (*In Memoriam*, cviii, p. 961)

> 'That type of Perfect in his mind
>   In Nature can he nowhere find.
> He sows himself on every wind.' ("The Two Voices," p. 534)

Ultimately, however, Tennyson comes back to simple human equations for his ideas, no matter how complex their ramifications may be. For him, as for Troilus, "What is aught, but as 'tis

8

valued?"[14] When our moods, inadequately disciplined by belief and selflessness, usurp our perceptive powers, we cast a gloom upon our entire ambience. One of the ironies of Tennyson's "Lucretius" is that the philosopher spent his entire life in learning to subordinate his emotions through a rigorous training of the will, based upon stern argument; and yet, the moods which could not break his self-command from within, violate him from without and turn his beautifully geometrical universe into chaos.

Tennyson's concern is not really with theology and philosophy, but with the individual's examination of his own powers. He would have recommended Socrates' dictum: "the life which is unexamined is not worth living."[15] However, he would have added that in that self-examination were the means to despair as well as salvation; though the risk was one that any serious man would willingly take.[16] His poetry concerns itself with the struggle of that self-examination, not with its presuppositions; its intellectual amplifications (though they are often included as part of the spiritual contest); or its consequences—which are rarely elaborated. The following lines from *In Memoriam* might stand as a suitable epigraph to most of Tennyson's moral poetry.

> If these brief lays, of Sorrow born,
>   Were taken to be such as closed
>   Grave doubts and answers here proposed,
> Then these were such as men might scorn:
>
> Her care is not to part and prove;
>   She takes, when harsher moods remit,
>   What slender shade of doubt may flit,
> And makes it vassal unto love. (xlviii, p. 905)

ACKNOWLEDGMENTS

I would like to express my gratitude to Wayne State University for granting me two Faculty Research Awards, which greatly facilitated the completion of this work. My thanks are due to my friend, Alan Barr, who read an early version of the manuscript and volunteered many useful improvements. I am grateful as well to Henry Kozicki—with whom I held numerous interesting conversations while directing his doctoral dissertation on Tennyson—for obliging me to re-examine many of the opinions I had formed in my own researches.

The University of Toronto Press has kindly permitted me to use my Tennyson article that appeared in the *University of Toronto Quarterly*. It appears here, in revised form, as part of Chapter One.

ONE

INTRODUCTION

"The Two Voices"

ALTHOUGH MY LEADING concern is the understanding of moral design and themes in the *Idylls of the King*, I feel that a convenient access to that poem is through the examination of earlier important poems that utilize a moral design and introduce thereby some of the themes that will later receive sharper attention. Such an introduction is necessary because, despite the growing sophistication in Tennysonian criticism, there remains a pronounced tendency to impose biographical simplifications upon Tennyson's poetry.[1] A poem that suffers particularly from such reduction is "The Two Voices," generally held to be an account of Tennyson's private emotions set in verse.[2] The same presumption imputes Tennyson in the fabricated narrator of "Supposed Confessions of a Second-Rate Sensitive Mind." In view of Tennyson's consciously dramatic sense of art, a more rewarding approach would minimize the cumbersome furniture of biography and concentrate upon the design of his poetry.

Constantly vexed by biographical interpretations of his monodramatic poems, Tennyson offered a clear statement of the poet's relationship to his creations.

11

"In a certain way, no doubt, poets and novelists, however dramatic they are, give themselves in their works. The mistake that people make is that they think the poet's poems are a kind of catalogue raisonné of his very own self, and of all the facts of his life, not seeing that they often only express a poetic instinct, or judgment on character real or imagined, and on the facts of lives real or imagined. Of course some poems, like my 'Ode to Memory,' are evidently based on the poet's own nature, and on hints from his own life."[3]

Tennyson did not deny that the poet employed his own experiences, but he did stipulate the importance of fashioning that experience into the final design of poetry. Poetry is utterance, but crafted utterance; and for Tennyson, the poem resides at some distance from the poet. Valuing what Keats called negative capability, Tennyson qualified his praise of Wordsworth by declaring that he " 'was great, but too one-sided to be dramatic.' "[4] Nor was Tennyson's own readiness to assume the dialectic manner limited to his poetry, for Hallam Tennyson remarks that his father frequently presented opposite points of view at different times.[5] "This was because from his firm sense of justice he had a dramatic way of representing an opinion adverse to his own in a favourable light, in order that he might give it the most generous interpretation possible."[6] In effect, Tennyson is doing just this in poems such as "Supposed Confessions," "The Two Voices," the Locksley Hall poems, *In Memoriam*, and *Maud*, among others.

Supposing an autobiographical voice in Tennyson's poems is a damaging presumption, for it hinders accurate analysis and full appreciation.[7] Tennyson is not, for example, the second-rate sensitive mind. The principal sin of the narrator of the "Supposed Confessions" is pride, though he, like St. Simeon Stylites, feels that his pride has been brought low, and that he suffers less from vanity than emptiness. His mother's assumptions were more accurate than his own, for she urged him to bow himself down in faith to God, and then "grace / Would drop from his o'er-brimming love, / As manna on [his] wilderness." (p. 200)

The second-rate sensitive mind, unable to bow down, reveals his pride by comparing his condition to that of the vexed sea, as opposed to the slumbering mountain tarn of simple fidelity. Obviously his agony has a grandeur for him that he will not relinquish for a banal faith. That Tennyson should be capable of so subtly rendering the second-rate mind's sin argues that he is not himself that second-rate mind.

The pattern of "Supposed Confessions" is roughly that of "The Two Voices;" ignoring his sin of pride, the narrator reflects upon his early aspirations. He had hoped to discover the "excellence and solid form / Of constant beauty," (p. 201) fixed beyond the force of change—a desire similar to Arthur's aspirations regarding Guinevere; toward this end he allowed himself the luxury of doubt, but doubt led him to confusion because he could not comprehend the possibility of a flexible and changing beauty. He is of those who may not doubt but must clasp idols, for, though he desires to be shadowed by God's love, and to have his sins forgotten, and to be taught "Somewhat before the heavy clod / Weighs" on him, (p. 202) yet he is unwilling to offer his own love to an ideal which is not certain, as an initial act of humble faith. In short, he demands that God should first stoop to him. He requires a changeless idol, not a living God. It was disillusionment with what was supposed a changeless idol that contributed largely to the decline of Arthur's Order as well. For Tennyson, love, whether directed toward a human or a divine object, is always an act of faith; analysis is inadequate to prove, verify, or endorse either. But love must also be selfless, for if pride prohibits the extension of love beyond the self, there can never be a true union.[8] The result of such pride is spiritual vacuity; life becomes empty and meaningless. The impoverished soul is left crying:

O weary life! O weary death!
O spirit and heart made desolate!
O damnèd vacillating state! (p. 202)

13

There is no reason to believe that this poem is an account of Tennyson's directly personal reflections and responses, though it is clearly the result of his speculations.[9] However, that he should have been capable of investigating and conveying the state of a soul impoverished through pride does not mean that he was, in fact, that impoverished soul. Such a reading diminishes the value of what Tennyson actually has accomplished in the poem. No one contends that Tennyson was a blindly proud St. Simeon, nor that he was a muddled Lucretius, a self-indulgent Merman, or a vain Mermaid, because, when exhibiting these figures dramatically in his poems, he presented views only slightly related to his own. When the sentiments of his narrators more closely resemble his own, critics seem impelled to dismiss the dramatic form acceptable in other poems. There is, in fact, some evidence that Tennyson was not describing his *own* state of mind in the "Supposed Confessions," but was detailing a *possible* state of mind. In an unpublished poem composed about the same time, he himself assumes the corrective function that the mother in the "Supposed Confessions" served; and this poem, unlike the "Confessions," is written undramatically in his own person.

> To _____.
> Thou may'st remember what I said
> When thine own spirit was at strife
> With thine own spirit. "From the tomb
> And charnel-place of purpose dead,
> Thro' spiritual dark we come
> Into the light of spiritual life."
> God walk'd the waters of thy soul,
> And still'd them. When from change to change,
> Led silently by power divine,
> Thy thought did scale a purer range
> Of prospect up to self-control,
> My joy was only less than thine.[10]

A similar case, with similar implications, can be made for "The

14

Palace of Art." Here again, it is unwise to read the poem as an autobiographical declaration at the expense of the poem's design. "The Palace of Art" follows a design much like that of "The Two Voices," but Tennyson made analysis easier and sought to avoid misinterpretation by placing at the head of the poem a summary statement of its theme, just as he was later to do in *In Memoriam*, fixing his statement of conviction at the opening of the poem to signify that, regardless of doubts expressed in the poem, the fundamental sentiments were faith and hope. In "The Palace of Art," Tennyson describes the subject of the poem as "a sinful soul possess'd of many gifts,"

> That did love Beauty only, (Beauty seen
> In all varieties of mould and mind)
> And Knowledge for its beauty; or if Good,
> Good only for its beauty, seeing not
> That Beauty, Good, and Knowledge, are three sisters
> That doat upon each other, friends to man,
> Living together under the same roof,
> And never can be sundered without tears.
> And he that shuts Love out, in turn shall be
> Shut out from Love, and on her threshold lie
> Howling in outer darkness. (pp. 399-400)

That the poet should urge the moral of his poem so earnestly suggests that he is beyond the limitations of its subject. A communication of Arthur Hallam's to Tennyson about the probable time of composition indicates that Tennyson was conscious of the need to love more than beauty only, though he loved beauty much.

> You say pathetically, "Alas for me! I have more of the Beautiful than the Good!" Remember to your comfort that God has given you to see the difference. Many a poet has gone on blindly in his artist pride.[11]

"The Two Voices" is a more sophisticated and more complete

rendering of the essential pattern of the "Supposed Confessions." The misery of the narrator in the former resembles the "misery of ignorance" that troubles the narrator of the "Supposed Confessions;" their mutual sin is pride, their fundamental discomfort, emptiness; both suffer a "divided will." "The Two Voices," however, completes the pattern of redemption. The poem can be appreciated productively if examined as a design rather than simple autobiography.

The titular change from "Thoughts of a Suicide" to "The Two Voices," was apt, and suggests that Tennyson wished to emphasize the dramatic nature of the poem. This is no mere outcry of a doubting mind, but a crafted rendering of a figuration which recurs throughout Tennyson's poetry. It is, perhaps, most evident in *In Memoriam*, but it is present as well in *Maud* and other poems, including the *Idylls of the King*, where it is more subtly presented.[12] The rudimentary pattern is this: a mind unsettled by doubts confronts the arguments which doubting reason offers, and, finding none sufficient to overbear an inner experience which discloses the perniciousness of self-absorption and pride, through love and an accompanying humility, he frees himself from selfishness and is made worthy, in his own eyes, of determined and selfless action toward an unchanged, but not unchanging, ideal. In "Supposed Confessions," the design is incomplete; though, as the contemporary lyric, "To ———," quoted above suggests, Tennyson was aware of the completed design when he wrote both poems. It is a belief in the incompleteness of the design that reveals the mind as "second-rate." In later poems, this design is embodied in a parable, a sequence of events, or a passage of time, but in "Two Voices," it occurs in the simpler means of the dialogue.

Unlike certain critics, I do not feel that Tennyson meant to give the "still small voice" of despair the sounder arguments in "The Two Voices."[13] The small voice has recourse to numerous sophistries, for he employs the unsound logical devices of argument by analogy and *argumentum ad hominem*, among other

16

equally specious techniques, in attempting to prove the necessity and convenience of suicide. The narrator, however, from his first response, is aware of these sophistries and dismisses the small voice's argument that the dragonfly's liberation from the cocoon is comparable to the soul's liberation from the body. What the narrator is finally driven to say outright, is assumed in all his resistance to the small voice's arguments:

> 'These words,' I said, 'are like the rest:
> No certain clearness, but at best
> A vague suspicion of the breast:' (p. 586)

The narrator remarks that that vague suspicion of the breast may be positive as well as negative, and goes on to prove it by citing his intimations of pre-mortality and immortality.

The truth is that the narrator is disappointed by the small voice's performance. He knows all of the arguments that it presents and counters them with similar arguments, verifying the attitude expressed by the Ancient Sage:

> Thou canst not prove thou art immortal, no
> Nor yet that thou art mortal—nay my son,
> Thou canst not prove that I, who speak with thee,
> Am not thyself in converse with thyself,
> For nothing worthy proving can be proven,
> Nor yet disproven: wherefore thou be wise,
> Cleave ever to the sunnier side of doubt,
> And cling to Faith beyond the forms of Faith! (pp. 1351-52)

Furthermore, "The Two Voices" is just that—a self in converse with itself. The small voice is the articulation of doubts in the narrator himself, just as the second voice he hears is the articulation of his hopes. The two voices are mutually exclusive products of the narrator's moods. Just as sad Mariana's ambience is sad, so the narrator's doubtful mood calls up a doubting voice. And, as the Soul in "The Palace of Art" learns that the imagina-

17

tion's grand edifice is mutable to her moods, and when she despairs grim scenes intrude themselves in what was once a luxuried region; so the narrator in "The Two Voices" discovers that no argument, but a change of heart, is the source of well-being. When his heart melts, his mood changes, and when his mood changes, nature wears the colors of a gayer spirit. This is not very startling, for we have Tennyson's later practice to consider, and know that something resembling this device was used in *In Memoriam*, of which Tennyson said:

> "The different moods of sorrow as in a drama are dramatically given, and my conviction that fear, doubts, and suffering will find answer and relief only through Faith in a God of Love. 'I' is not always the author speaking of himself, but the voice of the human race speaking thro' him."[14]

We also know that *Maud* is dramatically conceived, though in more unusual terms. " 'The peculiarity of this poem' [Tennyson said,] 'is that different phases of passion in one person take the place of different characters.' "[15] This is a technique not far removed from what happens in "The Two Voices." The fascinating subtlety in the latter poem is of a different kind, for it is expressed in the narrator's consciousness of the dramatic projection of his own feelings, and, guise of intellection notwithstanding, despair and hope, in the poem, are only feelings. The conflict of doubt and hope is not really an intellectual dialectic, but a dramatization of antagonistic moods.[16]

That the narrators of the poems I have mentioned should be so oppressed by doubt does not signify that they are despairing, but, on the contrary, that they are struggling to overcome the doubts they must face. It will not do to avoid dubiety by retreating into an unquestioned faith; only by meeting each doubt that arises and combatting it, as the narrator of "The Two Voices" most certainly does, can a convincing faith be achieved. For Tennyson himself, there was the model of Arthur Hallam, who,

18

if we may depend upon section xcvi of *In Memoriam*, experienced the same design in his life that Tennyson described in his poetry.

> Perplext in faith, but pure in deeds,
> At last he beat his music out.
> There lives more faith in honest doubt,
> Believe me, than in half the creeds.
>
> He fought his doubts and gathered strength,
> He would not make his judgment blind,
> He faced the spectres of the mind
> And laid them: thus he came at length
>
> To find a stronger faith his own;
> And Power was with him in the night,
> Which makes the darkness and the light,
> And dwells not in the light alone. (p. 948)

The narrator in "The Two Voices," wearying of the ineffective dramatic hypostatization of his own doubts, exclaims:

> 'O dull, one-sided voice,' said I,
> 'Wilt thou make everything a lie,
> To flatter me that I may die?' (p. 531)

"That I *may* die," he says, revealing the small voice as no more than an intellectual ruse by which the narrator hoped to provide himself with an excuse for suicide. But, being a weak projection of the narrator's depression, the voice inevitably fails, for the narrator "*cannot* hide" (implying that, in his gloomy mood, he would like to hide such optimistic evidence) that what he aspired to has been achieved by others. This external and quasi-historical evidence, in company with his inner experience, makes certainty in despair impossible. Ironically, it has been the failure of the voice of despair to articulate adequately the vague suspicions of the narrator's breast that directs the narrator away from suicide. The intellective attempt to prove despair has, instead,

19

revealed the narrator's true failings. The small voice defines the narrator's sin of pride: " 'Self-blinded are you by your pride: / Look up through night: the world is wide,' " (p. 524) and suggests a remedy by describing the narrator's dilemma as a divided will which is incapable of achieving its aims because it lacks " 'thought resigned, / A healthy frame, a quiet mind.' " (p. 527) Accordingly, instead of seducing the narrator to self-destruction, it shocks him back to a love of life. When the narrator perceives these consequences, he treats the small voice with dismissive contempt.

> 'But thou,' said I, 'hast missed thy mark,
> Who sought'st to wreck my mortal ark,
> By making all the horizon dark.

> 'Why not set forth, if I should do
> This rashness, that which might ensue
> With this old soul in organs new?

> 'Whatever crazy sorrow saith,
> No life that breathes with human breath
> Has ever truly longed for death.

> ' 'Tis life, whereof our nerves are scant,
> Oh life, not death, for which we pant;
> More life, and fuller, that I want.' (p. 539)

Instead of decrying the narrator's pride, the proper course was to indulge it; instead of proposing an end to unsatisfactory indulgence, the small voice should have promoted a desire for an unknown but great indulgence. Though the small voice has failed in its purpose, it has achieved another, which, without it, might have been very slow in coming. The dialogue has brought out positive sentiments that a morbid mind would evoke hesitatingly, for the narrator has been obliged to recollect his earlier, rewarding values and aspirations.

In a long passage developing metaphors of battle, the narrator explains that what he had desired was a purposeful action for his life. He proceeds, maintaining the metaphors, to the core of his ideal:

'As far as might be, to carve out
Free space for every human doubt,
That the whole mind might orb about—

'To search through all I felt or saw,
The springs of life, the depths of awe,
And reach the law within the law:

'At least, not rotting like a weed,
But, having sown some *generous* seed,
Fruitful of further thought and deed,

'To pass, when Life her light withdraws,
Not void of righteous self-applause,
Nor in a merely *selfish* cause—

'In some good cause, *not in mine own*,
To perish, wept for, honored, known,
And like a warrior overthrown;

'Whose eyes are dim with glorious tears,
When, soiled with noble dust, he hears
His country's war-song thrill his ears:

'Then dying of a mortal stroke,
What time the foeman's line is broke,
And all the war is rolled in smoke.' (pp. 528-29)[17]

As the words I have underlined suggest, the action he desired was one that would bear him outside himself; this, he then understood, would provide a rich and full life. His failing has been to lapse into a proud, self-absorbed state, a condition that reveals Tennyson's "vision of self-consciousness as self-imprisonment."[18] He has ensnared himself within himself, making himself his only reference and consequently reducing himself with the illusion of space that mirrors reflecting one another offer. His emptiness of spirit is consequent upon his absence of love.

Love is the power that fills out the shadowy forms of material

21

existence. Love transfigures and sustains all of phenomenal existence. But the mere rationalist or materialist, in Tennyson's view, perceived the world only with senses too coarse to appreciate the transfiguring power. To such as these, who doubt divine love and its force, the world is nothing more than dust ingeniously arranged. Tennyson, on the other hand, was sometimes so much convinced of a transcendent spiritual force in the universe that for him the forms themselves lost their boundaries and became no more than shadowy parts of a greater design. It is with a like recognition that the narrator happily discovers what will evict the small voice—"More life, and fuller." At the same time, he has learned that he can achieve this aim only if he passes the boundaries of his own self.[19] The narrator, sensing confinement, has coveted the freedom death might bring. Despair promised transformation like that of the dragonfly; however, the narrator's authentic escape is not from life, but from himself. The escape he makes is not from life to death, but from the self to life, much in the manner of the narrator of *Maud*. To choose what God would have him choose is not only real freedom, but it leads to genuine happiness. He chooses to hear the voice that cries: "Rejoice! Rejoice!" and choosing so, he may rejoice.

Accordingly, it is not the simple religious faith of a family on its way to church that revives the narrator's hopes, but the emblem of a proper exercise of emotion. The mildly firm father, signifying self-control; the mother, "faithful, gentle, good," representing tenderness and moral conscience; and the little maiden, indicating the unity of love that such disciplined good evokes, constitute a domestic Trinity which furnishes the narrator with a paradigm worthy approximation in his own life. Blessing them, he is released from proud self-absorption, and, without delay, another voice is at his ear.[20] The voice the narrator hears was heard by other poetic characters during these same years. In Arthur Hugh Clough's "Fragments of the Mystery of the Fall,"

Adam also hears two voices within him, and one is a grim despairing voice.

> But oftener far, and stronger also far,
> In consonance with all things out and in,
> I hear a voice more searching bid me, 'On!
> On! on! it is the folly of the child
> To choose his path and straightway think it wrong,
> And turn right back and lie on the ground and weep.
> Forward! go, conquer! work and live!' Withal
> A word comes, half command, half prophecy,
> 'Forgetting things behind thee, onward press
> Unto the mark of your high calling.' Yea,
> And voices, too, in woods and flowery fields
> Speak confidence from budding banks and boughs,
> And tell me, 'Live and grow,' and say, 'Look still
> Upward, spread outward, trust, be patient, live;'
> Therefore, if weakness bid me curse and die,
> I answer, No! I will not curse myself,
> Nor aught beside; I shall not die, but live.[21]

The hopeful voice of "The Two Voices" presents no arguments, no rhetoric; it only says that there is cause for hope, but feels no obligation to elaborate or justify the accompanying sensation. Whereas the small voice of despair presented numerous and prolonged appeals and was unsuccessful in its aim, the voice of hope gives only the slightest—though sweet—grounds for confidence; yet the narrator yields. In an instant, his blank existence assumes color and motion:

> From out my sullen heart a power
> Broke, like the rainbow from the shower,
>
> To feel, although no tongue can prove,
> That every cloud, that spreads above
> and veileth love, itself is love.
>
> And forth into the fields I went,
> And Nature's living motion lent
> The pulse of hope to discontent. (p. 541)

Nature offers no threats; man is no longer a mote in a waste universe, but has become the center of a bounteous and benign world in which "There seemed no room for sense of wrong" where everything was "so variously wrought." (p. 541) The narrator's life is suddenly rich and full once more. His revelation resembles the familiar pattern in "The Palace of Art" where a similar argument is framed in aesthetic terms. Pride leads the Soul to a selfish indulgence which, while excluding possible objects of love, also hardens the Soul against love. The result is barren despair. Parallel to the sin described in "The Vision of Sin," it is " 'a crime / Of sense avenged by sense that wore with time.' " (p. 725)

The self, isolated in indulgence, lacks the outflowing force of love to animate its existence. As Tennyson so often indicated, we see what we are. A beautiful landscape becomes so through the outrushing of emotion. Without such an emotion, even nature pales and diminishes. It is mainly through his contact with other human beings that man becomes aware of the boundaries of the self. These restraints, in turn, direct man's attentions outward from the self. In the sequestered imagination, there is no time, no space. It is an elegant and seductive domain, but potentially as wild as any pagan kingdom. Contiguity with other men convinces the self that Arthur's pronouncement at the end of "The Holy Grail" is correct. Despite the visions that entertain the yearning imagination, a man must do his work in *this* world, fitting the ideal to the substance. It is love that takes man out of his husk of self-consciousness and sets him at large in a world of beauty.

Through love, a feeling, the narrator of "The Two Voices" has been redeemed; whereas all doubting intellection has failed to damn him. Through love his youthful dream revives and his world is re-animated. He is prepared to engage in the selfless metaphorical battle that he once envisioned, just as the narrator of "Locksley Hall" is prepared to take action against evil, or the narrator of *Maud*, having been instructed by love, is anxious to exert himself in metaphorical and real battle. Here, as in *In Memoriam*, the prolonged argument of doubting reason is erased by the inner experience of love. An inconclusive dialogue of self in converse with itself forces an emotional and intuitional leap to redemptive awareness and conviction.

If *In Memoriam* was The Way of the Soul, then other poems, employing the same design, are alternate routes to redemption, and "The Two Voices" is a forthright utilization of that design. Furthermore, that this design should be repeated in several poems over a period of years suggests that it was not merely an autobiographical effusion, but a craftsman's device to present an important theme that he could describe dramatically from the private standpoint of conviction.

The Princess

It is possible to see in *The Princess* aspects of the design with which I am concerned. There is a reasonable resemblance between *The Princess* and "The Palace of Art," as well, for Princess Ida withdraws from common society out of intellectual pride to perfect herself in luxuriant and, to some extent, self-indulgent seclusion. Such a withdrawal is, in itself, a sign that Tennyson disapproved of her behavior, and, though he might consider her declared motives admirable, he did not consider Ida's practice correct, for we are told that she wrote "rhymes / And dismal lyrics, prophesying change / *Beyond all reason.*" (p. 755, my italics) Ida has placed all of her confidence in knowledge, but we are aware of the dangers of such exclusiveness, recollecting the admonition in the prologue to "The Palace of Art," that "Beauty, Good, and Knowledge are three sisters," (p. 399) all to be worshiped in fitting proportion.

The Princess, though obviously about love and ostensibly about the place of woman in the human community if not in

25

Victorian society, is also about proportion.[22] Tennyson is as concerned about mutuality in love as Dickens was, and, whereas Dickens employed a recurrently motivic contrast between the uneven jurisdiction in most marriages, and the balanced respect and affection of his nuptial heroes and heroines, so Tennyson felt inclined to conclude many of his works with the discovery of an authentic proportion within the individual, or, in other cases, the failure of that proportion, as in "Balin and Balan." I hope that I have made this evident already in discussing "The Two Voices," where the emblem of mutuality in love at the conclusion of the poem provides the model for the narrator's own personality.[23]

As in the *Idylls of the King*, one proportion to be achieved in *The Princess* is between substance and ideality. Ida is described as "All beauty compass'd in a female form," (p. 760) resembling the more obviously parabolic Sleeping Beauty who was "a perfect form in perfect rest," soon to be awakened and put to service by the questing Prince. (p. 628)[24] The Prince in *The Princess* is characterized by his weird seizures which dissolve reality or make it seem a hollow pretense. Material life is shadow and mirage until love fills and cloaks it with the highest aspirations of man's soul.[25] The Prince's seizures end, of course, when he is united with Ida. The Prince can never depreciate Ida as other characters do, for he is aware of her true merits—what she stands for. To the Prince, Ida's is a simple error of intellectual pride, for he declares that she "wears her error like a crown / To blind the truth and me." (p. 776) If her mood could be altered, her pride humbled, her heart touched, then beauty could combine with idea and the proper mutuality would exist. Even Ida's athletic brother, Arac, admits, "She flies too high, she flies too high!" (p. 809) Pride here is also confused, through the image of the crown, with an irregular assumption of authority. A woman craving absolute dominion is more than unusual, even in a nation ruled by a Queen. She is unnatural and invites retribution.

The necessary fall takes place ironically in the Prince's combat with Arac. It is when the representative of spirit is in danger that beauty yields.

> And then once more she looked at my pale face:
> Till understanding all the foolish work
> Of Fancy, and the bitter close of all,
> Her iron will was broken in her mind;
> Her noble heart was molten in her breast;
> She bowed, she set the child on the earth; she laid
> A feeling finger on my brows, and presently
> 'O Sire,' she said, 'he lives: he is not dead: (p. 821)

It is as though Ida's humility has revived the Prince, though there has never been any genuine threat to his life. It is not in the nature of this poem to have its characters die. It is a far different composition from those to follow—such as *Maud* or the *Idylls of the King*—where the tests are more severe, just as the offenses are graver. Before long, Ida is able to admit that "she had failed / In sweet humility; had fail'd in all," and she realizes that she "sought far less for truth than power / In knowledge." (p. 837) Love has redeemed her, and she and the Prince now pledge themselves to mutual reverence and mutual assistance.

It would be convenient if I could assert that Tennyson intended this as a manifestation of the moral design I have described, but I would rather say that the design is implied here only in a shadowy way. That it was not entirely inconsequential is suggested by Tennyson's addition of the Prince's seizures to emphasize his association with ideality, and by the extension of the lessons of the poem in the "Conclusion," where the virtues recently championed in the fable are now given a social significance. One of the characters praises England, saying it has

> Some sense of duty, something of a faith,
> Some reverence for the laws ourselves have made,

> Some patient force to change them when we will,
> Some civic manhood firm against the crowd. (p. 843)

And the narrator, taking not only the themes of the preceding poem but some of its furnishings and manner as well, provides the consolatory affirmation of the great design within which all men labor to fulfil their part.

> 'Have patience,' I replied, 'ourselves are full
> Of social wrong; and maybe wildest dreams
> Are but the needful preludes of the truth:
> For me, the genial day, the happy crowd,
> The sport half-science, fill me with a faith.
> This fine old world of ours is but a child
> Yet in the go-cart. Patience! Give it time
> To learn its limbs: there is a hand that guides.' (p. 843)

Ida, who has presumed beyond the present powers of her sex, has violated an order, but the Prince is not entirely free from rebuke. As much as she lacks obedience and the will to serve humbly, he lacks the virtues of authority, confusing his masculinity—noticeably gentler than his unreasonable father—with forbearance. Tennyson's final recommendation to the couple, while sounding like domestic advice, is just as much a recipe for excellence.

> Yet in the long years liker must they grow;
> The man be more of woman, she of man;
> He gain in sweetness and in moral height,
> Nor lose the wrestling thews that throw the world;
> She mental breadth, nor fail in childward care,
> Nor lose the childlike in the larger mind;
> Till at the last she set herself to man,
> Like perfect music unto noble words. (p. 839)

Man, while maintaining his attributes of authority, which include "wrestling thews," must attain less brutal attributes, while woman is to develop her mind with no injury to her natural feelings. Wed, these two represent the proportions each individual should feel within himself. As in the emblem of the happy family that concludes "The Two Voices," we have in the Prince and Princess the diagram of an ordered self. Moreover, if we keep in mind Tennyson's alertness to language—a subject we shall take up later in this study—the image signifying attained proportion is excitingly apt, for woman will "set herself to man, / Like perfect music unto noble words."

The Princess was admittedly an attempt to merge the genial and the serious, and consequently we should not expect in it the same intensity that we find in more consciously serious poems by Tennyson. The "wildest dreams" of Ida may later become the impossible scheme of the Round Table, still only a prelude to an ever-engendering truth. The self full of social wrong might soon become the self ultimately willing to admit the necessity of patience—not to mention humility—and the acceptance of "a hand that guides," in the narrator of *Maud*. If the design was no more than a shadow, possibly not even a conscious imposition, in this case, in *Maud*, it seems to me, it is undeniable.

Maud

No serious scholar would deny the importance of biographical evidence for the interpretation of poetry, but most would disfavor an approach that sacrificed technical excellence and concinnity to a biographical reading. I have suggested this much in discussing "The Two Voices." It is clear that certain poems must be read with the poet's biography in mind; for example, George Meredith's *Modern Love*. But it is equally clear that even these poems may alter facts to perfect a design.[26] Tennyson's monodrama, *Maud*, has suffered greatly from attempts at biographical interpretation and, consequently, has often been misunderstood and misvalued. The poem is not an excited avowal of social, political, or emotional values, but a poetic figuration, conveying by means of a parable, a moral conviction.

If we suppose that the narrator of *Maud* speaks in Tennyson's voice, or is merely his mask, we must assume that Tennyson here reverts to a state of mind which preceded the composition of such poems as "Supposed Confessions of a Second-Rate Sensitive Mind," "The Palace of Art," "Locksley Hall," and "The Two Voices," not to mention *In Memoriam,* for, in *Maud,* Tennyson utilizes once more the design employed in these earlier compositions. In most of them the design is complete, moving from a mood of darkened doubt to one of bright affirmation. The pattern of thought is by no means uncommon, as I have indicated earlier, and parallels, for example, Carlyle's scheme describing the growth of the soul from an Everlasting Nay, through the Center of Indifference, to an Everlasting Yea.[27] The repetition of such a moral pattern does not persuade me that Tennyson was forever stumbling back into agonizing doubt, then painfully struggling toward faith and conviction once more, but rather that, having found a satisfactory design for the presentation of an enduring moral problem, he exploited that design time and again within the framework of his own moral conviction.[28] Arthur Hugh Clough's "Fragments of the Mystery of the Fall," already cited, describes a similar moral design as the very curve of human existence. Describing Cain, Adam says to Eve:

> This child is born of us, and therefore like us;
> Is born of us, and therefore is as we;
> Is born of us, and therefore is not pure;
> Earthy as well as godlike; bound to strive—
> Not doubtfully I augur from the past—
> Through the same straits of anguish and of doubt,
> 'Mid the same storms of terror and alarm,
> To the calm ocean which he yet shall reach,

He or himself or in his sons hereafter,
Of consummated consciousness of self.[29]

It seems necessary to defend Tennyson's broader poetic skills at present because recent criticism has emphasized biographical readings of *Maud*. Ralph Wilson Rader's *Tennyson's Maud: The Biographical Genesis*, for example, enthusiastically explores the biographical rather than the technical features of the poem and thereby arrives at what I consider a mistaken evaluation. After a worthwhile examination of biographical possibilities, Rader concludes that *Maud* fails because the "hidden emotional dimension" of the poem is not adequately conveyed in the dramatic story of the hero, and that the poem falls awkwardly between lyric and drama in consequence. The hidden import to which Rader refers mainly concerns Tennyson's association with Rosa Baring, an association which, if actually pertinent to the poem, is, I contend, subordinate to the poem's design. In the same way, Tennyson's sources for the *Idylls of the King* are less consequential than what he does with them. Rader assumes that Tennyson has been unwilling to present in *Maud* the immediate experience that was still too intensely close to him. By contrast, he approves the direct presentation of *In Memoriam*, although Tennyson himself declared that he had diligently fashioned his private experience into something quite removed from direct expression.[30]

Although biographical information is always important in literary criticism, what seems paramount in a work such as *Maud* is not biographical allusion, but the manipulation of the poem's parts to fashion a unified design. And the design of *Maud* is firm. Like *In Memoriam*, it moves from darkness to light, from negation to affirmation, from self-concerned indolence and withdrawal to selfless participation. The notable difference between the two poems is that *In Memoriam* was ostensibly presented in Tennyson's own voice, whereas the narrator of *Maud* is conspicuously unlike Tennyson. The narrator of *Maud* has been said to resemble a spasmodic hero, and Tennyson admittedly had respect for some features of spasmodic poetry.[31] This, however, does not mean that Tennyson became such a hero; only that he found in the type of passionate but confused youth one means for presenting a familiar design. Had reviewers accepted this distinction from the first, as Tennyson's friends did, they might have avoided fruitless speculations on Tennyson's character and politics, and read the poem as the moral lesson it was meant to be.[32]

The moral design is the familiar one, moving from self-absorbed pride, through a liberating love and consequent suffering, to a higher knowledge of God's purpose and a humble suppression of self to that purpose. It is, of course, a variation upon the design of *In Memoriam*, where a lost love leads the poet-narrator from grief to conviction. Hallam Tennyson, paraphrasing for the most part, described his father's summary of the poem's import as follows:

> "This poem is a little *Hamlet*," the history of a morbid poetic soul, under the blighting influence of a recklessly speculative age.   He is the heir of madness, an *egotist* with the makings of a cynic, raised to sanity by *a pure and holy love* which elevates his whole nature, passing from the height of triumph to the lowest depth of misery, driven into madness by the loss of her whom he has loved, and, when he has at length passed through the fiery furnace, and has recovered his reason, giving himself up to *work for the good of mankind* through the *unselfishness* born of his great passion. My father pointed out that even Nature at first presented herself to the man in sad visions.

> And the flying gold of the ruin'd woodlands
> drove thro' the air.

> The "blood-red heath" too is an exaggeration of colour; and his suspicion that all the world is against him is as true to his nature as the *mood* when he is "fantastically merry." "The peculiarity of this poem," my father added, "is that *different phases of passion* in one person take the place of different characters."[33]

32

Like "The Two Voices," *Maud* is a poem governed by mood, not intellection. At the opening of the poem, the narrator's mood is understandably morbid, and he projects that mood first into the natural world and subsequently to the world of men, discovering in human nature features most likely to reinforce his mood. Moreover, by finding all men sinful, he extenuates his own sinfulness, which is, as with earlier narrators in Tennyson, a self-absorbed pride.[34]

> We are puppets, Man in his pride, and Beauty fair
>   in her flower;
> Do we move ourselves, or are moved by an unseen
>   hand at a game
> That pushes us off from the board, and others
>   ever succeed?
> Ah yet, we cannot be kind to each other here for
>   an hour;
> We whisper, and hint, and chuckle, and grin at a
>   brother's shame;
> However, we brave it out, we men are a little breed.
>   (One. IV. v., pp. 1049-50)

The narrator goes so far as to imagine in Maud his own worst inclinations, viewing her as cold, self-confined, and failing in affection. At the same time, however, Maud is presented from the first through the narrator's memories which predispose us in her favor as an ideal character, and which war against his temporary, unfavorable view of her.

Though he realizes that he should avoid surroundings congenial to his morbidity (One. I. xvi), the narrator decides instead to sink more deeply into them; so far, in fact, as to the depths of his own self. "I will bury myself in myself, and the Devil may pipe to his own." (One. I. xix.) However, his withdrawal into himself is the result of what he conceives of as an external threat—the beautiful Maud.[35] Becoming aware of the object of his fear, he declares "And most of all would I flee from the cruel madness of love." (One. IV. x., p. 1052) His impulse to hide himself is both a desire to pamper his luxurious melancholy and a cowardice in the face of the nobler but demanding emotion. Love threatens to draw him into a world of action and responsibility, and he resists it.

If, in *The Princess*, it was proud beauty that withdrew into self-caressing isolation, in this instance it is simple pride understandably afraid of the emotion most likely to pry him from his self-indulgent melancholy. But the narrator's heart is not entirely hardened, and Maud is as much the manifestation of his own desire for redemption as she is a character in her own right. "Maud is both individual woman and ideal beauty, an inhabitant of the sensual, the moral and of the dream world;"[36] moreover she embodies the narrator's true, or higher self, which only becomes clear to him later in his identification with an exquisite seashell.[37] Maud's military song, for example, associates her with the narrator's smouldering desire for a cause through which he may expend his energy in the service of Good and Truth. (One. I. xii-xiii) Maud's voice, unlike her ostensibly cold appearance, represents a warmth strongly in contrast with the "sordid and mean" world that the narrator inhabits. (One. V. i-ii.) Experiencing a gradual thawing , the narrator still wishes to silence the lovely voice which suggests a delight impossible to him and an unachievable goal. (One. V. iii.) The concurrence of the narrator's gradual mollification and the growing influence of Maud may be explained in terms of the love story of the poem, but there is no reason to overlook the possibility that the narrator's perception of Maud, as ideal, becomes more accurate the further he emerges from the distorting haze with which his mood of dismal selfishness and pride has enveloped him. When it becomes evident that Maud is not cold and indifferent as he had supposed, the process accelerates, a hope emerges, and he begins to regret his bitterness.

> Ah, what shall I be at fifty
> Should Nature keep me alive,

If I find the world so bitter
When I am but twenty-five?

He even begins to imagine the world as less than wholly wicked.

Yet, if she were not a cheat,
If Maud were all that she seemed,
And her smile were all that I dreamed,
Then the world were not so bitter
But a smile could make it sweet. (One. VI. v., p. 1054)

Remaining distrustful, in his wariness he mistrusts his mistrust, admitting that he may be deceived by pride. (One. VI. vii.)[38] This is nearer the truth than he supposes, though it is not the superficial pride he observes that endangers him, but a subtler subterraenean pride that will require severe humiliation to effect his salvation. In *Maud*, as the submerged patterns of imagery and allusion suggest, there are increasing depths of virtue and sin which appear gradually and unevenly to the tormented consciousness of the narrator. To penetrate through appearances to one awareness is merely to confront another illusion which the self participates in forming, until, the material world finally discovered as secondary, the narrator places his faith in a higher "dream," and moves confidently toward salvation.

Having been largely convinced of Maud's goodness, and thereby of the existence of goodness in a world he hoped to believe entirely corrupt, the narrator is obliged to examine himself and his motives, and, what is more important, is capable of doing so as a result of the waxing of his embodied ideal. In a passage with suggestive echoes of "Mariana," a poem about imputation of mood, the narrator articulates an awareness of his pernicious tendency to project private moods into the world at large. He knows that his mood is the result of

Living alone in an empty house,
Here half-hid in the gleaming wood,

> Where I hear the dead at midday moan,
> And the shrieking rush of the wainscot mouse,
> And my own sad name in corners cried,
> When the shiver of dancing leaves is thrown
> About its echoing chambers wide,
> Till a morbid-hate and horror have grown
> Of a world in which I have hardly mixt,
> And a morbid eating lichen fixt
> On a heart half-turned to stone. (One. VI. viii. p. 1055)

What has happened is simply that the voice of Hope has had an opportunity to speak against the voice of Despair. In "The Two Voices," the attitudes were mutually exclusive; but in *Maud* the two moods, objectified less abstractly, contend, reflecting an internal warfare. Despair and earthly wickedness constitute the darkness striving against the light of love and hope, signified by Maud.

Here again is a character snared in himself, uncertain whether to attempt a total incapsulation, or to admit the sentiments which in their overbrimming richness will prove the hollowness of his protected self. That he should later compare a shell to mankind is appropriate, given his defensive attitude regarding participation in the world. Again, the narrator of *Maud* is, at this point, ignorant of all proportion. Ungoverned himself, he yet hopes to be his own authority; but he is the slave of his moods. To resolve the battle in himself he must acknowledge, as the narrator of *The Princess* did, that "there is a hand that guides," (p. 843), there is a "purpose of God," and a "doom assigned." (Three. VI. v., p. 1093)

But the narrator, in spite of Maud's growing influence, continues at war with himself.

> At war with myself and a wretched race,
> Sick, sick to the heart of life, am I. (One. X. ii., p. 1058)

The narrator is far from having extirpated his fundamental

sin of pride and selfishness. At the beginning of the poem, he railed against the acquisitive society around him, though his railing possibly arose largely from his own frustration at being denied acquisitions himself. He even entertained the suspicion that Maud's brother, with the coming election in mind, had encouraged her to feign interest in him, in hopes that "A wretched vote may be gained" thereby. (One. VI. vi., p. 1054) When the narrator learns of a rival for Maud's love, his internal contest is postponed once more. Still inadequately aware of his own selfishness, he remains emotionally infirm until violently freed from the malady of self-concern. Until Maud is beyond possession, his aims are tainted. The young man who so wildly condemned the world's greed and that of Maud's father in particular, contains in himself the taint of acquisitiveness. Like the venal world around him, he views Maud's wealthy suitor almost as a commercial competitor. For both, Maud is a valuable object. The narrator, having previously described Maud in terms of precious stones, now fears that the wealthy suitor has "found [his] jewel out." (One. X. ii., p. 1058) At the same time, however, he has associated Maud with planetary bodies, and it is this less material function that must ultimately prevail. When she is beyond his grasp, she becomes his guide; until then, his motive remains to some degree selfish. If he can love, he cries, "I shall have had my day." (One. XI. ii., p. 1061) Here, as elsewhere, there is no mention of Maud having her day. Maud is important mainly insofar as she evokes one or another of the narrator's moods. In Part Two, this becomes abundantly evident when Maud, no longer a physical presence, becomes a shifting phantom projection of the narrator's guilt—a perversion of her true function as an enduring, stellar guide. But in the early part of the poem, she is a manifestation of accessible earthly beauty. When she is finally removed to an ideal sphere, the narrator's values will have assumed their proper proportion. It is necessary for him to ascend from a merely sensuous perception of the world (which, as we have seen, is largely distorted by his prejudiced senses), to an intellectual comprehension of his condition (which is likewise colored by his emotions), and finally to a spiritual understanding of his place in a greater scheme. He must learn that things of the flesh and of the phenomenal world are ambiguous, deceptive, and dangerous. Only when he understands them from a spiritual or ideal perspective will they become trustworthy; only then will he "embrace the purpose of God."

Though yet in a state of selfishness, and contemptuous of himself and the world, the narrator comprehends the nature of his disease. He lacks spiritual authority. The private chaos must find order before the public chaos can.

> Put down the passions that make earth Hell!
> Down with ambition, avarice, pride,
> Jealousy, down! cut off from the mind
> The bitter springs of anger and fear;
> Down too, down at your own fireside,
> With the evil tongue and the evil ear,
> For each is at war with mankind. (One. X. iii., p. 1059)

Divided by hope and despair, he wishes a worthy leader would arise to guide his confused, corrupted nation, and admits an equal need for a guide within himself, a constitution of discipline and self-control.

> And ah for a man to arise in me,
> That the man I am may cease to be! (One. X. vi. p. 1060)

The narrator is by no means ignorant, though his passionate nature prevents him from always acting upon his better decisions. He attempts to conclude his internal conflict and wishes to display amity toward Maud's brother, but his passions overwhelm him when the brother's pride offends his own. (One. XIII. i.) He smears his own dark issue upon the landscapes through which he moves, yet his darkness has been so far illuminated by Maud's image that he understands the part his own moody imagination plays in painting the world about him in dismal colors. This awareness leads him to acknowledge the necessity of acquiring self-reverence through a pure love. If pure love is possible, if the world bears such goodness, then there is hope for redemption and fruitful participation in the world. It is some time before the narrator apprehends the final implications of such redemptive action; at first even redemption is a selfish goal.

> So dark a mind within me dwells,
>   And I make myself such evil cheer,
> That if *I* be dear to some one else,
>   Then some one else may have much to fear;
> But if *I* be dear to some one else,
>   Then I should be to myself more dear.
> Shall I not take care of all that I think,
> Yea, even of wretched meat and drink,
> If I be dear,
> If I be dear to some one else. (One. XV. p. 1065)

He recognizes the *utility* of Maud's love.

> I know it the one bright thing to save
> My yet young life in the wilds of Time,
> Perhaps from madness, perhaps from crime,
> Perhaps from a *selfish* grave. (One. XVI. i., p. 1065; italics mine)

The more obvious Maud's beneficent effect, the more enamored of her and the effect he becomes, turning, like the narrator of "The Two Voices," and the poet of *In Memoriam*, from death toward life; and the world, reanimated, resembles the "more life, and fuller" of the former poem. (One. XVIII. vi.) His new affirmation through love he expresses simply.

> Not die; but live a life of truest breath,
> And teach true life to fight with mortal
>   wrongs.[39] (One. XVIII. vii., p. 1069)

Gradually disengaging himself from his own gratifications, the narrator determines to be rid of "this dead body of hate," which afflicts him, and finds himself relieved of melancholy through his desire to beguile Maud's melancholy. (One. XIX. x. and One. XX. i.) Through a selfless act, he escapes his morbid sorrow.

Unfortunately for the narrator, however, having been brought from the morbid projection of a morbid mood at the beginning of the first part of the poem to an ecstatic projection of his ecstasy at the end—going so far as to declare that the roses and lilies stayed awake all night for Maud because he did—his pride, which he has not yet commanded, occasions a relapse to the state of mind with which the poem opened. Although the narrator has been aware that Maud was "not blind / to the faults of [her brother's] heart and mind," (One. XIX. vii., p. 1072) he has not been alert to similar defects in himself. Although he despised Maud's brother for his materialism, the narrator himself has been living in an overwhelmingly physical world throughout Part One of *Maud*. The physical act of violence that closes this section of the poem initiates a crisis of self-consciousness in him. The physical being, whose dreams were too much of the flesh, whose hopes were too dependent upon the senses, is unmasked. The narrator discovers that the identity of Part One is not his true identity at all, but only a disguise. His own physical being is a mask and prevents him from recognizing the higher self of the spirit. Part Two will offer the narrator a similar discovery regarding the untrustworthiness of the mind. Eventually mind and body must be humbled and the spirit exalted.

At the opening of Part Two, as at the opening of Part One, the land is dark, hate is afoot, and violence is the cause.

> For front to front in an hour we stood,
> And a million horrible bellowing echoes broke
> From the red-ribbed hollow behind the wood,

And thundered up into Heaven the Christless code
That must have life for a blow. (Two. I. i., pp. 1078-79)

Not only are location and mood the same, but the new violence underscores the early violent associations. In the first situation, the narrator was the victim of violence; he himself was passive. Now he is the agent of violence and the cause of Maud's suffering. At first he experienced a "silent horror" at the "dreadful hollow," but now he hears "a million horrible bellowing echoes." The parallel is exquisite since he has supposed himself at the threshold of deliverance from his internal conflict when the conflict becomes real, with real and tragic consequences. As in *In Memoriam*, progress toward faith and selflessness does not come in an easy progression, but the ascent, having reached a high point, retreats to rise again. In both cases, however, there is not total relapse, for much has been learned by the preceding struggle. Gareth, too, must face new antagonists, new struggles, after each victory. In this case, the narrator of *Maud* has at least been led out of his stupefying melancholy into the range of action. Thus far, unfortunately, his actions, like his thoughts, are distorted and misdirected.

The narrator's misery is increased by evidence that his view of the brother was perhaps too severe. The man proves noble in death, " 'The fault was mine,' he whispered, 'fly!' " (Two. I. i., p. 1079) The narrator later remembers the ring that Maud's brother wore, probably containing a lock of his mother's hair. Surely a man with such filial affection could not have been the monster he initially seemed. The conseqence of these oppressive ironies is that the narrator, beyond projecting his bleak or merry moods, now projects his guilt itself. But this is an advance upon his earlier excusatory mood, for now he is aware of his own specific participation in evil. Maud, once the jewel he hoped to obtain, and the star that guided him, becomes a phantom figure, "a lying trick of the brain," (Two. I. ii., p. 1079) an image that "moves with the moving eye," (Two. II. v., p. 1080) a

41

"blot upon the brain / That *will* show itself without." (Two. IV.
viii., p. 1085) But in spite of such mighty persuasion, the narrator is not yet fully instructed. Still lacking self-knowledge, he
palliates individual guilt by applying it to mankind generally.
Though his joys were private, his evils remain universal.

> Arise, my God, and strike, for we hold Thee just,
> Strike dead the whole weak race of venomous worms,
> That sting each other here in the dust;
> We are not worthy to live. (Two. I. ii., p. 1079)

Nevertheless, he realizes that, like the shell on the Breton coast,
he is a work "Frail, but a work divine," and has, as the shell has
not, a "spark of will," yet in him. (Two. II. i. and vii.) The
shell is, moreover, a point of juncture for his material and higher
natures and recapitulates his earlier responses to Maud. His description of the shell as "pure as a pearl," with a "diamond
door," recalls his association of Maud with precious ornaments;
but, at the same time, both Maud and the shell are emblems of
his "first and highest nature." So long as Maud loves him, his
heart may be dark, but unextinguished. At this point, for the
first time, the narrator truly overcomes his selfishness, subordinating his own concerns to Maud's.

> However this may be,
> Comfort her, comfort her, all things good,
> While I am over the sea!
> Let me and my passionate love go by,
> But speak to her all things holy and high,
> Whatever happen to me!
> Me and my harmful love go by;
> But come to her waking, find her asleep,
> Powers of the height, Powers of the deep,
> And comfort her though I die. (Two. II. ix. pp. 1081-82)[40]

In spite of his overt crime—perhaps we may conclude because of it—his attachment to his ideal becomes more intense.

But Maud dies. The narrator is left alone with his anguish and his guilt, something like a wildly disillusioned Balin. Not having entirely outrun his selfishness, he misses Maud largely because there is no longer one to love him. This is another trough in the pattern, resembling the first reversal occasioned by Maud's brother's death. Having approached so near to selflessness, the narrator reverts to an extreme and frenetic desire for withdrawal within himself, reversing the action which Maud's love had initiated.

> But the broad light glares and beats,
> And the shadow flits and fleets
> And will not let me be;
> And I loathe the squares and streets,
> And the faces that one meets,
> Hearts with no love for me:
> Always I long to creep
> Into some still cavern deep,
> There to weep, and weep, and weep
> My whole soul out to thee. (Two. IV. xiii. p. 1086)

Believing that he has lost the image of goodness, like the Lancelot who loved his Elaine but was nonetheless denied her, the narrator despairs. Madness ensues. What the narrator feels as burial is his actual retreat into himself. It is the ultimate self-absorption that will prove the vanity of self-concern, for the narrator discovers that retreat provides no peace, that agony attends his supposed escape. Nevertheless, the withdrawal, as representing the long-postponed internal combat, is also necessary and morally hygienic, like Geraint's excursion in the wilderness.

The narrator's madness is but the obverse of his dream. In a world of mystery and enigma, belief may convert illusion to fact. But belief is manifold, and believing love futile and the ideal lost is madness; believing love immortal will be salvation. The narrator's railings become more hysterical than in his early dark mood, but now, despite madness, they move with a clear direction, focussing inevitably on his crime, and finally forcing an open admission. This admission is itself a qualification of his rudimentary belief that outer war was the same as inner war. The distinctions between actions governed by pride and actions governed by justice constitute further abrasive rebukes for the narrator's conscience.

> Friend, to be struck by the public foe,
> Then to strike him and lay him low,
> That were a public merit, far,
> Whatever the Quaker holds, from sin;
> But the red life spilt for a private blow—
> I swear to you, lawful and lawless war
> Are scarcely even akin. (Two. V. x., p. 1090)

He now feels more impelled to escape the consequences and conclusions of his own admission and the second part of the poem closes with his raving request to be buried yet deeper.

The narrator's madness is both practical and emblematic. Julius and Augustus Hare, Tennyson's contemporaries, subscribed to the view that "temporary madness may perhaps be necessary in some cases, to cleanse and renovate the mind; just as a fit of illness is to carry off the humours of the body."[41] Still, the narrator's recovery from madness is not the result of therapy or intellection, but a change of mood. (Three. VI. i.) Having gone as deeply into himself as possible, he is obliged to acknowledge the futility of retreat and abruptly changes his course. It is the narrator of "The Two Voices" once more, who, having found the arguments of despair unconvincing, is seduced to joy, not by arguments but by an altered mood. And, whereas the narrator of "The Two Voices," emerging from the confines of self finds the correlative of his recovered hope in the Sabbath dawn, the narrator of *Maud* finds his in a heavenly light, which, in his dream, is the spirit of Maud, who "spoke of a hope for the world in the coming wars." (Three. VI. i. p. 1091) As the narrator of "The Two Voices" finds the paradigm for action in the emblem of love represented by the serene family group, so the narrator of *Maud* finds his cause in the war which promises to establish a discernible battlefront between good and evil, a battlefront that will provide a convenient means toward the alignment of moral forces. Furthermore, since Maud, the narrator's image of good, is no longer an immediate, substantial object, he is obliged to recreate that image within himself. Now, with the image of Maud external no longer, and his soul no longer embrangled in selfish concerns, the narrator's eye is cleared with his clearing mind. The inward ideal glorifies the external world. The higher vision provides a new authentic mode of perception.

Before Maud's influence, the stars, as projections of the narrator's own self-disgust and despair, were "tyrants in [their] iron skies,"

> Innumerable, pitiless, passionless eyes,
> Cold fires, yet with power to burn and brand
> His nothingness into man. (One. XVIII. iv., p. 1068)[42]

But Maud, star-like herself, made them warm and harmonious.

> And ye meanwhile far over moor and fell
> Beat to the noiseless music of the night!
> Has our whole earth gone nearer to the glow
> Of your soft splendours that you look so bright?
> *I* have climbed nearer out of lonely Hell.
> Beat, happy stars, timing with things below,
> Beat with my heart more blest than heart can tell.
> (One. XVIII. viii., p. 1070)

In Part Three they resume their function as guides and lead the narrator out of his lonely hell, shorn not only of pride—for he has been humbled by his salubrious madness—but of selfishness as well, for he now devotes himself to "a cause that I felt to be pure and true." (Three. VI. iii.)[43] The war is not merely a convenient means of acting out his aggressions, just as the family going to church in "The Two Voices" is not a sign of the narrator's desire to attend church services. The war is far more significant and is, while real in the fable of the poem, symbolic in the moral design. The narrator has liberated himself from himself and has waked "to the higher aims." (Three. VI. iv.) He escapes the madness of self-involvement, just as the narrators of "The Two Voices," "The Palace of Art," "Locksley Hall," and *In Memoriam* do. The narrator of *In Memoriam* finds his proper action in poetry, but the narrator of *Maud*, not being a poet, though a poetic and passionate soul, finds his adequate correlative for moral action in battle. He discovers that life is not hollow, but is filled with energy under the direction of his will, which in turn derives its strength from subordination to a higher purpose and a higher will. Like the other narrators, he has escaped the fetters of self, moved from darkness and death to light and life, through the agency of love, which has transformed his despairing madness into a vision of faith. Now he is at one with the divine plan.

> Let it flame or fade, and the war roll down like
> a wind,
> We have proved we have hearts in a cause, we are
> noble still,
> And myself have awaked, as it seems, to the
> better mind;
> It is better to fight for the good than to rail
> at the ill;
> I have felt with my native land, I am one with
> my kind,
> *I embrace the purpose of God, and the doom
> assigned.* (Three. VI. v., pp. 1092-93; italics mine)

It is as though Arthur had newly established himself in his realm, and, guided by that ideal, all of his previously warring senses worked together with one will. The civil war is ended; the narrator, having acquired a humbled and proportioned view, is finally ready to direct his concentrated energies outward. /

The design is once more completed. The passionate soul, revealed as usual first in its gloomy mood, strives to preserve that gloom and a hard heart; but the argument of hope melts the heart and lays it open to love's benevolence. The heart is thereby rendered vulnerable, or feeling, though the soul is not yet worthy of the grace love offers. Through pride, the narrator of *Maud* inadvertently abolishes his first human hope, but when the loved object is beyond possession, he realizes that his sin was in his selfishness. Having, on the brink of manumission, been cast back into the dungeon of his self, he emerges once more, purged of his selfish motives, capable of accepting a divine plan to which he can subordinate his will, thereby discovering a harmony and beauty in the world which remain forever hidden to the proud and self-captured.

The familiar incidents of romance in *Maud* are merely a framework, a parable employed to higher purpose: the presentation of a moral design with a message not bound to its author by personal allusions, nor to its age by military topicality, but addressed to a less confined audience, forever acute to the dialogue of two voices within itself, and forever cherishing the skillful figuration of a desired resolution whether in dialogue, elegy, or parable.

TWO

IDYLLS OF THE KING

The Design

Examinations of the *Idylls of the King* have been concerned, for the most part, with structural and technical features of the poem, or they have investigated the psychology of its characters where they have not tried to make of it a social programme. Consequently, I shall have little occasion for reference to secondary sources in my study of this poem. For me, the *Idylls* are thoroughly consistent with Tennyson's earlier great works. Hopefully, my method of reading the work, though by no means an attempt to replace other readings, will encourage a more sympathetic interpretation and credit Tennyson with greater skill than he has so far been allowed.[1]

It is quite clear that the *Idylls of the King* is, while a fine narrative poem, also an allegorical poem with a moral point. The allegory, well-explained in F. E. L. Priestley's article, "Tennyson's *Idylls*,"[2] is, in Tennyson's words, "the dream of man coming into practical life and ruined by one sin."[3] Beyond the narrative and the allegory, however, there is another important dimension in the *Idylls* that relates them intimately to the major drift of moral signification in Tennyson's poetry. Beyond the narrative and the allegory is the moral design of the poem; a de-

sign we have seen manifested in earlier poems to varying degrees, though always with the same purpose.

The design, in the *Idylls*, may be observed in the completed
poem, or in its emerging parts. It is implicit in the several parts
of the poem, though the separate idylls emphasize different features of the design. The fundamental moral figure involves, as
always, the conflict of faith and doubt in which pride struggles
with humility. Only through humility can the human soul attain
selflessness and love, and thereby acquire the conviction in faith
and a sense of hope that makes the constant flux of the natural
world endurable, comprehensible, and acceptable. This pattern
appeared in relatively simple terms in *In Memoriam* and other
earlier poems, but with the *Idylls* it is developed in greater detail. Besides revealing the significance of certain circumstances
in the poem, the design provides an authentic unity complement-
ing the narrative and allegorical structure of the poem.

The first of the idylls to be composed was "The Passing of
Arthur," originally "Morte d'Arthur," which was first published
in 1842; it later appeared, adapted to the larger scheme of the
Idylls, in the 1869 edition. The earlier version was evidently not
conceived in precisely the same terms as the *Idylls*. I intend, in
this chapter, to examine the idylls individually in chronological
order, before generalizing on the *Idylls* as a whole. The moral
design that emerges in the idylls composed in 1856 and after,
though not necessarily a fully conceived idea from the first, was
implicit in the poems because it was the pattern of Tennyson's
own belief.

Merlin and Vivien

"Merlin and Vivien," originally entitled "Nimue, or The
True and the False,"[4] was the first of the idylls that Tennyson
took up when he decided to return to his Arthurian material.[5]
Familiar materials of the design are already evident in this
idyll. The poem is essentially a seduction scene, and, to some

extent, resembles the dialogue of "The Two Voices," without the earlier poem's sunny conclusion.

At the outset Merlin's condition is perilous, for he is sunk in a melancholy state of mind, resulting from his vision of "A doom that ever poised itself to fall," a premonition of the last weird battle in the west that will leave "the high purpose broken by the worm." (p. 1601) In spite of his melancholy, Merlin, like the narrator of "The Two Voices," is capable of answering the various doubts that the voice of despair and doubt, in this instance embodied in Vivien, presents. It is clear that the danger is more complex than that faced by the narrator of "The Two Voices," for Merlin is at the stage in his doubt where he is about to lapse into self-indulgent ease and abdicate hierophantic authority in favor of selfish comfort, though he realizes what the consequences of such a submission will be. Indeed, it is Merlin's very self-consciousness that constitutes the greatest malady. Were his lapse of will a question of ignorance and circumstance, it would be more endurable. But Merlin, like many another figure in the *Idylls*, advances to his fall conscious of his own imaginative participation in it.

It is a sudden recognition of the need to pursue a more active and fuller life that saves the narrator of "The Two Voices," but it is just this desire to participate that is lacking in Merlin and ultimately leads to his collapse. The intense desire for participation in the cause of truth springs from a hope in its outcome, but Merlin's vision has made him doubt that outcome. Merlin is capable of countering Vivien's slanders and penetrating her flatteries; he is even proof against her fleshly wiles. Yet, in the end, his negative stand defeats him, and he yields out of weariness. The storm and the wild forest of Broceliande represent forces of undisciplined emotion. At the conclusion of the poem, the storm finally breaks, and then passes,

> its burst of passion spent,
> Moaning and calling out of other lands,
> Had left the ravaged woodland yet once more

To peace; and what should not have been had been,
For Merlin, overtalked and overworn,
Had yielded, told her all the charm, and slept. (p. 1620)

The final collapse is anticipated in Merlin's intellectual capitulation earlier. After he has witnessed Vivien's vileness and correctly interpreted her motive, he is yet unable to free himself from her,

> And the dark wood grew darker toward the storm
> In silence, while his anger slowly died
> Within him, till he let his wisdom go
> For ease of heart, and half believed her true. (p. 1618)

Merlin's infirm mood, the result of his melancholy, is suggested by his *half* disdaining, *half* believing Vivien, in being *half* indignant, and having his words *half* suffocated, as well as in his realization that fame is *half* disfame. He lacks singleness of mind and purpose, and, being troubled by a doubt, lapses into his idle and pernicious melancholy. Ironically, in his idle state, confronted by the gravest threat to his utility, Vivien, he constantly explains that what he most dreads is rather "the loss of use than fame." (p. 1609) It is as though he hopes to employ utterance, like some magical charm, to fulfil what he no longer can induce himself to accomplish through acts. There is, in this feeble reliance upon language, a disturbing analogy with Vivien's "charmed" tongue, for Vivien's characteristic "action" is slander. What irony that the grand magus who once raised a mystic city, now lamely mouths formulaic words that are at once excuse and escape. Moreover, the entire idyll is given over to language. Merlin tells Vivien she will not be able to read his charm, yet her language ultimately lulls him. Significantly enough, the charm consists of "woven paces" and "waving hands," but no words. (p. 1620) It is as though all of the words that Merlin and Vivien utter accumulate like a gigantic wave to climax not in a tremendous roar, but in a pantomime silence. As we shall see in the next chapter, the *Idylls* as a whole pre-

51

sents a weird contention between utterance and silence, breaking occasionally into acts of violence or governed purpose. In this idyll, Vivien may perhaps be seen as the intellect's loquacity pre-empting useful thought and action. By dwelling on trivial spec-ulations in a valueless dialogue, Merlin lays waste his powers, though that he would engage in the dialogue at all reveals that he is half in love with easeful abdication of control. Merlin knows that his proper sphere is in Camelot, where he may be of use. Like Tiresias, Merlin realizes the importance and moral opportunity of deeds, and unlike Ulysses, he does not feel com-pelled "To strive, to seek, to find, and not to yield," (p. 566) for the conclusive action of the poem is, characteristically enough, a yielding.

The desire for ease, whether intellectual or physical, is just as voluptuous and reprehensible as excessive or immoral sexual indulgence—the crime of Lancelot and Guinevere—for it is fun-damentally the same sin of selfish gratification; "The Lotos-Eaters" is an early indication of this attitude, notably in its re-vised form. Merlin shares this characteristic of inclining to ease with the narrator of *Maud*, a poem written not long before this idyll. Like the melancholy narrator of the monodrama, Merlin wishes to withdraw from the world, to escape the demands of active participation; but this withdrawal is itself the first step toward inevitable defeat. The narrator of *Maud* has a human object that acts redemptively upon him; but Merlin has only Vivien. In telling Vivien the tale of the hart with the golden horns, Merlin describes a superabundance of energetic desire to pursue the ideal and the good, a desire common enough in noble spirits at the inception of the Round Table, but in sharp contrast to the present moody indolence that possesses the wiz-ard. Then, the young knight, whom his companions "could not keep silent . . . flashed . . . into such a song" that all craved ac-tivity. (p. 1606) Now, repining Merlin's unmusical conversa-tion leads him further and further from redemptive action.

Though Merlin's withdrawal is the first step toward defeat, all withdrawal is not necessarily so. Confrontation with the self might require such isolation. This is made clear in other idylls, but within this idyll there is an example of useful isolation in the character of the old wizard in the tale of the king who wished to keep his queen to himself. The wizard, unlike Merlin, did not retreat from society in order to abandon action, but in order to intensify the one act that gave his life its purpose. He was

> A little glassy-headed hairless man,
> Who lived alone in a great wild on grass;
> Read but one book, and ever reading grew
> So grated down and filed away with thought,
> So lean his eyes were monstrous; while the skin
> Clung but to crate and basket, ribs and spine.
> And since *he kept his mind on one sole aim,*
> Nor ever touched fierce wine, nor tasted flesh
> Nor owned a sensual wish, to him the wall
> That sunders ghosts and shadow-casting men
> Became a crystal, and he saw them through it,
> And heard their voices talk behind the wall,
> And learnt their elemental secrets, powers
> And forces. (pp. 1611-12; italics mine)

Merlin cannot claim to be so liberated from the flesh. The very mood he wishes to break by fleeing Arthur's court pursues him, and Vivien, who *seemed* the very agent of his loss of use and name and fame, follows only to become the *real* agent of his loss of use and name and fame. But the senses would have no force against the intellect if the intellect were not itself partly inclined to yield. Could he, like the old wizard in the tale, keep his singleness of purpose, as Arthur must do, he would be proof against the temptations of uncontrolled emotions and the senses. But, in his growing lethargy, Merlin wavers, and Vivien, skillful in her craft, works upon his mood here just as, in the midst of the storm, though frightened, she did not forget "her practice in her fright, / But wrought upon his mood and hugged him close." (p. 1620) So in Merlin's divided mood, his mere half disdain—which mirrors the court's pretermission of Vivien's slander—Vivien sees the means to overcome him. For

> the old man,
> Though doubtful, felt the flattery, and at times
> Would flatter his own wish in age for love,
> And half believe her true: for thus at times
> He wavered; but that other clung to him,
> Fixt in her will, and so the seasons went. (p. 1601)

It is significant that Merlin's melancholy and his vision of doom follow immediately upon this description of his broken purpose. His vision is as much imputation of his private state as it is actual prophecy, for he participates in his own collapse. Vivien lacks the intellectual or seductive powers to overwhelm the wizard; the secret of her victory is provided by Merlin's metaphorical version of the case.

> But since you name yourself the summer fly,
> I well could wish a cobweb for the gnat,
> That settles beaten back, and beaten back
> Settles, till one could yield for weariness. (p. 1605)

The corruption of the intellect by sense comes about, not through its force, but through its persistence. The besieged intellect is undone by a traitorous will that longs for the peace that surrender will bring. Duped by his irenic fantasy, Merlin has lost the significance of the moral declaration with which Tennyson closed *In Memoriam*. It is the purpose of the human will to provide the guidance by which man learns self-control and thereby comes to faith, which is his defense against all temptation.

Like "The Two Voices," or *Maud*, "Merlin and Vivien" describes the importance of mood in the struggle against doubt and temptation. The narrators of the two earlier poems do not overcome doubt and despair through reasoned arguments, but through intuitional change of heart which enables them to find an emblematic representation of their newly recovered faith in the circumstantial world. Merlin finds no such objectification of faith, for he experiences no redemptive hope. He has failed in the very first step of the moral design, and by doing so, forecasts the inevitable failure of the intellect in combatting doubt independently. There is no shortage of evidence in Tennyson's poetry and private comment to indicate that Tennyson distrusted the intellect and placed his reliance upon intuition, nor was he alone in this attitude during the Victorian period.[6] Merlin, representing mind, is the type of intellect unsustained by hope and faith.[7] Without these aids, Merlin resembles the narrator of "The Two Voices" before his change of heart.

In the initial stage of the moral design, man is confronted with the choice between faith and doubt. Faith will come if man can humbly submit himself to the purpose of God and offer himself actively in the selfless service of his fellow man through love. Merlin, himself, is aware of the ultimate function of the champion of faith in his description of the uses of fame:

> but Fame with men,
> Being but ampler means to serve mankind,
> Should have small rest or pleasure in herself,
> But work as vassal to the larger love,
> That dwarfs the petty love of one to one. (p. 1608)

Merlin, however, can no longer put his fame to such use, for he is no longer capable of combatting doubt. In order to combat doubt, he must remain pure and vigorous, supported by singleness of purpose and undivided will. The model in *In Memoriam* was Hallam, who "fought his doubts and gathered strength," who, unwilling to yield and unwearied in the struggle, "faced the spectres of the mind / And laid them." (p. 948)

His purpose divided, his mood blackened, Merlin is easy prey to the temptations of the sense, to the lust for ease. All else he understands—the necessity of overcoming pride, the function of humility and love; but such knowledge is worthless without the corresponding energy and determination to combat doubt and the temptations of the flesh.

"Merlin and Vivien," as I have suggested, is a poem largely concerned with the psychology of mood. The mind itself is the slave of the emotions, for they govern the nature of its processes. But both should be vassals to an imagination glorified by a high ideal. Merlin, echoing *In Memoriam*, where doubt was to be made vassal to love, declares that fame should "work as vassal to the larger love." The question of mastery is central in this poem, for, in reality, it is the intellectual Merlin who is imprisoned by the emotionally volatile and irresponsible Vivien. But this constraint is half allowed by its victim because conviction is lost. Arthur needs Merlin, as spirit requires mind, but Merlin can no longer live in the Idea as though it were possible. With no indomitable intent, the mind eddies into backwaters of melancholy and sloth, and, entrapped in this unsavory condition, easily finds the whole world lost or tainted.

Tennyson had dwelt upon this theme as early as "Mariana" and as recently as *Maud*, but in "Merlin and Vivien" he made explicit what was implicit, though as important, in the earlier poems, especially *Maud*. Just as mood governed thought in the individual, in society self determined perception of others. Belief was precarious for those who interpreted existence through the senses. The more authentic mode of perception transcended the senses and proceeded from the more stable realm of ideas. All humanity is, to some extent, subject to this failing, but some fashion the world coarsely, some nobly. Nonetheless, all men are bound by the limitations of material existence to view the world through the modulations of their own natures. Though Merlin is not specifically indicative of this characteristic, Vivien and Arthur are. While Arthur "in the highest / Leavened the world, so Vivien in the lowest," (p. 1600) for Arthur, himself the highest, imputes his values to others, while Vivien, herself base, imputes baseness. Merlin sees this tendency in Arthur "Who wouldst against [his] own eye-witness fain / Have all men true and leal, all women pure." (p. 1616) He likewise sees the tendency in Vivien, and reflects upon it at length.

'And they, sweet soul, that most impute a crime
Are pronest to it, and impute themselves,
Wanting the mental range; or low desire
Not to feel lowest makes them level all;
Yea, they would pare the mountain to the plain,
To leave an equal baseness; and in this
Are harlots like the crowd that if they find
Some stain or blemish in a name of note,
Not grieving that their greatest are so small,
Inflate themselves with some insane delight,
And judge all nature from her feet of clay,
Without the will to lift their eyes, and see
Her godlike head crowned with spiritual fire,
And touching other worlds. I am weary of her.' (p. 1617)

This might stand as a warning even to those who merely attend to slander, and who suffer so grievously later in the *Idylls* for it. Such self-imputation as Merlin describes, whether noble or vile, has the tendency to confirm the self in its own character, for each enhanced or tainted perception reaffirms the mood that engendered it. Hence, Vivien, though hypocritical and slanderous, is herself intensely sensitive to slander, and Arthur, led by a noble ideal, idealizes himself in others.

What Merlin does not perceive is the relationship between his own mood and his spiritual weariness. If he would struggle against the horrible vision rather than retreat from it, he might not be obliged to enact privately what he has foreseen as a universal cataclysm. When the mind envisioned beauty, great cities rose to music and a magical authority irresistibly assumed command of his domain; but when that same mind's visions, following a faltering will, picture disaster, the spirit is entranced and the kingdom knows an irreplaceable vacancy. This is the experience described in "The Palace of Art."

In "Merlin and Vivien," Tennyson described the failure of the mind to make its first step in the progress of salvation, thereby endangering the salvation of the soul itself. Understanding the nature of moral demands, but yielding through weariness to the petty naggings of the flesh, imaginative intellect is lost to use and name and fame. Lacking determination, insight is valueless. The mind, unbuttressed by hope, makes an unsteady ally, too easily inclined to treason.

Geraint and Enid Idylls

If "Merlin and Vivien" described the collapse of the will in the struggle of faith against doubt and the temptation to retirement from the battle, the Geraint and Enid idylls, which were originally composed as one, illustrate the proper function of that withdrawal as a contest with the self. They elaborate, as well, the first stage of that struggle; the conquest of pride.

Geraint, hearing and supposing true the rumor about Lancelot and Guinevere's sin, selfishly determines to retire from the court in order that Enid, his own wife, shall not be tainted. He is inordinately sensitive of his own vanity and good name and at the same time unjustifiably doubtful of Enid, who, on the other hand, is the very model of humility and trust. In short, Geraint and Enid represent opposing forces in the conflict of faith and doubt, and Geraint's withdrawal, which begins as a selfish attempt to keep Enid true to himself, becomes the necessary descent into the wilderness of the soul to root out the poisonous plants that have begun to burgeon there.

Geraint is another of those figures in Tennyson, who, dreading the persistent assault of experience upon their cherished emotional "possessions," prefers an equally difficult retreat into a private domain to straightforward combat. Like the jealous king who seeks a charm to veil his beautiful queen and succeeds in disanimating her, or like the Soul in "The Palace of Art," discovering the futility of isolated beauty, Geraint, in his wilderness, will learn that not beauty, but the valuing eye, is morbid and false.

Unlike the weary Merlin, Geraint is young and powerful and capable of the ordeal. However, he is among those who, unable to conceive of the world objectively, interpret all life through the medium of their fears and their desires. And, somewhat in the manner of Sir Percivale in a later idyll, as soon as his faith is shaken, he finds himself in a wilderness, under constant assault by hostile forces.

Geraint, in spite of his self-imputation, is no male Vivien, for his failing proceeds not from malice and voluptuous pride, but from vanity, or pride of nature. That is, he remains manly even in his discourtesy and will not assume a hypocritical manner to gratify his desires, as Vivien so readily will do. Geraint's is an ignorant pride, and his random quest an authentic deed, which, while ostensibly a retreat, actually emerges as the most fundamental of all encounters, the confrontation with the self.[8]

To emphasize the nature of Geraint's action, Tennyson provides us with an earlier adventure wherein Geraint overcomes the obvious representative of simple pride, Edyrn. Edyrn, too, lacks the deviousness of a Vivien, and has been forthright in his crimes; furthermore, these crimes proceed from an untempered love of beauty and the desire to possess it, not from destructive envy or malice. When Geraint and Edyrn meet in combat, they struggle with equal force so long as Enid is the object of both men's desires, but when Geraint is reminded of the great insult done the Queen, his devotion to an ideal raises him above himself and he overthrows Edyrn with ease. There are no

complications to this conquest. An offensive and external representative of pride has been vanquished by a selfless act. Geraint's
power is largely attributable to his fidelity to Arthur's code.
As Tristram admits later, the vows were capable of making
men, for a time, greater than they were. This episode in Geraint's
career suggests how important the commitment to, and faith in,
the vows really is, for it is only through the vows that Geraint
triumphs. Having learned this much of the lesson, Geraint has
yet to learn that the values and beliefs represented in the vows
must be made a part of each individual's life. If they are not,
and remain simply an external code, as they do for Pelleas, the
individual has no internal voice to coax him to "Rejoice! Rejoice!" when that official code is made suspect. So unquestionable
is the source and quality of Geraint's might, that even the defeated Edyrn acknowledges it, remarking,

> 'my pride
> Is broken down, for Enid sees my fall!'
> And rising up, he rode to Arthur's court,
> And there the Queen forgave him easily.
> And being young, he changed and came to loathe
> His crime of traitor, slowly drew himself
> Bright from his old dark life, and fell at last
> In the great battle fighting for the King. (p. 1544)[9]

It was Enid who reminded Geraint of his duty to the Queen,
enabling him to overthrow Edyrn by fixing his concerns upon
high ideals. Hers is a voice of wisdom and humility, for when
Geraint first hears her, she is singing the song, " 'Turn, Fortune, turn thy wheel and lower the proud.' " (p. 1536) And
while Edyrn boasts, Enid, the image of humility and constancy,
"lay / Contemplating her own unworthiness." (p. 1542) Her
one fear, having accepted Geraint, is that she "shall discredit
him," by appearing in shoddy garments. (p. 1545) But Geraint
demands that she wear her oldest clothing, thereby testing her
obedience and finding her sound. Enid suppresses her desire to

appear in a beloved and lovely dress, demonstrating not only her lack of vanity, but her devotion to Geraint, as well. Geraint is greatly pleased by her manner and prematurely exclaims,

> 'then I felt
> That I could rest, a rock in ebbs and flows,
> Fixt on her faith. Now, therefore, I do rest,
> A prophet certain of my prophecy,
> That never shadow of mistrust can cross
> Between us.' (pp. 1549-50)

On Enid's part, this is true; but it is not long before Geraint violates his own prophecy.

The metaphor of clothing serves a greater role in the idyll than I shall explain in detail here, but it is worthwhile to observe that whereas Enid is constantly obliged to clothe herself in faded silks, our first view of Geraint is hardly a dim one.

> A purple scarf, at either end whereof
> There swung an apple of the purest gold,
> Swayed round about him, as he galloped up
> To join them, glancing like a dragon-fly
> In summer suit and silks of holiday. (p. 1531)

Though he is capable of conquering Edyrn, he is not himself free from vanity. In his encounter with Edyrn, Geraint is provided a glimpse of the truth that his antagonists will embody his own weaknesses. As with the narrator of *Maud*, other characters are as much phases of his own nature as they are figures in their own right, and Geraint's encounters with them embody a general struggle between pride and humility, a baser and a better self. Combatting Edyrn, it is Geraint's promise to the Queen that gives him aid. Subsequently, only powers personal to himself will supply his armory.

The function of the second part of the idyll, then, is to describe the means through which Geraint learns to command his own passions and subjugate his pride to a higher authority within him. Without sufficient cause, Geraint conceives a mistrust of Enid's fidelity. His imagination tainted by traducers of the Queen and Lancelot, he extends doubtful evidence to behavior that has never given him appropriate cause for suspicion. The inclination to attend to slander is a weakness. In "Merlin and Vivien," the principal failing of the court was its negligent indifference to Vivien's practices, despite its realization that she was a dangerous gossip. Later, it becomes clear that the strong individual, though he be forced to accept unsavory evidence as true, does not allow it to pervert or corrupt his own values. For those who are influenced by slanders, especially regarding the crime of Lancelot and the Queen, the false is taken for true; that is, the material representative and model of virtue, Queen Guinevere, is mistaken for the immaterial and spiritual reality —the abstract quality of fidelity and chastity. For Geraint, the material emblem of virtue proving doubtful, all flesh becomes suspect. Because he has failed to fix his attention on the abstract ideal, and has confused matter and spirit, he is unable to perceive clearly what would be evident to a less muddied, less earthly nature. His response is not reasoned, for his reason has been overshadowed by his feelings. Geraint, in his disillusionment, interrupts his own reflections, breaking "the sentence in his heart / Abruptly, as a man upon his tongue / May break it, *when his passion masters him.*" (p. 1552; italics mine)

It is important that there be two stages to Geraint's withdrawal. The first is to "his princedom," where he hopes to preserve his treasured wife from all worldly stain. But such self-concerned withdrawal proves unsatisfactory; not only do Geraint's people become aware of the change in him, Enid does as well.

> He compassed her with sweet observances
> And worship, never leaving her, and grew
> Forgetful of his promise to the King,

Forgetful of the falcon and the hunt,
Forgetful of the tilt and tournament,
Forgetful of his glory and his name,
Forgetful of his princedom and its cares.
And this forgetfulness was hateful to her. (pp. 1527-28)

In this stage of retirement, the self attempts to bury itself in itself and let the devil pipe to his own. Fortunately, Geraint is too manly and good yet to lapse into idle self-concern, and so, his doubt stronger yet, he undertakes the second stage of his withdrawal—the actual contest with himself.

Though Geraint may be foolish and mastered by his passions, Enid remains her humble, well-ordered self. She will not, however, fulfil the Griselda syndrome and be an unwisely patient, long-suffering, and passive wife. She disobeys Geraint in order to spare him. Selflessly ignoring possible retribution upon herself, she insists upon warning Geraint of the dangers surrounding him, even against his direct orders to be silent. Moreover, she acts as a model that Geraint might well imitate in her treatment of the horses she is given charge of, for these responsive animals "felt / Her low firm voice and tender government." (p. 1556) Geraint's behavior is egregiously lacking in tender government, yet Enid stops to attend her fallen lord, refusing to desert him in any adversity. It is she who exercises a subterraenean government upon Geraint. Her faithfulness is never questionable. It is clear that the wasteland into which she has been led by force is not her wasteland, but Geraint's, for it is he who requires governance within himself. It is he who must meet the agents of his disorder here in his wilderness and master them.

The bandits that Geraint first encounters are comparable to uncontrolled passions, but the two major antagonists in the wilderness are Limours and Doorm, both of whom represent facets of Geraint's character. Limours, "Femininely fair and dissolutely pale," is characterized by a "pliant courtliness." By outward evidence and his own admission, he is both "wild" and civil:

> I call mine own self wild,
> But keep a touch of sweet civility
> Here in the heart of waste and wilderness. (p. 1559)

Limours is, at once, a perversion of the courtesy that Arthur aims to foster, and a foretaste of what happens to courtliness in later idylls, when Gawains and Tristrams become more common than Gareths and Lancelots. What Limours calls civility is nothing more than an outward style graced with facile speech and easy manner. In fact, he too is vassal to his passions, and under his sweet civility behaves in the most devious manner, soliciting Geraint's wife while partaking of his hospitality, and planning his host's demise while enjoying his good will. Limours is, in short, the embodiment of all that is false in courtliness, and Geraint, aware of how false courtliness may be, wishes no further contact with it. "I know, God knows, too much of palaces!" (p. 1557) Nevertheless, he himself has misunderstood one function of true courtliness—reticence. In Limours, reticence is connivance; in Geraint, it is the easy avoidance of combat with what he fears most. Like Limours, he acts secretly, and is as unjust to Enid as Limours is dangerous to himself. Geraint only becomes more persistent in his severity toward Enid as he realizes his inability to confront his dread openly:

> he fain had spoken to her,
> And loosed in words of sudden fire the wrath
> And smouldered wrong that burnt him all within;
> But evermore *it seemed an easier thing*
> At once without remorse to strike her dead
> Than to cry 'Halt,' and to her own bright face
> Accuse her of the least immodesty. (p. 1554; italics mine.)

Geraint's unwise imitation of a courtly manner is mirrored in

Limours' false courtliness, and, when the wild Lord has attacked
Geraint "all in passion," and been unhorsed, Geraint's persistent underlying nobleness emerges in his refusal to strip the
fallen knight of his armor. Even so, the encounter with Limours has had its effect, and Geraint is wounded in the conflict.
His injury is entirely appropriate to the cause, for the unwisely
reticent Geraint, struck by the hypocritically secretive company
of Limours, acts out a small recapitulation of his own failing.

> But as a man to whom a dreadful loss
> Falls in a far land and he knows it not,
> But coming back he learns it, and the loss
> So pains him that he sickens nigh to death;
> So fared it with Geraint, who, being pricked
> In combat with the followers of Limours,
> *Bled underneath his armor secretly,*
> And so rode on, *nor told his gentle wife*
> *What ailed him, hardly knowing it himself,*
> Till his eye darkened and his helmet wagged;
> And at a sudden swerving of the road,
> Though happily down on a bank of grass,
> The prince, without a word, from his horse fell.
> (p. 1564; italics mine)

Now Geraint's uncommunicativeness has reacted against himself. As he would not confess his injured pride, he now does not
confess his physical hurt. His collapse is prelude to recovery.

Geraint's reticence is not consistent with his willingness to
listen to others and accept their delinquencies of speech. If
Merlin was undone by misguided conversation replacing necessary action, Geraint is imperilled by a confused regard for language. The essence of courtesy, not to mention love, is trust;
yet Geraint never opens his heart to the woman he has had most
ample cause for trusting. He does not attempt to redeem his
failure through language that meekly imitates a lost enchantment, but he wastes himself in dangerous audience. Like Merlin,

he does not test the doubts he so easily credits. Even the occasion for his expedition into the wasteland is an overhearing and a confusion of speech. The reticence of courtesy and the silence of cowardice have nothing but outward similarity. The adventure with Limours offers Geraint this knowledge. Geraint remains unable to deal with the ambiguities of phenomenal existence. He must discover the highest in himself and fix his faith upon that. Then the material world will assume meaning in terms of the spirit.

If Geraint had a mistaken concept of courtesy, he has another equally distressing fault in his obstinate pride, and this aspect of his character is embodied in Earl Doorm. Doorm and his company exist at the bestial and alimentary level of existence. Both qualities, though demonstrated elsewhere, combine when the Earl and his followers sit down to dinner.

> And none spake word, but all sat down at once,
> And ate with tumult in the naked hall,
> Feeding like horses when you hear them feed;
> Till Enid shrank far back into herself,
> To shun the wild ways of the lawless tribe. (p. 1567)

But Earl Doorm's outstanding quality, aside from his crude brutality, is his outrageous and proud assumption of total mastery, reminiscent of the Prince's father in *The Princess*, who could exclaim:

> Look you, Sir!
> Man is the hunter; woman is his game:
> The sleek and shining creatures of the chase,
> We hunt them for the beauty of their skins;
> They love us for it, and we ride them down. (p. 806)

Doorm is pleased by Enid's beauty and offers to marry her; an act which he considers an excess of benevolence. The burden of his manner he expresses, "For I compel all creatures to my will." (p. 1567) When Enid, remaining faithful to the fallen

66

Geraint, who by now is merely feigning death in order to test Enid to the uttermost, refuses Doorm's offer, he exclaims: "Amazed am I, / Beholding how ye butt against my wish." (p. 1568) When Enid persists in her refusal, Doorm, demonstrating a pronounced contrast to the falsely courteous Limours, abjures all courtesy and slaps Enid. Geraint, by now convinced of Enid's faithfulness, and fearing for her, leaps up and murders Doorm. In rising from his supposed death, he rises in fact from a spiritual death through which he has shed the qualities least consistent with his manhood. The Limours and Doorm in him are dead, his secret injury no longer troubles him, and he no longer doubts his Enid. "Henceforward I will rather die than doubt," he exclaims. (p. 1570) And he promptly leads Enid out of the wasteland into which she was forced to accompany him. He has taken what is dearest to him—his image of goodness—into his private wasteland, to undergo severe trial. That goodness emerging from these trials thoroughly vindicated, Geraint's spiritual restoration is assured. Like the narrator of *Maud*, he has transferred his image of goodness from without to within himself, though he, unlike that character, still has the reification of his spiritual values with him. He has achieved his proportion, and Enid is the signification of the mutuality lacking in his models, Arthur and Guinevere.

Appropriately enough, as they leave the wilderness, Geraint and Enid encounter the reformed Edyrn, now a trustworthy knight because he has overcome his pride and subordinated his passions to a grander and more elevated purpose than self-gratification. As Edyrn had been cast down by Geraint to rise purified, Geraint has been cast down and has risen in a similar manner. But whereas Geraint's combat with Edyrn was external, the struggle in the wilderness was the type of the necessary internal victory. This victory, on the other hand, has been made possible because Geraint has had a fixed object in the material world which serves as his guide. He has been able finally to distinguish her value from a generalized condemnation of womanhood. When Enid informs Geraint of Limours' intention to steal her from him, Geraint's response is " 'Your sweet faces make good fellows fools / And traitors.' " (p. 1561) He reveals in his use of the plural number that he is missing the point of the specific case before him. But after Doorm's death, and as soon as they are alone together, Geraint promptly addresses his wife by her name once more, promising to trust her without questioning, and clothing her once more with the identity he first knew in her. Her specific name implies a precise identity. Enid is love and service in a defined form, not all women. It is possible, Geraint now realizes, that the ideal may be false in one form, yet manifest itself truly in another. Enid is both woman and ideal, she is Princess Ida and Maud, but most important she is Geraint's image of love and goodness. She is the gentleness wedded to his manhood, and she represents his achieved humility. His vanity and doubt have been tested, and through his fall he has been liberated from his own moody projections. He is capable now of love and faith, and, what is more, useful action in the King's cause.[10]

Edyrn is a rare example of self-command and self-redemption, and, ironically enough, it is the very court from which Geraint fled in dread that has proved the model upon which Edyrn has reconstructed himself. Moreover, the qualities he has attained are the true form of those which Geraint has encountered in a debased and false form in the wilderness of his doubt.

> And all the penance the Queen laid upon me
> Was but to rest awhile within her court;
> Where first as sullen as a beast new-caged,
> And waiting to be treated like a wolf,
> Because I knew my deeds were known, I found,
> Instead of scornful pity or pure scorn,
> Such *fine reserve and noble reticence,*
> *Manners so kind, yet stately, such a grace*
> *Of tenderest courtesy,* that I began

> To glance behind me at my former life,
> And find that it had been the wolf's indeed:
> And oft I talked with Dubric, the high saint,
> Who, with mild heat of holy oratory,
> Subdued me somewhat to that gentleness,
> Which, when it weds with manhood, makes a man.
>
> > (p. 1573; italics mine)

Arthur, meanwhile, explains that it was Geraint's example that prompted him to set forth on an expedition of purification in his realm. Geraint's assault upon the chaotic world within himself, is, of course, identical to Edyrn's achievement, and is extended to the kingdom at large by Arthur's purpose.

> The world will not believe a man repents:
> And this wise world of ours is mainly right.
> Full seldom doth a man repent, or use
> Both grace and will to pick the vicious quitch
> Of blood and custom wholly out of him,
> And make all clean, and plant himself afresh.
> Edyrn has done it, weeding all his heart
> As I will weed this land before I go. (p. 1574)

And Arthur goes on to do exactly as he plans, establishing a proper authority throughout the land. Geraint, now having achieved self-control, can return to his own land and keep the justice of the King. Though he may still doubt the Queen, he has learned that it is in the individual soul that the seeds of hope or disaster lie. He has overcome the dangers of slander and learned to found his faith upon the bedrock of his own soul and its images of the high ideals; consequently, in his realm "the spiteful whisper died," and his people "called him the great Prince and man of men." (p. 1575)

Guinevere

The "Guinevere" idyll, which was next in order of composition, may justifiably be viewed as the central idyll in terms of the moral design with which I am concerned, and this may help to explain the particular fondness Tennyson and his auditors felt for it. The poem opens with another instance of withdrawal; like Merlin and Geraint, Guinevere flees from a threatening environment. Nor is it the last case of such a withdrawal. Later, Lancelot will find such retreat expedient, and, in "The Holy Grail," retreat becomes a major theme. But Guinevere's withdrawal is occasioned by fear, and she is inadvertently led to self-knowledge. Under any circumstances, retreat becomes a challenge, for, if you cannot face an external antagonist, you must face the internal combatant; retreat may be cowardice or an aspect of humility and a means to grace. For the Queen, it is an opportunity for salvation.

Guinevere's external antagonist, the antagonist of Arthur's entire order, is Modred, described here as a beast, a caterpillar, a worm, and a little bitter pool. (pp. 1725-26) Modred is evil with no qualifications and is insanely proud. Like Arthur, who represents ultimate human good, Modred remains a more or less shadowy figure in order that his evil qualities may remain vague and largely unassigned. It is enough to know that his ambition is to overthrow Arthur and assume his place. Modred is the enemy of Guinevere, Arthur, and Lancelot; yet it is through Guinevere and Lancelot that he finds his opportunity to strike at Arthur, for it is when Arthur leaves to war with Lancelot that Modred usurps the kingdom. In short, the inclinations to evil in man's nature require some conscious participation (as of the will or the senses) before they achieve any degree of mastery.

In a beautifully emblematic scene reminiscent of Milton's *Paradise Lost*, Tennyson describes the relationship of good, evil, and fallen virtue. Modred has climbed onto the garden wall

> To spy some secret scandal if he might,
> And saw the Queen who sat betwixt her best
> Enid, and lissome Vivien, of her court

70

The wiliest and the worst; and more than this
He saw not, for Sir Lancelot passing by
Spied where he couched, and as the gardener's hand
Picks from the colewort a green caterpillar,
So from the high wall and the flowering grove
Of grasses Lancelot plucked him by the heel,
And cast him as a worm upon the way;
But when he knew the Prince though marred with dust,
He, reverencing king's blood in a bad man,
Made such excuses as he might, and these
Full knightly without scorn. (p. 1726)

This is the apparently Edenic garden that—to employ Arthur's image from the previously composed idyll, "Geraint and Enid" —must be kept weeded just as the realm must be kept clean and the individual man must "pick the vicious quitch / Of blood and custom wholly out of him." (p. 1574) The gardening image does not end there, but appears occasionally throughout the poem. In this scene, it is Lancelot, most conscientious of Arthur's company in rooting out evil, who plucks the "worm" from the garden wall. The ostensible Eden is not so pure as it seems, however, nor is the knightly defender untainted. Nonetheless, that we may understand and excuse Guinevere to some extent, and that we may be prepared for her repentance, Tennyson has placed her in a pictorial tableau resembling a medieval illustration. Guinevere sits between Enid, "her best," and Vivien, "the wiliest and the worst." It is as though a good and a bad angel are contending for her soul. All that is fine in Guinevere inclines toward Enid, but her lubricity and pride attract her equally toward Vivien. Guinevere is not a faithful Enid, but she is likewise no false Vivien. Her virtues and her sin keep her precariously suspended in a threatened Eden. Meanwhile, the "worm" greedily awaits the outcome when this tableau is unsettled and forced into action.

Of her sin Guinevere has become amply conscious; she has sensations of foreboding and experiences a prophetic dream which indicates the extensive consequences of her failing. (p. 1727) When the sin is finally uncloaked and Guinvere and Lancelot are forced to part, Guinevere responds to Lancelot's offer of sanctuary by crying, "Would God that thou couldst hide me from myself!" (p. 1728) This is the signal that her sin is ended; there remains now the confrontation with the self, and sequestration in the convent represents that confrontation. The little maid that Guinevere encounters at the convent, "Who pleased her with a babbling heedlessness / Which often lured her from herself," (p. 1729) in fact becomes the agent most effectively revealing herself to herself. She is another Ambrosius, eliciting even those responses that her companion would rather not express. Even in her song, "Late, so late!" which mirrors Guinevere's spiritual despair, the little maid serves as an articulate conscience. (p. 1729) As with Enid, whose songs and appearance are a reproach to Geraint's bad conduct, the maid indicates that, because men are self-conscious of their sins, they will always find reproachful emblems of conscience around them. It is worthwhile observing that there are no notable examples of heedless sinning in the *Idylls*.

When Arthur appears, Guinevere throws herself grovelling on the floor before him and hides her face. Arthur's address to her is restrained and summarizes both his aspiration and her part in defeating his purpose. A bard had once proposed that could Arthur find "A woman in her womanhood as great / As he was in his manhood, then, he sang, / The twain together well might change the world." (p. 1732) But Guinevere has not proved worthy. She has not been Princess Ida to her Prince. What is more, she has jeopardized and finally corrupted one of Arthur's most worthy ideals—pure love as a means to noble acts. One of Arthur's vows was a declaration of fidelity to one pure love

for indeed [he] knew
Of no more subtle master under heaven

Than is the maiden passion for a maid,
Not only to keep down the base in man,
But teach high thought, and amiable words
And courtliness, and the desire of fame,
And love of truth, and all that makes a man. (p. 1737)

The same ideal is expressed in other poems of Tennyson's, for example, "The Gardener's Daughter," *Maud*, and *The Princess*, but even within the *Idylls*, we see salvation worked out through the agency of a pure human love. Enid is the principal example; she forcibly obliges Geraint to love her only by manifoldly demonstrating her worth; and Gareth, in his innocence, assumes a maiden love which quite literally leads him to noble acts. There are, however, instances in which this maiden love fails; perhaps because the object of love is false, like Ettarre. And when it fails, as it almost does with Geraint—but for Enid's strength and goodness—its failure is either wholly or partially attributable to Guinevere's sin. In short, her sin is not so much a sin against Arthur as it is a subversion of his morality, and Arthur, attempting to make this clear, declares that though he personally loves Guinevere yet and might hope to be rejoined with her in heaven, he cannot accept her again as his Queen. This is no failure of love on Arthur's part, but an acknowledgment of a moral necessity. Forgiveness he can offer, but he cannot expunge the effect of her sin upon his community, and should it be re-established, it must be done without Guinevere. Arthur leaves, having forgiven Guinevere and provided her with his blessing.

Of course, just as Enid was not simply a pure young lady, Guinevere is not only a tainted Queen. She is material beauty through which Arthur's idea was to have found its highest execution. Just as the soul, being firm within itself, must maintain its faith despite the failure of its incarnate forms, so Arthur's faith is not unseated by the liabilities of his Queen. She is still the highest earthly beauty, but having proved a poison to moral excellence, she must be dismissed. There is a sad but hopeful irony also in Arthur's "waving of his hands" to bless Guinevere, for this blessing, in a sense, cancels Vivien's charm of "woven paces and of waving hands" that trapped Merlin in himself. Now Guinevere, immured in a convent, can break free from the confinement of her own self-absorbed sin. As she directs her interests and energies outward, she will achieve the liberating sense and power that Merlin abdicated.

Once Arthur is gone, transformed now in Guinevere's imagination from a cold, prudish husband, to a feeling and noble man and lord, revelation batters her painfully. Her reluctant recognition of wrongdoing now checks itself no more and breaks forth like "a stream . . . spouting from a cliff." (p. 1740) Just as the narrator of *Maud* can only properly evaluate Maud when she is beyond possession and prescinded out of the flesh into the spiritual realm, so Guinevere can only correctly estimate Arthur's worth when she realizes she can never have him near her again. Guinevere's first reaction is to consider her own shame and the inevitable scandal forever to be associated with her name, and, in so doing, she relapses for a time into the state of mind that she exhibited at the opening of the idyll. Finally, putting considerations of herself aside, she dismisses the vanity of reputation: "I must not dwell on that defeat of fame. / Let the world be; that is but of the world." (p. 1740) Instead, she begins to speculate upon the hope that Arthur has offered for redemption and reunion in eternity. Her mind turns from the earthly Eden that proved so baleful for her to the spiritual city in which she may be united once more with her true lord.

> And blessèd be the King, who hath forgiven
> My wickedness to him, and left me hope
> That in mine own heart I can live down sin
> And be his mate hereafter in the heavens
> Before high God. (p. 1740)

Having expressed her fervent desire that this hope may have substance, she proceeds to acknowledge Arthur's true nature and the quality of her sin, for Arthur was as "the conscience of a saint / Among his warring senses," and she, through her "false voluptuous pride, that took / Full easily all impressions from below," but failed to take impressions from above, failed him in his need of her. (p. 1740) Her pride was treason to his love, for in yielding to voluptuous pride, she became a fifth column from the warring senses, an instrument that was ultimately to deliver the valued fortress to an enemy who would lay waste the entire realm.

It is too late for retribution, but not for redemption. Guinevere now sees the extent to which she might have served as Arthur's partner in virtue and good action.

> "Ah my God,
> What might I not have made of thy fair world,
> Had I but loved thy highest creature here?
> It was my duty to have loved the highest:
> It surely was my profit had I known:
> It would have been my pleasure had I seen.
> We needs must love the highest when we see it,
> Not Lancelot, nor another." (p. 1741)

Two of Tennyson's later poems express the mood of Guinevere's trial in a direct and traditional manner. In "Doubt and Prayer," the poet says that sin, when smitten, may simply rail and pine; however, it is possible "From sin thro sorrow" to pass to God. He asks that his reason not fail him before he has learned "that Love, which is, and was / My Father, and my Brother, and my God!" He pleads to God, "Steel me with patience! soften me with grief." In the second poem, "Faith," the tone is consolatory and reassuring.

> Doubt no longer that the Highest is
> the wisest and the best,
> Let not all that saddens Nature blight
> thy hope or break thy rest. (p. 1455)

Guinevere may now pursue her redemption steeled by patience

and softened by grief; having experienced humility, she will not rail or pine, nor longer doubt the Highest, though she may not see it face to face until she joins with it in heaven. Instead, she gives herself to charity and love. A further passage might have served not only as a warning to Guinevere, but to all those waning spirits in the later days of Arthur's reign.

> Neither mourn if human creeds be lower
> than the heart's desire!
> Through the gates that bar the distance
> comes a gleam of what is higher. (p. 1455)

Guinevere's was no intellectual pride, like that of the narrator of "The Two Voices," or "Confessions of a Second-Rate Sensitive Mind;" hers is a voluptuous pride that wilfully overlooked its principal duty and thereby doomed itself. Just as intellectual pride can harden the heart and shut out, through mere vanity, the hope that reasoning despair denies; so the voluptous heart can shade itself against pure light, while it inclines to the ruddier colors more idly appreciated and enjoyed. Guinevere's duty was something more than merely to love Arthur; it was to labor with him for the good of this "fair world." But voluptuousness solicits ease and readily ignores those duties which demand exertion. Far easier to imagine the castle garden as an Eden where some remote yet familiar Lord provides all necessities and luxuries as well. But what vanity to suppose that we should inhabit such a paradise through no labor but that of singular beauty. Reward in the realm of the spirit comes not for what we are, but for what we do. Tennyson's moral activism would have scorned the claims of beauty for its own sake, as his prefatory poem to "The Palace of Art" explicitly shows.

Guinevere's pride hardened her heart against her rightful Lord. She did not believe in him, nor in her proper office. Her concerns were for herself. But when her pleasures are threatened and she admits the necessity to remove herself from the source of her temptation, a temptation that is already tainted more by selfishness than satiation, the struggle for redemption has begun. Guinevere flees to the convent to protect herself; she remains to aid others. She comes to the convent in transports of selfish fear and suspicion; she remains humbly to serve others. The symbolic moment of redemption is the moment when she humbles herself before her proper Lord and throws herself at Arthur's feet. It is her acknowledgment of her sin and her liberation from the concerns of self. Nowhere else in the *Idylls* is the symbolic movement from pride to humility more clearly presented. The tableau having started into action, Guinevere swings toward all that Enid represents, and the slanders of Vivien are reduced to the innocent queries of the little novice in the convent. The still small voice at Guinevere's ear is gradually transformed to one that says "Rejoice! Rejoice!" and hope sanctifies her world once more.

Since Arthur is lost to her forever, Guinevere has no selfish reason for maintaining her masquerade of virtue, and her subsequent behavior—the tending of the poor and the infirm, the subordination of herself to the regimen of the convent—is a manifestation of her authentic recovery. Furthermore, Tennyson goes so far in this poem as clearly to imply that Guinevere recovered her spiritual inheritance in heaven.

In this idyll, then, the withdrawal from the external campaign occasions the most intense private struggle, for pride is faced with the very embodiment of love and duty; the consequent humility and selflessness sternly prove the value of a qualified participation in life. Guinevere never returns to the great world; she no longer feels the attraction of that world. Her only concern with this world is to tend its suffering inhabitants; her own aspirations are directed "To where beyond these voices there is peace." (p. 1742)

Lancelot and Elaine

The next idyll that Tennyson composed was "Lancelot and Elaine," (in the *Memoir*, variously referred to, in its early form, as "The Fair Maid of Astolat," "The Lily Maid," "The Maid of Astolat," and "Elaine") which was written during 1858 and published in 1859. Aside from the action, which centers upon the diamond jousts, the primary concern of the poem is in the contrast between Guinevere and Elaine, and the effect of that contrast upon Lancelot. In the "Guinevere" idyll, Tennyson had already indicated that the Queen's sin was in her "voluptuous pride," and wilful indifference to Arthur's excellence. In "Merlin and Vivien" he had shown the pernicious effect of slander, and he had suggested, in the Geraint and Enid idylls, that that effect can be counteracted by a moral assurance within the self. Slanderous talk about the Queen need not make the whole world false. All of our strength should not derive from others; they are but models upon which we form ourselves. If the substantial model prove false, the ideal is not necessarily so. In this idyll, it is that model, once so contemptuous of rumor, who now reveals the weakness of pride that makes acceptance of rumor not only easy, but congenial to her most self-destructive passions.

Near the beginning of the idyll, when Guinevere says she is not well enough to attend the jousts, Lancelot, thinking to please her, also claims indisposition and plans to stay at home with the Queen. He is surprised by her response:

> 'To blame, my lord Sir Lancelot, much to blame!
> Why go ye not to these fair jousts? the knights
> Are half of them our enemies, and the crowd
> Will murmur, "Lo the shameless ones, who take
> Their pastime now the trustful King is gone!" '
> Then Lancelot vext at having lied in vain:
> 'Are ye so wise? ye were not once so wise,
> My Queen, that summer, when ye loved me first.
> Then of the crowd ye took no more account
> Than of the myriad cricket of the mead,
> When its own voice clings to each blade of grass,
> And every voice is nothing. As to knights,
> Them surely can I silence with all ease.' (p. 1624)

78

Later, when Arthur informs Guinevere of Lancelot's identity as the mysterious knight at the jousts, and declares also that he wore a maiden's favor, she withdraws to her own room to rage against the 'Traitor,' "Then flashed into wild tears, and rose again, / And moved about her palace, proud and pale." (p. 1638) It is Guinevere's pride that is offended; but more important yet is the rapidity with which she concludes that Lancelot has been false. All of Lancelot's prior behavior makes betrayal unthinkable, yet Guinevere's suspicious imagination willingly accepts what is largely its own creation. Just as substantial appearances usurp the true immaterial reality of spiritual things, so, ironically, insubstantial rumors and irresponsible language assume more apparent reality than deeds. Set against the vows, which are verbal formulas for deeds, and which become real only through enactment, are rumors, which assume reality by depriving deeds of their virtue. Language, never sufficient to create belief, has now been transformed from anthem to insult. In belief, harmonious song breaks from the heart, as with the young knight in Merlin's tale of the hart with the golden horns; but, in doubt, the mind involuntarily accepts the cacophonous wooings of innuendo. A false courtliness, characterized by irresponsible converse, replaces a reticent courtesy.[11]

So sensitive to rumors about herself, knowing her own falseness to Arthur, Guinevere now readily believes the rumors about Lancelot and suffers from the open acknowledgment of them in court, being obliged all the while to crush out "the wild passion" that others may not observe her agony. These wild passions hint at the transformation that is in process within Guinevere. Virtue is not, for her, mere pretense. Even Ettarre, after all, is touched by the example of innocence. Guinevere is still drawn as much to Enid as to Vivien, but at this stage of her career she has begun to feel the discomfort of her suspended state.

When Lancelot, recovered from his injury, returns to court, he speaks to Guinevere immediately regarding the false rumors.

'Our bond, as not the bond of man and wife,
Should have in it an absoluter trust
To make up that defect: let rumors be:
When did not rumours fly? these, as I trust
That you trust me in your own nobleness,
I may not well believe that you believe.' (p. 1653)

Of course, Guinevere does believe them, and breaks into a pas-
sionately jealous denunciation of Lancelot's behavior, announcing at the same time her belief in Arthur's superiority, and parad-
ing her own value in stipulating the sacrifice that she has made
for her unworthy lover. But if it was a sacrifice—and her later admission of voluptuous pride suggests that it was no such thing
—that sacrifice is surely obscured by the valuation she places
upon it, in that it derives its excellence from the comparison
with the supposedly faithless Lancelot. It is necessary, in short,
to insult the beloved in order to exalt the lover. In a fit of spite,
Guinevere throws the gift of the diamonds out the window,
and at this climactic moment in Guinevere's ugly passion, the
barge bearing the dead Elaine appears. More than diamonds
has been lost forever.

Lancelot, counting on Guinevere's trust, has been disappointed. There has been an earlier hint of the direction in which
Lancelot should properly have offered his trust when Arthur,
upset by Lancelot's unconfided disguise, says to Guinevere:

'Far lovelier in our Lancelot had it been,
In lieu of idly dallying with the truth,
To have trusted me as he hath trusted thee.' (p. 1637)

Far lovelier, perhaps; certainly far wiser, since his trust in
Guinevere ultimately proves to have been misplaced. The King
is not vain, nor is he falsely proud. Guinevere is both, and pas-
sionately so. Material beauty is fickle in a way that ideal values
cannot be. The wise man may worship and admire the former,
but his trust should rest always with the other.

"Lancelot and Elaine" is about misplaced trust and misplaced love. Imprisoned as much by the code he respects as by his love for the Queen, Lancelot cannot escape the constraint of his attachment, though it now shows signs of failing. There is room too for speculation upon why he comes to Astolat, for it is when he takes the "green path that showed the rarer foot . . . among the solitary downs," that he finds it, and we are told that he travelled in a forgetful manner, and "Full often lost in fancy, lost his way." (p. 1625) That his fancy should lead him to Astolat and the pure Elaine might suggest something about the nature of his fancies. Just as Elaine is to live in fantasies about the mysterious and wonderful knight who has left her his shield to guard, Lancelot might have been musing upon a dream that he had had another time (though it appeared in an idyll as yet unwritten). In the last of the idylls that Tennyson composed, Lancelot, walking among the flowers in Guinevere's garden, describes his dream.

> 'Last night methought I saw
> That maiden Saint who stands with lily in hand
> In yonder shrine. All round her prest the dark,
> And all the light upon her silver face
> Flowed from the spiritual lily that she held.
> Lo! these her emblems drew mine eyes—away:
> For see, how perfect-pure! As light a flush
> As hardly tints the blossom of the quince
> Would mar their charm of stainless maidenhood.' (p. 1583)

Guinevere responds to this account by stating her preference for the rose, "Deep-hued and many-folded," or the "wild-wood hyacinth." (p. 1583) What Lancelot craves is purity, and Elaine is that; his true fancies draw him toward an ideal he will neither recognize nor accept when he finds it. Just as Guinevere saw the highest and failed to love it, Lancelot now is shown the purest, and fails to accept it, although it makes itself fully available to him.

Lancelot himself is still an admirable man, and his inclination to purity is part of that admirability. He has true courtesy, and, when asked by the Lord of Astolat to spare Elaine by being discourteous to her, the most he can manage is to leave without saying goodbye. Discourtesy simply isn't in him. Moreover, he is humble and does not exploit his greatness. For him, the family at Astolat is as valuable as the court.

> Then the great knight, the darling of the court,
> Loved of the loveliest, into that rude hall
> Stept with all grace, and not with half disdain
> Hid under grace, as in a smaller time,
> But kindly man moving among his kind:
> Whom they with meats and vintage of their best
> And talk and minstrel melody entertained. (p. 1628)

He can be mirthful, "but in a stately kind," and is neither proud nor priggish. Furthermore, his admiration for Arthur has not abated; he still recognizes excellence, and, but for his one flagitious sin, strives to emulate it. It is much otherwise when Gawain, the representative of a declining order, appears at Astolat. He is disdainful of the people he finds there and is attracted to Elaine only because of her "wild flower" beauty. His is a "Courtesy with a touch of traitor in it;" (p. 1639) it is a courtesy of manner, not meaning. He is courtly after the fashion of the courtier who, in bringing the news of Lancelot's return to the Queen, sees through the Queen's cold manner to the quivering passion that really moves her, and departs "laughing in his courtly heart." (p. 1653)

Gawain has reluctantly accepted the quest to find the wounded Lancelot, and he gives it up easily, having delivered the diamond to Elaine. Furthermore, while he himself is unsteady in love and takes Arthur's rules rather lightly, he facilely assumes the same of others, and, although he thinks it unlikely that Lancelot's affections have altered, he considers it possible. "Must our true

82

man change like a leaf at last? / Nay—like enow." (p. 1640)
Arthur is fully aware of the threat revealed in Gawain's behavior. When that knight returns, having carelessly and incom-
pletely performed his task, Arthur expresses his disappointment.

> The seldom-frowning King frowned, and replied,
> 'Too courteous truly! ye shall go no more
> On quest of mine, seeing that ye forget
> Obedience is the courtesy due to kings.' (p. 1641)

Of course, Lancelot too is guilty of disobedience to the King;
yet, in this, as in other ways, Lancelot is the admirable half of
the parallel with Gawain. Gawain, intent upon pleasing himself, rarely considers the effect of his pleasures upon others. He
is not an evil figure like Mark or Vivien, he is simply the thoughtless form of what can only be maintained through careful
thought and constant examination. Lancelot has sinned more
seriously than Gawain, but he has not forgotten his duty to the
King, and his agony of awareness, though it has not cleansed
him, has kept him noble. In this idyll, Lancelot is characterized
by a conversational reticence but a private eloquence of the
heart. His discourse is mainly with himself. Gawain, on the contrary, escapes as quickly as he can from intimations of reflection.
Appropriately enough, he is not much wounded by the King's
correction and hurries off to spread the rumor about Lancelot and
Elaine.

Though Lancelot is still an excellent man, he has been affected
by his sin, and more by his knowledge of that sin.

> The great and guilty love he bare the Queen,
> In battle with the love he bare his lord,
> Had marred his face, and marked it ere his time.
> Another sinning on such heights with one,
> The flower of all the west and all the world,
> Had been the sleeker for it: but in him
> His mood was often like a fiend, and rose

83

And drove him into wastes and solitudes
For agony, who was yet a living soul. (p. 1628)

Lancelot is more typically human, according to Tennyson's usual terms, than any other knight in the poem, for, when confronted with sin, he struggles with it. The very fact that he suffers intensely from his sin is more than the simple Victorian convention of having illicit lovers exist in constant misery. His suffering is an indication of his alert conscience that will not be lulled by verbal enchantments, and yet must strive unendingly against the demons in its own wasteland. Had Merlin possessed this endurance, he might not have failed in his melancholy mood. The narrators of "The Two Voices" and "Locksley Hall" found the metaphor of battle suitable for describing their states of conflict with doubt and evil; the narrator of *Maud*, having settled his internal war, found salvation in an external combat against more than personal enemies. Lancelot, a noble but sinning man, maintains a constant warfare within himself against a mood which is "like a fiend." But the fiend is never triumphant; whereas in "Balin and Balan," moods are no longer *like* fiends, but become fiends in fact which destroy the spirit.

There is a melancholy parallel between Lancelot's disguise and Gareth's. Lancelot's supposedly manifests a certain humility and a reasonable desire for glory, but is a necessary deception to mask his sin. Gareth's is a genuine act of humility, and it leads to virtue. There is, however, a further resemblance, for Lancelot's deception indirectly leads him back to virtue's footpath. Through the disguise, he encounters Elaine, an example of goodness, fidelity, and purity, who values him, not for his reputation as a great warrior, but for his qualities as a good man. At the tournament, the ironic corollary of this acceptance is in his knightly rejection. His power, usually the source of affection in others, now becomes the cause of his very kinsmen's anger, and they turn upon him. It is a foretaste of the internecine combats yet to come and is an outward expression of the combat within Lancelot. The motif of the crown is utilized in a similar manner.

Two brothers battled one another to possess the crown, and in the struggle for mastery both were destroyed. Now, through this same crown, flesh and spirit contend once more, and so do Guinevere and Elaine. Again, both warring factions lose, for Guinevere's love is seriously compromised and Elaine's is removed from the earth. Soon Lancelot and Arthur, in their war, will reenact the theme.

Lancelot's kinsmen fell him with brute power, hinting the quality of his nature which has so far undermined him. Arthur has tried to combine, in his vows, two sets of codes—the knightly and the moral. Chivalry, the active form of courtesy, demands virtues of the flesh, but morality demands virtues of the soul. Until now, Lancelot, by means of his assured identity and recorganized position as mightiest in strength and virtue, has remained unvanquished. But, having masked that identity, his nature reveals its terrible division, and he is abruptly overthrown. His apparent rôle was the real mask, the assumed identity the more accurate. His fall becomes symbolic of the genuine act of humbling that he requires. Similarly, the narrator of *Maud* must undergo the humbling process in his madness before he returns, alert once more to a spiritual reality beyond man's capacity for possession and valuable only as an ideal.

The next step in Lancelot's moral exercise is the withdrawal from the world occasioned by his salubrious illness. Like Pip's redemptive illness in *Great Expectations*, where an unquestionable representative of authentic love attends him, Lancelot's necessary illness revives for him the values that he once honored. He, too, is tended by a genuine representative of love. Lancelot is still a good man, and Elaine embodies his goodness. She is his unacknowledged ideal, despite his acknowledged passion. In more senses than one she sustains his life, for, without what she represents, he would lose not only his body, but his soul as well.

> And never woman yet, since man's first fall,
> Did kindlier unto man, but her deep love

Upbore her; till the hermit, skilled in all
The simples and the science of that time,
Told him that her fine care had saved his life.
And the sick man forgot her simple blush,
Would call her friend and sister, sweet Elaine,
Would listen for her coming and regret
Her parting step, and held her tenderly,
And loved her with all love except the love
Of man and woman when they love their best,
Closest and sweetest, and had died the death
In any knightly fashion for her sake.
And peradventure had he seen her first
She might have made this and that other world
Another world for the sick man; but now
The shackles of an old love straitened him,
His honour rooted in dishonour stood,
And faith unfaithful kept him falsely true. (pp. 1644-45)

It is the code of courtesy to which Lancelot remains committed, simply because it is this code to which he has first so deeply
engaged himself. He would die the death "In any knightly
fashion," for Elaine, but he will not love her and take her unto
himself. But it is insufficient to be knightly with an ideal; a
man must make it a part of himself. Lancelot's behavior with
Elaine repeats the pattern of his life. He would die the death
in any knightly fashion for Arthur's ideal, too, though he has
failed to make it a part of himself, as his violation of trust
signifies. He is the good man believing in the good, and defending the good, but unable to enact the ideal which remains
a concept at a distance and not a reality in his blood. His case
directly opposes Arthur's, for Arthur has never faltered in his
adherence to the ideal, and has certainly made it a part of himself. His predicament is to make the ideal real and impart it to
the flesh. The one possesses the ideal, but loses the fidelity of
the flesh; the other has the doubtful fealty of the flesh, but remains estranged from the ideal. Were Arthur to suspect Guinevere, the ideal might have collapsed before it could begin; but

86

his faith was firm. Were Arthur not firm, Lancelot would have fallen. Model and fallible performer of that model's highest purpose require one another, yet ultimately, the division made clear, they too must do battle.

Arthur, when fully acquainted with the history of Elaine's love for Lancelot, wishes that it might have been possible for Lancelot to love her because she seemed shaped by God for him alone. This was the intended plan: that Arthur should have his faithful Guinevere, the spiritually excellent wed to worldly beauty; and that Lancelot should have his Elaine, the physically excellent wed to ideal purity. Significantly enough, whereas the guilty Guinevere quickly accepts the rumors about Lancelot, Elaine refuses to doubt him even against the testimony of her family. It is also interesting that Lancelot, who wonders at the Queen's sensitivity to rumors, is especially tender in regard to Elaine's reputation. The court may not yet have lapsed so far as "Mark's way," but it behaves in Vivien's manner. The court seems crowded with sniggering knights and ladies delighting to find their own failings justified through the transgressions of peers and superiors. But Elaine, like Lancelot, remains resistant to this most insidious of enemies. Lancelot is never mean; even to his sin he is faithful. His reticence is the true courtesy, but it is almost the last example. And, as the purity of the court dies away in the murmur of traducing voices, Elaine is shepherded from the world by two of the last assuredly unsoiled knights.

As with the narrator of *Maud*, Lancelot is made acutely aware of Elaine's real significance only when she is removed from the physical realm—when she is beyond possession and taint. As an ideal and spiritual recollection, she becomes a more successful guide. Lancelot can now say of Elaine

> 'Ah simple heart and sweet,
> Ye loved me, damsel, surely with a love
> Far tenderer than my Queen's.' (p. 1659)

87

He declares, moreover, that Guinevere's jealousy in love looks far more like "jealous pride." Her fear of slander suggests to him more a love of self than a love of Lancelot. Lancelot now feels a genuine remorse, for he realizes the significance of Elaine's epistolary farewell. She loved him and could not live without his loving her. In this way did Justice leave the earth to reign over men from heaven only as an abstraction. Purity cannot linger long where it is not beloved, therefore it must depart the earth and man's presence.

Elaine's death, in the complete structure of the *Idylls*, is sadder than we ordinarily acknowledge, for it signifies the passing of innocence. What follows in the final sequence of the *Idylls* is the flight of purity in "The Holy Grail," its corruption in "Pelleas and Ettarre," and its death in "The Last Tournament," which is fittingly the tournament of dead innocence. But it is with Elaine that that ideal purity first fails; it is not long before the fact follows.

Lancelot's remorse is more productive than he knows, and the guidance of the now ideal Elaine genuinely active, for he is led not only to question Guinevere's affection and motives, but also to reapproach his own identity. Like Merlin, he is preoccupied with the idea that he must serve some use in Arthur's scheme. Also like Merlin, his use is impaired by his yielding to a seduction, though with Lancelot, the seduction is more rudimentary. In masking his identity from others, Lancelot has revealed himself to himself. His redemptive illness having brought him close to death and shown him which graces attend man in his suffering and humiliation, he can never return to the mode of his earlier existence. He has seen his purity die because he loved an impure beauty. He has seen his love disfigured by distrust and pride. He has felt his own profound dismay. Finally, he is obliged to reconsider his own identity. Is he the lover of the Queen, a model knight, or is he only an anonymous warrior battling against his own kind and himself?

For what am I? what profits me my name
Of greatest knight? I fought for it, and have it:
Pleasure to have it, none; to lose it, pain;
Now grown a part of me: but what use in it?
To make men worse by making my sin known?
Or sin seem less, the sinner seeming great?
Alas for Arthur's greatest knight, a man
Not after Arthur's heart! I needs must break
These bonds that so defame me. (p. 1660)

The poem ends with Lancelot unsure of how those bonds might be broken, though his very perception of the need signals the onset of the fiercest struggle he has yet endured—the real struggle with himself brought finally to the surface. He has, by inadvertently stepping outside his customary identity, been humbled in the flesh. He has the opportunity to see that the flesh itself is the disguise, the "mortal veil and shattered phantom of that infinite One," ("De Profundis," p. 1283) and that he himself is more than lover or invincible warrior. This is Lancelot's opportunity to see his truest function as a name, a force, a spirit, or a sign—all parts of a larger design and elements of "that infinite One." Being brought low, and weak in the flesh, he has a clearer perception of the ideal he has failed to espouse. Now, the ideal no longer actually attainable, he realizes the true nature of his struggle toward redemption.

In Lancelot's case, as in numerous other cases throughout the *Idylls*, the concept of bondage, slavery, or constraint plays an important part.[12] It was crucial to Merlin, afflicted Geraint, and will trouble others to come. It was an urge for liberty that occasioned the dispute of "The Two Voices," and in that poem true freedom was manumission from the self. In the *Idylls*, the accumulating references to entrapment, containment, and confinement, whether actual or metaphorical, create an image of a being writhing in fettered agony, attempting to slough off intangible chains which prevent its soaring free. Never is anyone entirely liberated, though freedom in the *Idylls*, as in earlier poems, is in the coincidence of the individual will with the eternal design, a harmony of each individual song of love in the total composition of the King's music. But, in the *Idylls*, far too few are capable of disprisoning themselves from themselves. In this idyll, Lancelot faces the quandary; and, to complete the design, which to this point remains unfulfilled, Tennyson appends the following two lines.

> So groaned Sir Lancelot in remorseful pain,
> Not knowing he should die a holy man. (p. 1660)

The Holy Grail

If "Lancelot and Elaine" removes actual purity to the realm of the ideal, "The Holy Grail" transfers active purity, embodied in Galahad, to the next world or confines it in a cloister. Sir Percivale, "called the Pure," has renounced the world, where purity is more and more a matter of jest, and where the Gawains, who can be tempted from the quest by a bevy of nubile ladies, begin to predominate. The pure Percivale does not favor the company of courtliness. The old courtesy is gone; the new courtliness repels him. The withdrawal of the pure to a realm of fastidious inactivity is predictably consequent upon the removal of purity from the active world.

The Quest, however, has another significance in terms of the moral design of the complete *Idylls*. In Percivale's career we may behold the same pattern of redemption, now gravely qualified, that was apparent in Geraint, Edyrn, and Guinevere, has only partially succeeded with Lancelot, has failed with Merlin, and will, find further elaboration in subsequent idylls.

Although only Galahad is qualified to pursue the Grail, a large number of knights determine to venture the quest because they wish to leap instantly to grace without the mundane struggles of the Round Table, believing that "if a man / Could touch or see" the Grail, he would be "healed at once, / By faith, of all his ills." (p. 1663) The consequences of such an encounter are excellent and even meritorious; it is the labor to achieve that encounter that is overlooked. The Grail is nothing more than the reward offered to those who have merited it. The same reward awaits any knight who labors for an entire life in the good and the just. That the Grail is the reward we all deserve according to our vision is indicated by Arthur at the end of the quest when he explains that each of those who has witnessed the Grail in his peculiar manner has seen the truth. Lancelot, entangled in his sin, which Arthur assures him is not all-encompassing, sees the Grail confusedly and "palled in crimson samite." (p. 1685) His vision is tainted by his sin, but that he should see the vision at all is earnest that Arthur is correct in assuming that no single sin defiles completely. The conclusion to "Lancelot and Elaine" hints at the same hope for Lancelot.

Sir Bors, the type of trusting and simple faith, is imprisoned by unbelievers but sees the Grail in the heavens anyway, and afterwards escapes through the assistance of a faithful believer. Percivale has seen the Grail, too, but at a distance, and not for himself so much as for Galahad. As Merlin's feckless mood betrayed him to eternal inutility, and Geraint's piacular journey assumed the shape of his moral dilemma, so here, each man views Faith in terms of his private faith. The Grail gives back to the mind what the mind has projected. It is, consequently, appalling that only three knights should have returned, having seen the Grail. But then, if most knights assayed the quest in order to avoid the struggles of faith, and to acquire a ready-made conviction, having projected no faith, they could find none.[18] Pure faith now passes from the earth. Only Arthur will still have his visions.

Buoyed by the conviction that he will surely find the Grail, Percivale sets out with the others upon the quest, but, before he has gone far, begins to meditate upon Arthur's caveat that this quest is not for everyone. The slight doubt swells until, like

Browning's Childe Roland, Percivale is surrounded by the externalized wilderness of his own doubt. It is Geraint's case once more. The wilderness into which Geraint withdrew was the wild confusion of his own heart. The conviction of inner unworthiness begets an ignoble landscape.

> Then every evil word I had spoken once,
> And every evil thought I had thought of old,
> And every evil deed I ever did,
> Awoke and cried, "This Quest is not for thee."
> And lifting up mine eyes, I found myself
> Alone, and in a land of sand and thorns,
> And I was thirsty even unto death;
> And I, too, cried, "This Quest is not for thee." (p. 1673)

Percivale's self-doubt calls all of the world and every value into doubt as well. All previous appearances of sense, family joy, fame and glory, now fall to dust before him. It is the narrator of "The Two Voices" persuading himself that he might conceive some manner of justly escaping a miserable life. But the same means to grace is available for Percivale as for these others. As the narrator of *Maud* required the humiliation of his madness, and Lancelot both illness and deliration, so Percivale must receive his lesson in humility; but Percivale, not having offended so intensely as these others, requires a milder reproof. Percivale moves from the high hill on which he experiences the ultimate ruin of his earlier aspirations, to "a lowly vale, / Low as the hill was high," and, in the lowest spot, finds a chapel and a holy hermit who is prepared to instruct him.

> ' "O son, thou has not *true humility*,
> The highest virtue, mother of them all . . .
> But her thou hast not known: for what is this
> Thou thoughtest of thy prowess and thy sins?
> Thou hast not lost thyself to save thyself
> As Galahad." ' (pp. 1674-75)

Once Percivale has acquired this knowledge, Galahad appears at the low vale and invites Percivale to accompany him on the quest. Now Percivale believes as Galahad believes—at least in kind, if not in quality. But when Galahad is borne off to his spiritual city, Percivale is left behind. Percivale is abandoned in the world, though he has glimpsed Galahad's destination. It is as though Lazarus were unwillingly revived to life, having been on the threshold of heaven. Nonetheless, Percivale understands the value of humility as he had not before. Lancelot, too, in spite of his sin and his madness, longed to lose himself in the great sea and wash away his sin, though in fact he neither lost himself nor washed away his sin; yet his fidelity to his ideals entitled him to see the Grail faintly. To escape the self is the means to salvation, as the soul in "The Palace of Art" discovered, and as Enoch Arden comprehended in his selfless dedication to the well-being of a family he dared not acknowledge.

To escape oneself is not, perhaps, so simple as it seems, and this is the import of the Siege Perilous. All men may hanker to escape the penitentiary of the self, as did the narrator of "The Two Voices," but that does not guarantee that each man will automatically adopt the correct means to that liberation. The greater part of "The Two Voices" is concerned with arguments for the liberation of the self through death, and only at the conclusion of the poem does the narrator realize that the true release from self is a dedication to life, a humble offering of love beyond oneself. To break the siege of self-concern a man must envision a purpose *out there*. But he does not hurry after a glorious relic that may provide him with facile redemption. The quest cannot be selfish. He must not imagine that Maud can ever be possessed. The purpose he discovers *out there* must not be a projection of private fears or cravings. Man escapes the self when he ceases to populate his ambience with ghosts of his own character. True humility will cure man of diseased self-imputation. His actions are unfettered from lower needs and the purpose becomes consecrated by love—an endowment, not a demand. In his melancholy, Merlin sat in the Siege Perilous and lost himself. Man may lose himself through selflessness which leads on to charity and love, the benevolent gift of the abundant and overflowing self to others. But one may lose one-self in another sense through self-abdication, the collapsing of the self in upon a void and abandoned spirit. In the first case, a hopeful mood presides and action is anticipated; in the second, a barren mood dominates, and quiet oscitancy succeeds. It is the contrast between "Ulysses" and "The Lotos-Eaters" in a profounder setting. Galahad has no doubts of himself or his cause, nor need he have them; hence he succeeds. Merlin not only doubts, but he is troubled by despair. Without a redeem-ing hope, he is lost. His collapse is a yielding to his own inertia, embodied by the seductive Vivien, for Vivien alone is no ade-quate temptress for the ascetic intellect.

Percivale, then, has followed the usual pattern of Tenny-son's moral design from pride, to doubt, to humility, and then to love. Percivale's love, however, is not the same active desire to participate in the world expressed by the narrators of *Maud*, "Locksley Hall," or *In Memoriam*, but is, rather, a quiet with-drawal, an unassuming offering of his love with spiritual con-sequences only. His struggle is over; knowledge and purity alone content him. He has found no object *out there* to inspirit him to action. Tennyson was not likely thoroughly to have approved this mode of combatting evil in the world. Later, in his "St. Telemachus," he will have God's voice upbrade the solitary eremite, " 'Wake / Thou deedless dreamer, lazying out a life / Of self-suppression, not of selfless love.' " (p. 1432) And in "De Profundis" he hopes that his own son will "Live, and be happy in thyself, and serve / This mortal race thy kin." (p. 1282) Percivale may be one who "has nailed all flesh to the Cross, till Self died out in the love of his kind," ("Vastness," p. 1348) but he has not been willing to live among his kind, serving actively as Ambrosius and Arthur serve.[14]

94

In "The Holy Grail," the inadequacy of Percivale's solution is illustrated through Ambrosius, the humble oblate to whom Percivale tells his story. Ambrosius serves the same function here that the innocent novice serves in "Guinevere"; he is Percivale's externalized conscience, obliging him politely to review the religious experience he has undergone. He even makes Percivale recollect passages that he would rather have suppressed, for Ambrosius, with his eye always to the human, elicits Percivale's account of the childhood sweetheart he might have married. Like Lancelot, however, Percivale turned from a woman who might have served as his guide in this world, favoring instead the abstract quest. There is a hint in this passage, and particularly in Ambrosius' comments upon it, that Percivale might have done well to marry the lady, live in harmony with her, and " 'be as Arthur in [their] land.' " (p. 1678)

If Percivale is all ideal and abstraction, Ambrosius' earthy humanity complements him nicely. He never had to learn humility, since he was never proud; furthermore, he is compassionate, as his behavior with Percivale shows. Like a somewhat less disciplined monk, Fra Lippo Lippi, Ambrosius is in constant participation with the circumstantial world he loves. He likes to "mingle with our folk," knows "every honest face," and is interested in all of their trivial concerns, saying to himself, "Rejoice, small man, in this small world of mine, / Yea, even in their hens and in their eggs." (p. 1677) Ambrosius began this exposition with his question to Percivale regarding the Grail. He says that he has found no accounts of it in ancient books, and, naturally he is right, since it is of the spirit. Ambrosius, too, will see his Grail, for he labors toward it daily. He will possess the Grail because he has faith, humility, and love, if not the high ideal that demands embodiment in the immediate.

The conclusion we derive from "The Holy Grail" is that one would do best, if he is no Galahad, to combine the Percivale and Ambrosius in him; to love this world, yet strive toward a higher. It is the lesson so often repeated by Browning in such poems as "Fra Lippo Lippi," "Abt Vogler," and "Andrea Del Sarto," though Browning's concern is often with the *poet's* means to grace. Man must love the world, then comprehend it, then reach beyond it to the spiritual, much as Wordsworth suggested in *The Prelude*. In secular form, it is Meredith's advice as well. Man must approach the Woods of Westermain with humility and shed the taint of self; only then is he prepared to rise by steps inclusively from blood, to brain, to spirit.

Tennyson does not leave this important tuition implied in the characters of Ambrosius and Percivale, but states first symbolically, and then unequivocally, that man's proper function is to work by gradual stages from this-worldliness toward the ideal. Commenting on this idyll, Tennyson said that he had expressed in it his "strong feeling as to the Reality of the Unseen. The end, when the king speaks of his work and of his visions, is intended to be the summing up of all in the highest note by the highest of human men."[15] As long as man is part of this world, he must engage it, though he dream of what follows. This is, as well, the desired programme for the entire *Idylls*, though it fails. The sculptures at Camelot show beasts slaying men, then men slaying beasts, then "warriors, perfect men," and finally "men with growing wings." (p. 1669) No one in Camelot reaches that final stage, unless it be Galahad on his way to the spiritual city. Even Arthur Henry Hallam, a warrior for the truth, stopped in this world at the third stage, and Tennyson knew no better model. Assuredly, then, that stage was in some future time when men should pass perfection. It is important that man must rise to that stage by gradual degrees. Tennyson's political caution was not an isolated sentiment, for he felt that all things, institutions, and men must fulfill themselves by steady progression. Perhaps he would have sympathized with Arnold's suggestion that God might conceivably be defined as that force which drives men and things to fulfill their nature, after all. The clearest testimony of this conviction is voiced by the purest representative of man Tennyson ever created. Arthur concludes "The Holy Grail" by explaining that even the highest himself must, in this world, despite visions and certainties of another world, labor practically toward the ideal in which he believes.

> ' "And some among you held, that if the King
> Had seen the sight he would have sworn the vow:
> Not easily, seeing that the King must guard
> That which he rules, and is but as the hind
> To whom a space of land is given to plow.
> Who may not wander from the allotted field
> Before his work be done; but, being done,
> Let visions of the night or of the day
> Come, as they will; and many a time they come,
> Until this earth he walks on seems not earth,
> This light that strikes his eyeball is not light,
> This air that smites his forehead is not air
> But vision—yea, his very hand and foot—
> In moments when he feels he cannot die,
> And knows himself no vision to himself,
> Nor the high God a vision, nor that One
> Who rose again: ye have seen what ye have seen." '

It is an indication of the inadequacy of Percivale's solution to the puzzle of salvation that he should, in his retirement, conclude: " 'So spake the King; I knew not all he meant.' " (p. 1687)

The Coming of Arthur

Certainly humility is important in "The Coming of Arthur," which was published in 1869 in the same volume with "The Holy Grail." In the "Dedication," Tennyson stated that Prince Albert reminded him of his own Arthur because he was "modest, kindly, all-accomplished, wise," and lived with "sublime repression of himself." (p. 1468) Arthur, aside from his proper decorum as a King, does not obtrude himself and is not vain. In fact, because he "rode a simple knight among his knights," Guinevere did not know him among his company. (p. 1471) He is capable of overcoming the petty rulers of his land because "each / But sought to rule for his own self and hand." (p. 1475)

Although humility is still a critical virtue, what is most important in this idyll is the establishment of Arthur's authority. At the beginning of the new order, Arthur is capable of overcoming the doubts of those around him; and Leodogran's dream of the triumph of spirit over sense, in which he envisions Arthur crowned in heaven, is a symbolic confirmation of that conquest.[16] Merlin's prediction of Arthur's immortality is another testimony of the ultimate triumph of spirit over sense. When Arthur speaks, he speaks "in low deep tones, / And simple words of great authority." (p. 1476) There is no wasted language now, for all ideal finds its fruition in deed. Language predominates when practice begins to flag. There is no mistaking the importance of this opening idyll, and surely Tennyson hoped that it would provide necessary expository material not only for his tale, but for his themes as well.

At the beginning of the new order, with hope high and doubt temporarily contained, Arthur is successful because he "and his knighthood for a space / Were all one will." (1483) There is no dissension within to divert the vital spiritual force, and Arthur's followers—for which, of course, we read human capacities—can sing "Blow trumpet" and prepare for the battle against evil with a true spirit, being confident not in a metaphor but a reality. Here is the enthusiasm of the narrator of *Maud* once he has found a selfless cause in which he may worthily struggle, embracing the purpose of God. Self-mastery is achieved; the highest qualities of man's nature assume authority, as they should. Arthur, as a character, is not imprisoned by self-concern, and the forces against which he struggles are not within him. His nature is obedient to him, and his high principles, his actions, are untrammeled. Arthur as ideal, however, is not so simple a matter, for although in its springlike hope the kingdom accepts him, certain features can not be extirpated. There is a Modred—and there is Guinevere.

This idyll is perhaps the most obvious of all, consequently requiring little explication, but one point is worth making in view of the emphasis upon persistent action in the material world which appeared in "The Holy Grail." It is in this idyll that Arthur allies himself with Guinevere, thereby supposing that they may "live and love and make the world / Other," (p. 1482) though, in reality, Arthur has admitted the element which is to destroy his grand design. It is his motive for wedding Guinevere that is important. In this there is a parallel with at least two earlier Tennyson poems. The Prince, in *The Princess*, loves Ida because she represents the height of earthly beauty, just as Guinevere is "all earth's beauty." (p. 1482) The Prince is too idealistic, too little of this world; hence his visionary questioning of the circumstantial world. To be joined with Ida would be to perfect the whole; to unite the highest earthly beauty with the highest earthly sense. What is more, it would lend purpose to that beauty. Gama, in recollecting his wife's judgment of Ida, stipulates the necessity for such control. The wife had said:

> "Our Ida has a heart"—just ere she died—
> "But see that some one with authority
> Be near her still." (p. 824)

The authority she required was not Lady Blanche, but the Prince.

The Princess is much more than an essay on women's rights or the value of feminine education. It is more closely allied to "The Day-Dream," in which the sleeping beauty, "A perfect form in perfect rest," represents once more earthly beauty, and the Prince, who seeks her "scarce knowing what he seeks," (p. 628) is a near relative to the Prince of *The Princess* and to King Arthur. In each case, an idealist hopes to fulfill his dream by wedding it to material beauty. Only in the first two poems is this fully successful. The Prince and Beauty of "The Day-Dream" go off together "In that new world which is the old," (p. 630) a world rejuvenated, a world of love in which the old order has definitely passed and the new order has begun. Once Princess Ida has followed the customary redemptive route, overcoming pride and achieving a "sweet humility," she discovers the capacity for love and she and the Prince come to an understanding. Although the hopeful picture they project of the new times is essentially social, there is, as well, a moral dimension wherein Ida is moral beauty and the Prince guiding authority.

> And so these twain, upon the skirts of Time,
> Sit side by side, full-summed in all their powers,
> Dispensing harvest, sowing the To-be,
> Self-reverent each and reverencing each,
> Distinct in individualities,
> But like each other even as those who love.
> Then comes the statelier Eden back to men:
> Then reign the world's great bridals, chaste and calm:
> Then springs the crowning race of human-kind. (p. 839)

In this Eden there are no Viviens and apparently no Modreds spying on the wall. It is an Eden, moreover, that lover and beloved share. Together, they approximate Tennyson's ultimate model for human authority—"the character of Christ, that union of man and woman, strength and sweetness."[17]

Arthur represents moral authority, but he feels that he must affiliate it with earthly excellence before he can accomplish his aims. Though his spiritual ideal is all very agreeable and admirable, it cannot entirely be fulfilled unless enacted in this world. In Arthur's marriage to Guinevere the precept becomes act. It must be so, Arthur says,

'for saving I be joined
To her that is the fairest under heaven,
I seem as nothing in the mighty world,
And cannot will my will nor work my work
Wholly, nor make myself in mine own realm
Victor and lord. But were I joined with her,
Then might we live together as one life,
And reigning with one will in everything
Have power on this dark land to lighten it,
And power on this dead world to make it live.' (p. 1472)

It is as though the Prince has come to wed Beauty and wake the sleeping city. Here, in the unity of hope, at the outset of the new order, all work with a united will. Humble authority is in control and expresses itself in the most appealing material form. As Buckley has pointed out, it is the absence of self-reverence, self-knowledge, and self-control that dooms most of the characters of the *Idylls*; but in this poem, Arthur's virtue holds the question in abeyance.

Pelleas and Ettarre

If Tennyson established clearly the purity, and innocence, and singleness of purpose that characterized the initiation of Arthur's plan in "The Coming of Arthur," and the passing of thorough innocence and purity out of the practical world in "The Holy Grail," in the third idyll published in 1869, "Pelleas and Ettarre," Tennyson demonstrated the impotence of superficial innocence, the evident effect of the tarnished ideal, and the usurpation of courtesy by courtliness—ideas which had been adumbrated in "Lancelot and Elaine." Furthermore, "Pelleas and Ettarre" provides a gloomy version of the Geraint and Enid idyll, where a lovely woman leads a strong but distrustful knight to salvation and service in the good. Although Enid's virtue is falsely questioned because of the Queen's sin, it is ultimately vindicated, and she and Geraint learn to live in their own realm, dependent upon their own strengths, regardless of what rumors tattle about their quondam paragon. But in "Pelleas and Ettarre," it is the willing knight who is deceived by the virtueless lady. Beyond Geraint's misunderstanding is the solid redemptive virtue of Enid; beyond Pelleas' misunderstanding is Ettarre's very real vice. And whereas Geraint, with his true Enid to serve him, can ignore the failings of the Queen; Pelleas, deprived of any material aid and of his ideal as well, falls back upon railing against the ills of his age. He, too, withdraws from the court, but to no realm of his own where he may labor in self-correction. Pelleas' withdrawal resembles Merlin's abdication, for he has had no inner strength to support him. He has lived on visions and found them wanting and once they have failed, he can only despair.

There is, moreover, an obvious parallel in the Pelleas-Ettarre-Gawain relationship with the Lancelot-Guinevere-Arthur triangle. Pelleas, with no actual person yet in mind, but longing for a substantial form with which to clothe his ideal, pleads

> 'O where? I love thee, though I know thee not.
> For fair thou art and pure as Guinevere,
> And I will make thee with my spear and sword
> As famous—O my Queen, my Guinevere,
> For I will be thine Arthur when we meet.' (p. 1688-89)

His craving will be fulfilled all too literally, though Pelleas' sword will not bring Ettarre fame, but, as a symbol of her immorality, will make her notorious. Ettarre will be just as fair and pure as Guinevere, which is saying very little and will deal with Pelleas as Guinevere did with Arthur. The difference, of course, is that Pelleas is incapable of approximating Arthur's behavior.

There is no doubt of Pelleas' innocence and virtue. When he first came to Arthur, "the sunshine came along with him;" (p. 1688) but to Ettarre and her sort, Pelleas' is a "fulsome innocence." (p. 1694) Still, Pelleas, as a novice knight, worships Arthur and all that he signifies, and is, furthermore, neither proud nor vain. Like Arthur, he imputes his own good qualities to others, as is evident in his first encounter with the beautiful Ettarre.

> But while he gazed
> The beauty of her flesh abashed the boy,
> As though it were the beauty of her soul:
> For as the base man, judging of the good,
> Puts his own baseness in him by default
> Of will and nature, so did Pelleas lend
> All the young beauty of his own soul to hers,
> Believing her. (p. 1689-90)

Also implied in this first encounter is the rudimentary error that engenders Pelleas' later agonies and discontents. Just as he has been quick to accept an unexamined virtue, so now he as quickly devotes himself to unexamined beauty. His trust in Arthur does him credit; but trust here proves false. Pelleas is unable to distinguish the spiritual from the physical, and there are too few models left to guide him. What is more, his failing is nearly allied to the usurpation of courtesy by court-liness, for there too the appearances of virtues merely cloak a growing cynicism. As superficial excellence slowly replaces spiritual admirability, there is greater need in the innocent and virtuous to derive strength from within themselves. As the Viviens invade the court, Merlins must not lapse into melancholy moods. The Round Table could contend adequately with bestial lords behaving obviously like beasts, but knights are less able to endure the gradual erosion of their will by the internal acquiescence in luxuries of spirit and sense. Pelleas, more than Gareth—who arrives at the dawn of the new order in the dawn of his youth and innocence—has need of private sources of strength to contend with a world that is more seeming good than good itself.

The speaker in Matthew Arnold's "Self-Dependence," in a

despondent mood, weary of himself, "and sick of asking / What I am and what I ought to be," casts "a look of passionate desire," at the distant stars. But their geometric, unhuman excellence is as impossible to accomplish as Arthur's perfect code is to maintain.[18] Though the speaker in Arnold's poem recognizes the vanity of hoping for such detached and self-assured calm, he feels that he may approximate the method of the stars. A voice within him recommends self-sufficiency.

'Resolve to be thyself; and know that he
Who finds himself, loses his misery!'[19]

But, in "The Holy Grail," we have already observed that to find himself a man must first lose himself. Pelleas has never questioned his motives, never tested his values, never met the ominous inner antagonist.

Pelleas is unselfconscious and considers virtue a kind of utensil. He has the proper admiration for what is good, but it is, for him, like a pattern in a lovely tapestry—something taken on trust and trusted in relentlessly. Virtue is a machine whose workings remain unknown, yet seem to operate the better for that ignorance. The paradigm in Pelleas' imagination obscures the flawed reality. He is led not by a spiritual Ideal, but by a material notion. And yet to blame Pelleas for his ignorance or condemn him for his simplicity is unjust and inappropriate; although he is simple and easily duped, his simplicity stems from essential well-meaning. It is a mixed fault, for, were he come to court at better times, when persons were what they seemed, his superficial view of virtue might have been amended. As it is, he lacks the opportunity. In better times even lesser men may be preserved, but in bad times only the finest persevere. And as the roll of disenchanted minor knights increases, the once monumental code proves unsteady, like images in delirium.

When Ettarre, having gained her object, drops her pleasant manner toward Pelleas, the young knight cannot understand that the mask of warmth is gone and now the cold nature of his beloved object is revealed. Never having been obliged to scrutinize his own identity by assuming an alien character, as Lancelot and Gareth have done, Pelleas is unequipped to fathom duplicity. If there are masks, then they must be benign. Unaware of the dark forces within himself, untested in his own unsteady innocence, he assumes that the cruel version of Ettarre is the performance, her selfish grace the true identity. To him, the pattern persists, and he interprets Ettarre's manner in terms of chivalric model in his imagination. When she prevents him from her castle, he concludes that she is not serious:

> 'for I have sworn my vows,
> And thou hast given thy promise, and I know
> That all these pains are trials of my faith,
> And that thyself, when thou hast seen me strained
> And sifted to the utmost, wilt at length
> Yield me thy love and know me for thy knight.' (p. 1694)

It is a parody of the real means to grace, whereby man must be tested before he achieves his ideal. Pelleas is equally trustful of Gawain when that doubtful knight offers his assistance. Again he is dealing with courtliness, and he cannot see the difference between manner and conviction.

When Gawain goes to Ettarre, Pelleas' real trial begins. Anxious with expectancy during the three days allowed for the success of Gawain's ruse, Pelleas wanders "aimless about the land, / Lost in a doubt." (p. 1698) Overcome by impatience, he investigates only to discover that Gawain has betrayed him, but the metaphors describing Pelleas' reaction imply something more profound than disgust, revulsion, or anger.

> Back, as a hand that pushes through the leaf
> To find a nest and feels a snake, he drew:
> Back, as a coward slinks from what he fears
> To cope with, or a traitor proven, or hound

105

> Beaten, did Pelleas in an utter shame
> Creep with his shadow through the court again. (p. 1700)

This is, truly, what Pelleas fears to cope with, for it demands
not a superstructure of rules, laws, codes, vows, and so forth, but
a deeply rooted conviction based upon inner feelings. Pelleas
followed Arthur because he admired his Order, but there is nothing to indicate that, like Gareth, he was urged by a forceful private morality. He is proven traitor to himself, for, as he previously imputed his excellence to Ettarre and made her represent
his ideal, now, in discovering her worthlessness, he reveals the
treason of his unjustified imputation. But even more consequential is his retreat, like a hound beaten, in utter shame. This is no
lesson to Pelleas, as Arthur's discovery is to him; this is a shame-
ful injury. It does not prompt him to review his own values and
reconsider their nature and application in terms of his experience; instead, it is the values he is prepared to disown. Tennyson's Athena offered to Paris power in life through self-reverence, self-knowledge, and self-control; it was a power "to live by
law, / Acting the law we live by without fear." ("Oenone,"
p. 393) But Pelleas' reaction is the reverse. Given an example
of behavior inconsistent with the code he has adopted, he credits
the behavior and discards the code. In his first real test Pelleas has
indeed proved coward, traitor, and beast, for no sooner has he
left the illicit lovers with a sign of his knowledge to frighten
them, but he lapses into disillusionment and repeals his trust in
Arthur.

> Fool, beast—he, she, or I? myself most fool;
> Beast too, as lacking human wit—disgraced,
> Dishonored all for trial of true love—
> Love?—we be all alike: only the King
> Hath made us fools and liars. O noble vows!
> O great and sane and simple race of brutes
> That own no lust because they have no law!
> For why should I have loved her to my shame?

106

I loathe her, as I loved her to my shame.
I never loved her, I but lusted for her—
Away. (p. 1701)

Here is the reverse of the pattern operating in such poems as
Maud, "The Two Voices," "Locksley Hall," and in many ways
In Memoriam. The mood until this point has been hopeful and
trusting, but, confronted with a serious challenge to sunniness,
it is darkened entirely. Now Pelleas no longer believes in love,
nor in any laws. Nor will he believe that he did love. Though
values are fickle, one's faith should not be so. The Ancient Sage
advised his auditor

> If thou would'st hear the Nameless, and wilt dive
> Into the Temple-cave of thine own self,
> There, brooding by the central altar, thou
> Mayst haply learn the Nameless hath a voice.
> ("The Ancient Sage," p. 1351)

But Pelleas is unwilling to make that descent into the self, for he
has ever been content to move upon an easy surface. Could he
now engage in the dialogue of "The Two Voices," he might find
cause yet for hope, but he makes no inquiry and longs instead for
the surcease of death, a suicidal tendency that occupied the
narrators of certain earlier poems. When he comes to the monastery where Percivale dwells, he exclaims, " 'Of Arthur's hall
am I, but here, / Here let me rest and die." (p. 1702) It is here,
also, that Pelleas, in the depths of his gloom, learns of Guinevere's falseness, and his disenchantment is complete.

Not realizing that his rage and anger are symptoms of pride;
not realizing further that his railings against the age lack point
unless he is willing—as the narrator of *Maud* ultimately is—to
act in some worthy manner to correct the evils of the time, Pelleas sets out on a course of destructive activity, determining to
scourge the Table Round. That Lancelot, obliged to battle with
Pelleas, easily unhorses him, and that Pelleas then requests his

107

victor to slay him, since his "will is to be slain," and that Lance-lot responds by reproving him as a "weakling," is sufficient evidence that Pelleas' behavior is an improper answer for his dilemma. Nor can he, when faced with the offense he so despises, offer any better remedy than to wish that he had a sword. He craves some external means of obliterating his shame and his injury; his impulse is to destroy, whereas the appropriate mode of redemption demands a humble reconstruction of what has been so brutally shattered. With Pelleas, "the form alone is eloquent;"[20] beneath is no substance. That he fails or fears to perceive this and rages only to aim destruction at what is beyond himself, thereby, of course, jeopardizing himself as well, is a lamentable consequence of the triumph of surface. This is a retreat, and a cowardly retreat at that. And Lancelot and Guinevere have as much cause for seeing the onset of bad times in the weakness of Pelleas' character as in the exposure of their sin. When knights of the Round Table behave in this fashion, less orderly types may be supposed to constitute a prodigious threat, as Tristram is soon to prove.

But "Pelleas and Ettarre" is not all blackness, for from Pelleas' fall, ironically, comes Ettarre's self-revelation. Ettarre was proud and scornful not only of Pelleas' innocence, but of Guinevere and even Arthur himself. She was unquestionably selfish and self-gratifying, considering deceit no grave fault, but a useful means of accomplishing her objective. Faced with the simple, though, as it turns out, unsteady virtue of her young lover, she realizes that she has been intimidated by something nobler than herself that makes her hate him. So long as she can recognize her distance from the good, there is hope for regeneration. When Ettarre discovers the sword at her throat, she discards Gawain and fastens her love, instead, upon the unattainable Pelleas, pining for him in vain. Here, again, is a parody of the usual circumstance in which the ideal woman, once beyond possession, becomes a guiding force for the abandoned admirer. This was the pattern of *Maud* and of "Lancelot and Elaine." Unfortunately, there is no evidence that Ettarre was redeemed, only that her affections veered in a more suitable direction, though, bitter irony that it is, when this happens, the virtues as embodied in Pelleas have evaporated. This sequence echoes Guinevere's tardy recognition of Arthur's merits; for Arthur is lost to her as Pelleas to Ettarre. Ettarre has been Pelleas' Guinevere in more ways than he supposed, but he was not secure enough in the values he professed to be Arthur in return.

The Order is certainly seriously challenged now from within by the defection of such promising young men as Pelleas, but the combat remains at a superficial level. It is still the external struggle of appearances in which the ever-advancing encroachment of courtliness gradually supplants true courtesy and virtue. There is no redemptive mode fulfilled in this idyll, there is only an empty parody of it, for there is neither genuine doubt (involving self-questioning), nor genuine humility (involving self-recognition), nor is there subsequent love and devotion to a selfless service of others. Instead, there is irresponsible ranting against the source of private injury. Surely, as Modred concludes, " 'The time is hard at hand.' " (p. 1704)

The Passing of Arthur

The "Morte d'Arthur" was primarily a story, though it clearly dealt with the vanishing of surpassing virtue from the world and rendered the confused nature of that termination. The "Authority [that] forgets a dying king, / Laid widowed of the power in his eye / That bowed the will," was really a general authority. (p. 1750) When incorporated as a part of the *Idylls*, that authority represented a source of command both profounder and more precise. The deepest statement of the early poem was the acknowledgment that God's design cannot be entirely known by man and that it operates eternally despite the apparent flux of the material world. So Arthur is capable of subordinating his desires to that design.

> 'The old order changeth, yielding place to new,
> And God fulfils himself in many ways,
> Lest one good custom should corrupt the world.' (p. 1752)

Tennyson thought it fitting to repeat the first line of this expression in "The Coming of Arthur," not only to give a symmetry to the total work, but to show that Arthur's order was only one of many ways in which God's full purpose might find operation.

The significance of the design of the *Idylls* is demonstrated to some extent in the additions Tennyson made to "The Passing of Arthur," which was published in 1869. Arthur's death is now clearly the death of man as well as the passing of virtue. The last great battle in the west is man's confrontation with mortality. In this case, doubt becomes more than a simple confusion of a wounded king and stands instead for the inevitable questioning of God's will. Arthur, having lamented that his ideal was to be found in natural phenomena but not in mankind, admits that his realm now "Reels back into the beast, and is no more," (p. 1743) and he exclaims, more than merely echoing Christ's cries upon the cross, " 'My God, thou hast forgotten me in my death.' " But instantly he recovers his faith. " 'Nay—God my Christ—I pass but shall not die.' " (p. 1743) Like the poet of *In Memoriam*, he is prepared to say "I curse not nature, no, nor death; / For nothing is that errs from law." (lxxiii, p. 924) There also appears to the virtuous Arthur, like an ascetic's verifying vision, the mournful ghost of dead Gawain who whines " 'I am blown along a wandering wind, / And hollow, hollow, hollow all delight.' " (p. 1743) Bedivere correctly interprets the significance of the ghost when he comforts Arthur, saying, " 'Light was Gawain in life, and light in death / Is Gawain, for the ghost is as the man.' " (p. 1744)

110

There is a great deal of implication in Bedivere's comment, for what he is saying is that a man's afterlife is what he makes it. Though not so simple as Galuppi's music would have it, saying that "The soul, doubtless, is immortal—where a soul can be discerned,"[21] yet it does resemble the stringent demand that Arnold posits in "Immortality."

> No, no! the energy of life may be
> Kept on after the grave, but not begun;
> And he who flagged not in the earthly strife,
> From strength to strength advancing—only he,
> His soul well-knit, and all his battles won,
> Mounts, and that hardly, to eternal life.[22]

If in life a man has not labored to fulfil himself, he may expect no remedy in an afterlife. What is more, the promised liberation that death should bring will not come for those who could not free themselves from themselves in life. All of eternity will become a prolonged confinement in the stale atmosphere of an untended self. However, Arthur, who has never sinned, scarcely need worry about his reward.

Following Arthur's doubts of divine support, and of the value of human existence, comes a more penetrating distress, for he realizes that "The king who fights his people fights himself." (p. 1744) Here is a dimension that the early version of the poem did not have. It clearly suggests the greater import of the amended idyll as a part of the total poem. The battle in the "death-white mist" is the contention of the human spirit with death, as it was not in the original form. It is the self against itself before the arbiter of mortality. Though, at the conclusion of the battle, Arthur feels confusion in his heart and does not know "what I am, / Nor whence I am, nor whether I be King," (p. 1746) when he sees Modred still alive, he easily asserts his command again: "King am I, whatsoever be their cry." (p. 1747) As Lancelot and other figures have been obliged to do, Arthur questions his identity. It is a necessity for all men; if not during life, then at its close. Like Arthur, Lancelot faced death and fought his internal strife. Arthur's conviction, however, is more assured, for no sin troubles his conscience.

If Modred, shadowy figure as he is, is meant to suggest all of the evil inclination within one's own dominion—be that self or kingdom—then it is necessary, in the virtuous man, that that force of selfish arrogance and cringing pride should be extinguished before death. It is necessary that Arthur destroy Modred in order that he *may* go to Avilion. The qualities that Arthur represents are the same qualities that Christ represented. They will reappear. In the early version of the poem, no clear suggestion of that reappearance is given, but in the amended form, after the recurrent phrase "From the great deep to the great deep he goes," (p. 1753) rings for the last time on Bedivere's ear, he hears a more agreeable sound.

> Then from the dawn it seemed there came, but faint
> As from beyond the limit of the world,
> Like the last echo born of a great cry,
> Sounds, as if some fair city were one voice
> Around a king returning from his wars. (p. 1754)

The soul has returned to its proper kingdom, no longer requiring the fleshly struggle that made its passage on earth a trial and small delight. These exclamations from the phantom island suggest the true reward of every Christian pilgriming toward the Heavenly City. And in order that hope be not appropriated to the immortal alone, when the barge carrying Arthur passed beyond vision, "the new sun rose bringing the new year." (p. 1754)

In the rewriting of this poem, Tennyson revealed the antetype in his mind for the moral design occuring so frequently in his work. Pride of the flesh, with all of its doubts—especially the doubts of the spiritual world which is the true reality—must be humbled. In this poem we see that the ultimate test, the ultimate combat, the ultimate humbling is in the encounter with mortality. What follows is liberation of all that is highest in man, if he prove worthy. However, it is insufficient that this paradigm should occur only once in a man's life, for constant humility, constant testing, constant rebirth are the constant message that Tennyson offers. The true Christian governs his life with the thought of death always in mind. In *Nicholas Nickleby*, Dickens presents a contrast between the evil Ralph Nickleby and his virtuous niece, Kate. The young woman's heart palpitates "with a thousand anxieties and apprehensions," while in Ralph's heart there is not "one figure denoting thought of death or of the grave," for it is nothing more than "a piece of cunning mechanism . . . yielding no one throb of hope, or fear, or love, or care, for any living thing."[23] It is as though by ignoring death man hopes to cancel the possibility of judgment; correspondingly, if one thinks of death and what that extreme test means, one sustains a persistent judgment. It is by this persisting judgment that strength of faith is nurtured, for who can think on death and not be humbled? And, once humbled, what the heart will cry for is not release, but "More life, and fuller," until death comes as part of a divine and perfect scheme.

The true sadness in the failure of the Round Table is not that it should fail. Like all things terrestrial, it was destined to pass. Even Christ only walked this earth for a time, Tennyson reminds us. The true sadness is in the image of youth and innocence gradually losing the power to recover grace through humility and love. Pride and doubt gradually triumph over faith and love. The form of belief yields to "Mark's way." But always, beneath this failure, is the clear implication that man, no matter how abandoned, still craves that which he violates. As numerous other poems by Tennyson suggest, man's truest suffering comes from a misguided vanity that will not permit him to accept what his hidden wish most covets.

Nor did Tennyson confine this theme to his better and profounder works, but offered it clearly in such poems as "Aylmer's

Field," which is structured upon the convention of the obdurate arrogance of wealthy parents who will not allow their daughter to marry for love beneath her station. The poem opens with lines that might have served several proud spirits well in the *Idylls*.

> Dust are our frames; and, gilded dust, our pride
> Looks only for a moment whole and sound. (p. 1160)

Averill, the brother of the beautiful Edith's lover, Leolin, after the latter's suicide, delivers a sermon against the confused pride of which the Aylmers are the representatives.

> 'Gash thyself, priest, and honor thy brute Baäl,
> And to thy worst self sacrifice thyself,
> For with thy worst self hast thou clothed thy God. (p. 1177)

Like the misguided figures of the *Idylls*, the Aylmers have confused their own failings with all existence. The narrator of *Maud*, finding himself base, determines that all mankind is therefore base—a questionable logic born of a morose and moody vanity. The Aylmers have confused their true desire for their daughter's happiness with the aims of their own vanity. When Edith is destroyed by their misapplied firmness, the consequences for themselves are madness and death. Beneath the false, apparent wish, was the genuine, unregarded desire. But the unexamined heart never acquaints itself with that desire. As "The Two Voices" suggests, it is pride that engenders doubt, yet it is that very doubt that tends to flatter pride into a position of irrevocable despair and self-destruction, and self-destruction is almost always the end to which such doubt drives. This too, of course, is the theme of the *Idylls*.

The Last Tournament

When Tennyson came to write "The Last Tournament," the design of the *Idylls* was complete. The poems added later are some of the best, but they are not necessary to the design in the way that "Guinevere" or "The Holy Grail" are. Nevertheless, they are rich in themselves and provide a deeper interpretation of the same themes that most of the earlier idylls exhibited. In the image of the carcanet of dead innocence there is an ironic parallel with the diamonds that Lancelot brings to the Queen, as, of course, there is a parallel between their romance and that of Tristram and his adulterous queen, Isolt. The greatest contrast in this parallel, however, is in the mode of correction that the offended king utilizes.

The ambiguity of the Tournament of Dead Innocence is apparent even to the characters within the poem, and the pun is made an open joke among the courtly wits. But dead innocence is, in more ways than one, suggestive of what might have been, and how Guinevere's sin might have been prevented, or, at least, corrected. The Queen says to Arthur that, in the tournament, she hopes "the purest of thy knights / May win them for the purest of my maids." (p. 1706) This is not to be. An openly impure knight redeems the carcanet for the most notoriously tainted woman; more pathetically, it is impossible to deny them. Guinevere has given up the carcanet because it "Vext her with plaintive memories of the child," Nestling, with whom the jewels were found by Lancelot and Arthur. (p. 1706) These memories are plaintive because they affirm Guinevere's potential for selfless affection, which, given the opportunity might have cured her voluptuous pride. That, in the end, can only be remedied by the loss of Arthur. When Nestling is given to Guinevere, the Queen is reluctant to take the child, being cold and proud; but gradually she warms to it:

> the Queen,
> But coldly acquiescing, in her white arms
> Received, and after loved it tenderly,
> And named it Nestling; *so forgot herself*
> *A moment, and her cares.* (p. 1705; italics mine)

In these arms, where innocence no longer rests, no innocence can live. As Lancelot could not accept the pure Elaine, the pure

115

Elaine must necessarily depart from the earth. So too with innocence and the Queen.

The world now is given up to hypocrisy, and open recognition of the failing order is evidenced in the Red Knight's insolent establishment of his own "Round Table in the North," a counter Round Table, full of sin and vice, but free from hypocrisy. Tristram resembles the followers of the Red Knight himself, for he also refuses to ape a courtesy he no longer credits; he has enough nobility in him not to sham a sentiment he cannot feel. Moreover, he sees himself as an utter worldling and rather delights in the rôle. Meanwhile, Lancelot, the noblest, though tainted, has lapsed into a moody trance reminiscent of Merlin's pernicious despondency, and allows the rules of the Tournament to be violated. Arthur himself is clearly aware of the decline that has set in and therefore leads the assault upon the Red Knight himself. The King has seen

> 'The foot that loiters, bidden go,—the glance
> That only seems half-loyal to command,—
> A manner somewhat fallen from reverence—
> Or have I dreamed the bearing of our knights
> Tells of a manhood ever less and lower?
> Or whence the fear lest this my realm, upreared,
> By noble deeds at one with noble vows,
> From flat confusion and brute violences,
> Reel back into the beast, and be no more?' (p. 1708)

Surely Arthur has seen correctly, but what he does not realize is that his knights' deeds are no longer at one with their noble vows. This is evident in the more raucous revelling of the court that annoys Guinevere, in the brutality of Arthur's army in the massacre of the Red Knight's company, and in Dagonet's comments to Tristram. But it is most apparent in Tristram himself, though he is not the confirmed skeptic he considers himself. Just as Vivien could not escape the discomfort of her sinning and was the most acutely sensitive to her own brand of offense, scandal, so Tristram, ostensible worlding, still craves what he no longer can accept. He is no Pelleas abdicating all contact with the court through a fallen hope. He is no Merlin lapsing into useless torpor. Maintaining the form of nobility, he lacks its inner motive.

Tristram amply illustrates the importance of moody pride and self-indulgence in the soul's demise. His disbelief in the vows is conditioned largely by the fact that his own behavior would be inconveniently restricted by them. After all, it was by using the model of Guinevere's sin that he seduced Isolt for his own pleasure. He took his pleasure with her and with Isolt of Brittany, and yet, libertine that he seems to be, he is not willing to allow Isolt the same freedom in love that he enjoys, for he quickly puts an end to their conversation when she entertains a fancy of offering herself to Lancelot, even though it seems no more than a jest. Nor has Tristram's supposed worldly wisdom given him any assurance of firm character, or decided mind, for, in investigating his feelings about the two Isolts, he can only conclude, " 'I know not what I would.' " (p. 1718) Like Gawain, his eye seeks its contentment anywhere, yet nowhere does it find fulfilment and certainty. Surely Tristram's ghost, too, will go wailing in the wind, "hollow, hollow, hollow all delight!"

Thomas Traherne, in his *Centuries*, captures with beautiful concision the predicament of Arthur's ideal and the difficulty of fixing it in this world. Traherne says that man's true desire is to love and honor God. But ignorant man, incapable of fathoming God, wanders through the material world seeking the means of contentment for his vague spiritual craving. All this Traherne summarizes in one sentence: "We lov we know not what: and therfore evry Thing allures us."[24] Arthur has offered men knowledge of what they love and capacities to attain it, yet they turn from him, allured still by substantial shadows, preferring illusions to ideals. This would be folly enough, but Tristram's sel-

117

fish indulgence has further consequences, for, as Dagonet indicates to him, he damns not himself alone, but others with him, unlike that "Paynim bard," Orpheus, whose music led his wife *outward* from Hell. It is the nature of Tristram's cynical sinning to dismiss its effects upon others, and it is this very neglect that leads to Tristram's own undoing. Tristram's neglect of the consequences of his sinning ironically amplifies the fact that the earlier sins of indifference and neglect that troubled Arthur's Order have now swelled into active hostility and contempt. The earlier *loss* of use and name and fame now becomes the *perversion* of use and name and fame in Tristram.

Tristram is spokesman for the convenience of doubt. Tristram was once, as Isolt reminds him, a greater man when he had genuine courtesy, but now he has "grown wild beast" himself. (p. 1721) It suits Tristram's purpose, as it did that of the narrator of *Maud*, to judge all men, all vows, by himself and his vows. He failed, and instantly the world was false. So with Pelleas' disenchantment. Again it is a question of mood. When we believe, our behavior follows our belief. The obstacle arises when our belief contends with sensuous drives; should the appetites triumph, for peace of mind we persuade ourselves that our belief was false. So Tristram.

> Then Tristram, pacing moodily up and down,
> 'Vows! did you keep the vow you made to Mark
> More than I mine? Lied, say ye? Nay, but learnt,
> The vow that binds too strictly snaps itself—
> My knighthood taught me this—ay, being snapt—
> We run more counter to the soul thereof
> Then had we never sworn. I swear no more.
> I swore to the great King, and am forsworn.
> For once—even to the height—I honored him. (p. 1721-22)

There is a pettish indictment of the self in this romantic rejection of virtue; yet it is Tristram's idle self-indulgence that makes innocence so irrecoverable. Guinevere knew, though she would not admit until past acting, that Arthur was the highest and she could turn to him if she willed it. She chose her voluptuous pride. Tristram, too, makes the selfish choice. In his railing against the vows, he misses the central point, though he himself expresses it.

> 'The vows!
> O ay—the wholesome madness of an hour—
> They served their use, their time; for every knight
> Believed himself a greater than himself,
> And every follower eyed him as a God;
> Till he, being lifted up beyond himself,
> Did mightier deeds than elsewise he had done,
> And so the realm was made; but then their vows—
> First mainly through that sullying of our Queen—
> Began to gall the knighthood, asking whence
> Had Arthur right to bind them to himself?' (p. 1722)

If the vows really did lift men out of themselves and above themselves, and helped them to perform deeds they never otherwise could have done, were these deeds and this excellence illusion? Tristram ignores the counter-argument of his account, that, denying the vows, we make ourselves less than ourselves. It is a question of belief, once more. Isolt acutely signifies as much when she exclaims, "'My God, the power / Was once in vows when men believed the King!'" (p. 1721)

The vows were never true nor false, but always merely the high ideal, assuming validity through being enacted. Tristram's very discarding of the vows proves them to have been all that Arthur meant them to be. The fault is not in the vows, but in those who fail to maintain them. The vows did not wear with time, becoming false; it was human endurance that weakened. The vows, after all, never were objects to suffer erosion, though Tristram assumes they are a form of weapon that has lost its edge. How barren the world is to the narrator of "The Two Voices" until hope prompts him to rejoice, and then, his heart

119

melted to love, his spirit humbled, the world is reanimate in his imagination. Beauty surrounds and supports him. It is men who prove the vows either true or false; the vows are neither in themselves, but only abstract guides. " 'Tuwhoo! do you see it? do ye see the star?' " Dagonet asks Tristram, who responds: " 'Nay, fool . . . not in open day.' " (p. 1714) But the stars gleam on, whether or not men perceive them through the glare of their immediate world of flesh and self-concern. If man's vision be flawed, does that compromise the stars?[25]

Tristram's worldliness, then, is not so adequate as it seems, nor is his doubt so certain as he would have himself believe. His argument, Tennyson suggests, is certainly inadequate. But if proof were needed of the falseness of Tristram's position, it is summed up in his fall. What Tristram has championed is a life of liberty; unprincipled, self-indulgent, uncontrolled. Accordingly, as he hands the symbol of dead innocence to his tainted queen, Mark—the embodiment of this undisciplined, unprincipled existence—strikes him dead. " 'Mark's way,' " he says. (p. 1724) Mark's way, indeed. Tristram has here his mortal lesson too late to utilize. What value in his nobility, his prowess, his strength, if there be no rules by which men contend? If he may violate by stealth, then Mark may exterminate him in a similar fashion. By surrendering himself to an anti-code of anarchy and self-indulgence, Tristram has been blinded by his own vanity, for he has failed to realize that this philosophy will operate for all men, and therefore against himself. If one allows that each man's hand is against his neighbor, he should have sense enough to beware his neighbor's hand. Tristram is, in fact, no worldling at all, though Mark is. Tristram is only self-outcast from the camp of virtue. Much as he rails against the vows, he does not truly see all the world consigned to the license he allows himself. He has contempt for Mark, and yet he advocates Mark's way. And, in the end, he has it. Furthermore, the liberty Tristram seeks in freeing himself from the supposed bondage of the vows is only license, which entraps him more surely than hopeful visions would have. He lives from moment to moment, sullen, brutal, and vacillating in nature. His fine qualities are valuable no more, for in a world ungoverned by rules, fine qualities compromised are easily defeated by the most base. Giving up the guidance of the stars, Tristram has plummetted into a swamp of self-concern, unlike Lancelot, who, while bound and confined by his one sin, is still capable of "gazing at a star" emblematic of the Ideal, though he continues bewilderedly "marvelling what it" is. (p. 1703)

If "The Last Tournament" is largely funereal in tone, it is not entirely so. Tennyson did not seem inclined to leave any composition without a hint of hope; and so, in Dagonet, Arthur's fool, he provides a tiny model of the redemptive design. Tristram scorns him, calling him a swine and saying he knew him when he wallowed like other men, though now he's vain at being nominated Arthur's fool. But Dagonet is, appropriately enough, the humble figure, while Tristram plays the proud fool. And Dagonet comprehends the values Tristram lightly mocks.

> Swine? I have wallowed, I have washed—the world
> Is flesh and shadow—I have had my day.
> The dirty nurse, Experience, in her kind
> Hath fouled me—an I wallowed, then I washed—
> I have had my day and my philosophies—
> And thank the Lord I am King Arthur's fool. (p. 1713)

Gareth and Lynette

"Gareth and Lynette," added to the *Idylls* in 1872, is a reasonable, and, in retrospect, necessary addition to the poem, for it is the only idyll in which a hero fulfils the ideals of Arthur's order. In adding a positive figure late in the history of the whole poem, Tennyson was able to show more clearly than he had anywhere else, except in the "Guinevere" idyll, what the proper mode of behavior was. Guinevere illustrates that mode only by having failed and by requiring redemption, but Gareth represents it in an unsoiled condition.

The imagery associated with Gareth indicates that he is both natural and innocent, but unlike Pelleas, who possesses the same qualities, he is morally mature before he goes to Arthur's court. His first interest is to serve God; Arthur's Order is to him not an ideal in itself, but the best means to fulfil God's will. In an apostrophe to a stream swollen with spring rain, he says,

> Thou dost His will,
> The Maker's and not knowest, and I that know,
> Have strength and wit, in my good mother's hall
> Linger with vacillating obedience. (p. 1484)

His intention in joining Arthur's company is not simply to emulate Arthur; primarily he wishes to be Arthur's knight so that he may work "out his will, / To cleanse the world." (p. 1485) His motivation is not fundamentally courtly, but moral. Later, in his attempt to coax his mother to release him from her benevolent tyranny, he summarizes his purpose.

> 'Follow the deer? follow the Christ, the King,
> Live pure, speak true, right wrong, follow the King—
> Else, wherefore born?' (p. 1487)

He does not fancy the usual chivalric career; to him, a lovely maid is yet an unconsidered consequence; his desire is to live well and to enact his values in appropriate incidents. Had Pelleas thought more of living pure, speaking true, and righting wrong, and less of fair maidens to whom he might offer his service, his disillusionment might have had far different consequences. Gareth, of course, is never faced with disenchanting facts such as Pelleas faces; but then, he has not contributed any false enchantment to his own career, as Pelleas most certainly has done. Nor is he interested in withdrawing himself from the world of action, for he vigorously refuses the life of ease that his mother offers to him.

The quality that most characterizes Gareth is his humility. Here is no pride to be brought low. Accordingly, Gareth need never be humiliated as Guinevere is, or as Lancelot is. For him, there is not humiliation, but endurance, since he must be tested. When his mother imposes upon Gareth the condition of serving as a menial in Arthur's court before making himself known, she assumes that her son will be too proud to concur, but he responds willingly, adding, " 'The thrall in person may be free in soul, / And I shall see the jousts.' " (p. 1488) This comment shows that Gareth is cognizant of what, for Tennyson, is the true liberty. When the soul is free, no material constraint signifies; but, no matter how free behavior may be, if the soul follows the enticements of sense or vanity, it is enthralled in a manner that only recovered humility can remedy. Follow the king by choice, and you are free; be captive of your desires, and you find bondage. Meanwhile, in fulfilling his duties as a drudge, Gareth ennobles the most humble toil, performing "All kind of service with a noble ease / That graced the lowliest act in doing it." (p. 1497) So later, as Lynette is finally obliged to admit, in performing noble deeds he exhibits an admirable humility and is "meek withal / As any of Arthur's best." (p. 1518)

If Gareth, as representative of the truly virtuous man, need not contend with his own pride, he is also appropriately free from moodiness and doubt. It is true that conditions at Arthur's court, being at their earliest and therefore most virtuous, are congenial to his excellence as they might not have been later; but we may also suppose that his untainted vision contributes to the purity he sees. When Gareth and his servants approached Camelot, the servants were frightened, dreading some enchantment; but Gareth said, truly enough, that he feared it not, having "glamour enow / In his own blood, his princedom, youth, and hopes," (p. 1489) to contend with any malign forces working there. That the city will be what each man is capable of making it is suggested in Merlin's comments to Gareth, though the young man finds them cryptic in spite of their direct application to himself.

Gareth's counter-enchantment consists of belief and hope. If disenchantment leaves Camelot a city of scarred neglect after the disastrous quest of the Grail, hope may, contrariwise, see it as the beautiful fabric it is meant to be. Faith in the Unseen, in the spiritual Ideal, conveys a power of perception unavailable to men submerged in the world of sensation and matter. This trust in the greater Will is Gareth's magic. And if Gareth has enchantment in him to combat evil forces, as he presumes, then, according to Merlin's account of Camelot, he should find the climate congenial.

> 'And, as thou sayest, it is enchanted, son,
> For there is nothing in it as it seems
> Saving the King; though some there be that hold
> The King a shadow, and the city real:
> Yet take thou heed of him, for, so thou pass
> Beneath this archway, then wilt thou become
> A thrall to his enchantments, for the King
> Will bind thee by such vows, as is a shame
> A man should not be bound by, yet the which
> No man can keep; but, so thou dread to swear,
> Pass not beneath this gateway, but abide
> Without, among the cattle of the field.
> For an ye heard a music, like enow
> They are building still, seeing the city is built
> To music, therefore never built at all,
> And therefore built for ever.' (p. 1491)

Here, again, is the image of thralldom, but now it is the proper service due the King and his vows. The alternative to such service is existence outside the city, "among the cattle." And associated with the voluntary acceptance of the vows is the concept of music. Freedom is like a cadence fulfilling itself, moving according to useful rules toward its resolution. There is no music when independent figures choose their own mode and create an aleatory composition discordant to the King's more classic ear. Such noise destroys all order and defeats itself.

Self-fulfilment, in Tennyson's view, involved the conscious discovery of that buried life that Arnold said could only be glimpsed rarely. To know oneself and the direction in which one longs to move is a truer and more harmonious freedom, than the aimless trailing after each allurement that presents itself. Tristram, Vivien, and others troubled Arthur's music with their sins, but for those who feel in harmony with Arthur's ideal, the visionary city is a-building still, for it is building always in the souls of those who believe. The city is not the reality; only the King is. This world derives its beauty from belief, and Gareth believes; hence, when he enters the enchanted city, enchanted as much by his vision as by Arthur's image, he sees, glancing from casements, "Eyes of pure women, wholesome stars of love," and the knights ranged about Arthur's throne display

> Clear honour shining like the dewy star
> Of dawn, and faith in their great King, with pure
> Affection, and the light of victory,
> And glory gained, and evermore to gain. (p. 1492)

Gareth sees the stars that Dagonet proved Tristram could not see. Here, for Gareth, are those stars shining in midday. Nor is Gareth's innocence the product of ignorance, but a disciplined resistance to corrupting influences. He will not find amusement in the low talk of his servile associates, but indicates his displeasure without giving offense, and gradually, by his good example, he has a beneficial effect upon his companions.

Gareth's disguise is a noble disguise, as Lancelot's was not; for Lancelot masked a lie with his pretence, while Gareth conceals his identity through obedience and humility, preferring to be tested not by name and lineage, but by act. Gareth, above all of Arthur's knights, has self-reverence, self-knowledge, and self-control, and so he succeeds.

If Gareth demonstrates the virtues of humility, faith, and worthy action, then it is Lynette who represents proud beauty. She is constantly designated through her pride, and when she and Gareth stop at a friendly baron's castle, it is before Lynette that "the peacock in his pride," is placed. (p. 1508) Like Princess Ida, Lynette is beautiful and worthy of obedience and service, but she is also proud and requires instruction in the proper method of controlling vanity. Gareth provides this education through his good example rather than with didactic disquisitions such as the Prince employed to convince Ida. Eventually, of course, Lynette accepts Gareth as worthy of her respect, even before she is informed of his aristocratic caste. Appropriately enough, Tennyson would wish that Gareth and Lynette —the one representing male virtues, the other adjusted feminine virtues—should be joined, and he concludes the poem with the apparently indifferent comment:

> And he that told the tale in older times
> Says that Sir Gareth wedded Lyonors,
> But he, that told it later, says Lynette. (p. 1525)

If Gareth need not contend with flaws of his own nature, he is provided with ample antagonists, nonetheless, for they are nothing less than the forces of Time as they operate upon man in general; they are the dirty nurse, Experience, who fouled Dagonet. Gareth, then, becomes the virtuous soul in contention with the generalized effect of experience, though, unlike Dagonet, he need not be washed. This much is perfectly evident through the allegory in the hermit's cave.

> 'Sir Knave, my knight, a hermit once was here,
> Whose holy hand hath fashioned on the rock
> The war of Time against the soul of man.

> And yon four fools have sucked their allegory
> From these damp walls, and taken but the form.'

In the rock are carved the names: Phosphorus, Meridies, Hesperus, Nox and Mors, and

> beneath five figures, armèd men,
> Slab after slab, their faces forward all,
> And running down the Soul, a Shape that fled
> With broken wings, torn raiment, and loose hair,
> For help and shelter to the hermit's cave. (p. 1519)

In the allegory, Time seems victorious, for the soul can only retreat. So will Merlin withdraw, defeated; so will Percivale withdraw, refusing further combat. But Gareth, having been unwilling to remain withdrawn at the beginning of his career, is even less inclined to repine and shrink from action now. There is no melancholy moodiness in him to make him dread himself and therefore incline to self-destruction. Sure of himself, hopeful always in his mood, he can, with a single purpose, direct his actions outward against obvious evil. This is more than his antagonists can do,

> Who ride abroad, and do but what they will;
> Courteous or bestial from the moment, such
> As have nor law nor king; and three of these
> Proud in their fantasy call themselves the Day,
> Morning-Star, and Noon-Sun, and Evening-Star. (p. 1501)

The other, of course, is Night, or Death. The first three are all that Gareth is not—self-indulgent, undisciplined, proud, and brutal, and they represent the manifestations of these qualities in the several stages of man's life, climaxing in Evening Star, with whom to do battle is "To war against ill uses of a life," (p. 1517) which we have allowed to usurp dominion over us. But this is not Gareth's case, and he defeats Evening Star as he did the others.

Gareth's tests, as one would expect, increase in difficulty to this point, but the gradual nature of his maturation is indicated even before he begins the combats. He takes a step forward when he leaves home, another when he overthrows Kay, demonstrating his knightly intent. Similarly illustrative of his progressive growth is the metaphor wherein Gareth's appearance in armor is likened to a butterfly emerging from its cocoon. These are necessary stages in his development, and the favorable end of the progression is indicated in Gareth's Cinderella image of himself. He tells Lynette,

> 'thou wilt find
> My fortunes all as fair as hers who lay
> Among the ashes and wedded the King's son.' (p. 1510)

Having advanced gradually from the most fundamental level of existence—for he was under the dominion of Kay, an alimentary figure, associated with the kitchen and the basic requirements of existence—to the conquest of death itself, Gareth has indicated the necessary mode of dealing with experience, or time. One conquers step by step. In *In Memoriam*, Tennyson had observed "That men may rise on stepping-stones / Of their dead selves to higher things." (i, p. 864) By the time of "Gareth and Lynette," he might say that men *must* rise in this manner, and in "The Progress of Spring," which appeared after the *Idylls* was completed, Tennyson recommended this same gradual advance.[26] "A simpler, saner lesson might he learn / Who reads thy gradual process, Holy Spring," says the poet, observing also that Spring's "scope of operation, day by day, / [grows] larger and fuller, like the human mind!" His conclusion has the same intent in this poem as in the Gareth idyll.

> Thy warmths from bud to bud
> Accomplish that blind model in the seed
> And men have hopes, which race the restless blood,

That after many changes may succeed
Life which is Life indeed. (p. 480)

Assumed in this attitude is the concept that redemption is gained through self-fulfilment, and that that self-fulfilment involves self-knowledge and a corresponding humility which enable the individual to recognize the persistent design that overrules the apparently random changes of material existence. Gareth's mode is the proper mode; his success will be complete. In "The Holy Grail," men try to leap to perfection, overlooking the necessity for constant labor in this world, as Arthur embodies it. The consequence is that many are lost, and the purest, Percivale, withdraws to isolation like the soul of the hermit's allegory.

Conquering all of the dangers that life offers to the soul does not guarantee that death will lose its mysterious dread, for it is silent, and in that silence is its greatest horror. That horror tested, however, it is revealed that death is "a blooming boy / Fresh as a flower new-born." (p. 1525) For one who has triumphed over the vices of this world, death becomes the promise of rebirth, not the horror of extinction. This is all too obvious, but what it implies in regard to Tennyson's permanent moral views is that hope is an essential quality in the very contention with life's vices.[27] Humility and hope provide Gareth with the enthusiasm to fulfil his quest, and whereas hope has created a sufficient and necessary strength, the benefit does not end there, for hope is fuel to further hope which begets a greater reward. A man who believes eternity available to him will not be a wailing ghost like Gawain. He, never thinking of eternity, is abandoned beyond death, which is, for him, a genuine horror. He who doubts, as the narrator of "The Two Voices" discovered, doubts to no rational purpose, since, as the Ancient Sage observed, nothing worthy proving can be adequately tested in terms of this world. Hope, then, is the wisest method, and Tennyson is suggesting here that it is the truest as well. For as doubt begets despair, and despair ennui and inaction, so hope begets further hope, conviction, and vigor in the struggle and beyond. In Gareth alone are the *virtues* of Tennyson's moral design victorious, and they provide the valuable touchstone against which all the failures may be tried. However, Gareth is not obliged to follow the *pattern* of the moral design and it is still a figure like Guinevere who enacts the entire scheme.

Balin and Balan

The last section of the *Idylls* was added several years after the poem seemed complete. Although it was composed at approximately the same time, it was more than a dozen years after "Gareth and Lynette," that Tennyson included the idyll of "Balin and Balan," because, as his son explains in the *Memoir*, "he felt that some further introduction to "Merlin and Vivien" was necessary."[28] The question remains: In what way was the new idyll to introduce "Merlin and Vivien"? If Merlin's collapse is principally that of the will yielding from internal inanition then perhaps Tennyson wished to show the step that leads to such internal collapse, and that stage is internal fragmentation. In earlier idylls, the self is secure, for even in doubting Geraint, the doubt is overcome and Enid is safely his; but in Balin and Balan we encounter the critical division of the self—the self no longer governed by a firm will to a single purpose.

Balin obviously represents the natural energy and force of human nature; if one were hard-pressed for terms, one might call it the Id. At any rate, he accepts the nickname, "the Savage," (p. 1578) and readily admits that it is his "heats and violences" that he must overcome. (p. 1581) These passions were the reason for his being ostracized from Arthur's court. Balan, on the other hand, is the governing faculty, controlling the undisciplined urges of its other half, even to the extent of guarding against the impulse to self-injury, for Balin declares that he "Had often wrought some fury on [himself], / Saving for Balin." (p. 1579) Balan protects his brother from the moods which are the greatest danger not only to others, but to himself. Would that such moody men as Merlin, Pelleas, or even Tristram, had such a brother to guard them from their own self-punishing moods.

Aside from his moods—his heats and violences—Balin is noble enough and wishes to improve; he even admits that Arthur's anger, demanding his temporary expulsion from the Order, was a "just wrath." (p. 1578) In desiring to amend himself, he takes as models for excellence Lancelot and Guinevere, hoping that their examples will assist him. But Balin does not find self-restraint easy, though it is essential to virtue; for, as the jaundiced eye sees everything yellow, so Balin's darkened eye sees all things darkly.

> Thus, as a hearth lit in a mountain home,
> And glancing on the window, when the gloom
> Of twilight deepens round it, seems a flame
> That rages in the woodland far below,
> So when his moods were darkened, court and King
> And all the kindly warmth of Arthur's hall
> Shadowed an angry distance: yet he strove
> To learn the graces of their Table, fought
> Hard with himself, and seemed at length in peace. (p. 1582-83)

Balin is aware of the dangers of such self-imputation, but, as Merlin's example reveals, self-awareness is no certain defense. Balin's fault is to be governed by moods arising from wild emotions, and he requires governance of those moods based upon reason and goodwill, as represented by Balan.

So uncertain is Balin of himself and of the forces that move him, that when he overhears the compromising conversation of Lancelot and Guinevere, he supposes that it is his own imagination imputing evil in what is really innocent speech. His anger is against himself and, rather than test the appearance, he flees from it. But retreat is never adequate, as Geraint learned to his salvation, and as Merlin learned too late. Running from evidence that might make us doubt our beliefs is no way of insuring them. Like Arthur Hallam, we must learn to face "the spectres of the mind / And [lay] them." (*In Memoriam*, xcvi, p. 948) Geraint learned that whether or not the Queen be true, he could be true himself. Balin is not prepared to make the same acknowledgment, though it would be the means to his redemption. Like Pelleas, he fears the collapse of his idols, for he has no other source of strength. His ideals are external; within him is the chaos of his moods and violences. So, fearing to face his fears, and in "gloom on gloom / Deepened," he speeds away, "mad for strange adventure." (p. 1584)

If the other idylls did not present adequate warning against retreat as a means of combatting moral evil, then the example of Pellam within this idyll does. Pellam's castle is "bushed about . . . with gloom," and he himself has taken to asceticism, hoping to outrival Arthur's holiness. In an irony not yet evident in the sequential scheme of the *Idylls*, Pellam "Hath pushed aside his faithful wife," thereby going Arthur one better. (p. 1580) How cutting that the wife of this humbug should be a faithful wife, and Arthur's what she is. Pellam's religious values are embodied in objects, such as relics and shrines, all external to himself. He has put his faith in material articles and relinquished the internal struggle, thereby lapsing into the sins of idolatry and presumption. Edward, in Tennyson's drama, *Harold*, was another eremitically inclined ruler who was excessively concerned with shrines and with purity through abnegation rather than engagement. The narrator of "The Supposed Confessions," feared that "All may not doubt, but everywhere / Some must clasp Idols." (p. 202) He does not add that those who clasp idols do so from weakness. To accept a code through conviction is one thing; to follow the same code for less profound reasons is still meritorious; but to reduce that code to relics and shrines for the simple purpose of insuring a moral profit is to reduce a spiritual reality to a commodity. If Balin could see his own failings intensified in the thoughtless Pellam, he might find redemption speedily, but he draws no lesson from that story.

Arthur had hoped that for Balin as for other men, such as Edyrn, his fall might prove a *felix culpa*. But Balin still finds it easier to rage against some external provocation, such as Garlon's insult, and then bemoan those violences with ecstasies of self-denigration. When he encounters Vivien, he is in one of his most madly volatile moods, overcome by shame for behavior he feels has defamed the idol he admires, his ideal Guinevere. He wishes only to be a brother to beasts, a creature "whose anger was his lord!" (p. 1589) When Vivien concocts new lies regarding Guinevere's virtue, Balin is persuaded with unaccountable expedition of their validity. The initial evidence, which before seemed insufficient, now appears concrete. His mood, still wrathful, veers wildly round, making his former idol the object now of his rage. There is no steadiness in him, no self-governance. When Vivien has goaded him further, "his evil spirit upon him" leaps, and he surrenders himself to anger, (p. 1590) trampling the symbol of Guinevere depicted upon his shield. In doing so, he releases a "weird yell, / Unearthlier than all shriek of bird or beast," and "Balan lurking there / (His quest was unaccomplished) heard and thought / 'The scream of that Wood-devil I came to quell!' " (p. 1590) And, indeed, it is the demon he sought, though it is Balin himself, for in his ungovernable rage he has been transformed into the beast he sought. Earlier, he had learned that the demon was supposedly the spirit of one injured by slander, who became hateful of his kind and struck always from behind. Balin, fleeing from his suspicions of Lancelot and Guinevere, is too enraged to observe that he is near the demon's cave, and it is then that the demon makes an assault upon him, for the fiend is a consubstantiated form of his own unmanageable mood. There has been sufficient evidence to indicate that this is so, for, when Balan set out on his quest to quell the demon, he admonished Balin,

'Let not thy moods prevail, when I am gone
Who used to lay them! hold them outer fiends,
Who leap at thee to tear thee; shake them aside,
Dreams ruling when wit sleeps! yea, but to dream
That any of these would wrong thee, wrongs thyself.' (p. 1580)

In effect, he is warning Balin that to believe in his angry moods is to reify them and to lead on to self-destructive doubt and despair. Likewise, for those who renounce Arthur's vows, the vows cease to operate, and a gradual loosening of discipline proceeds. It is the human will that is of consequence, and when the will is blind or undisciplined, only sorrow and destruction can follow. But when the will places its trust in a higher purpose it can work with conviction and discipline. When Balin sets out to contend with the wood-devil, he exclaims, " 'To lay that devil would lay the Devil in me,' " (p. 1584) but he does not succeed, for his "evil spirit" ambushes him after all. Because he looks inward while overwhelmed by his passions and his senses, Balin's vision is imperfect, and he betrays himself by trusting what he should realize are ambiguous forms of the material world. In thus submitting to the visible world, he betrays as well the invisible world, which, paradoxically, provides the truer vision.

So Balan, in fulfilling his quest, must destroy Balin, who now is the demon. But in destroying him, he quenches himself as well. When the passions become so unruly that they will destroy themselves, self-control, in contending with them, may be obliged to extinguish them totally and thereby end the entire man. It is not suicide, but the cancellation of all vitality. This is the outcome of internal dissension—the inability to govern the rudimentary man. If Gareth never experienced such division, and Geraint went into the wilderness to discover the means of avoiding it, all those who follow are to be aware of this quandary. And the realm itself progressively discloses the effects of internal weakness as the passions begin to challenge spiritual authority, and knights and ladies turn toward superficial forms, like Pellam's shrines, instead of trusting the reliable values residing only within the human individual which make possible the enchanted city built to music that never was and therefore always is.

Summary

The *Idylls of the King*, in completed form, presents very much the same pattern that Tennyson had revealed in numerous other poems, though more intricately, and, I believe more profoundly. Nevertheless, a simple description of the design can be hazarded, in spite of the ultimately irreducible nature of that scheme, which relies upon the evocation of its parts rather than upon any rational explication of the phantom paradigm that arises from them. If we may qualify by imagining the moral design as a sort of smoky ideogram rising out of the matter of the poem itself, some simple description may be justifiable. Like faith, the design is not material, but ideal.

In "The Coming of Arthur," Tennyson describes a world newly won from the bestial elements of human nature, yet there are already suggestions that this triumph will not be permanent. Even so, we are made aware of the need for certain crucial values. Faith must overcome all doubt; actions must be performed in humility and governed by an undivided will. The consequences will be peace, contentment, and joy; all made available through the victory that hope inspirits and insures. "Gareth and Lynette" offers an illustration of the perfect state, where no contention is demanded; faith, humility, and hope are never questioned from within. With the Geraint idylls, doubt begins to trouble this certainty and drives the soul into its own wilderness, where it is obliged to vanquish its particular spectres

—mainly projections of its own worst qualities. Yet in these idylls the contest is successful, and pride, having been the principal offender, is temporarily contained. With "Balin and Balan," an equally serious dilemma arises—the necessity of controlling the passions which form our moods, which in themselves may resurrect a moody pride either of spirit or of flesh, and thereby lead us to doubt, despair and self-injury. This idyll may be considered the initiation of the downward movement in the poem, for, although Balan never doubts Guinevere's innocence, the fact remains that Balin and Balan destroy themselves. It is a draw of sorts.[29] Given this model for internal division, the nature of Merlin's failure in "Merlin and Vivien" becomes more obvious. It is less a seduction of the flesh than an undefended ennui of spirit that dooms the magus. As with Balin, it is the inability to control a doubting mood that dooms him. Here there is no stand-off, but an outright defeat. We have not got beyond the first voice in "The Two Voices."

With "Lancelot and Elaine," the yielding is certainly to the flesh, and the consequence of a marred will struggling to remain noble is still the loss of purity. Once the image and ideal of purity, represented by Elaine and Galahad, lose substance, actual purity only persists through withdrawal, though such retreat has been shown throughout the *Idylls* to be a step toward a potentially weakened will (though a favorable transformation may easily occur). In "Pelleas and Ettarre," the superficial, waxing from "Balin and Balan" onward, has usurped control. Courtliness now replaces courtesy, and the motive force is external in Pelleas as it was internal and genuine in Gareth. Doubt easily overcomes belief, for it is easier now that belief is so poorly grounded. With purity gone and belief a form, all innocence is dead, and in "The Last Tournament," the corrupted knight, Tristram, tries to console himself with self-indulgence, not recognizing that he dooms himself through his own false values.

"Guinevere" is the low point of the design, but also the point of salvation, for Guinevere now sheds her voluptuous pride—an act that the preceding idylls have gradually been preparing us for—and achieves authentic humility. The necessary fall now leads back to redemption through humility, love, and selflessness. Appropriately enough, it is the earthly representative of the royal couple who is redeemed, since earthly beauty remains sublunary and must be purified for the next visitation of the spiritual idea; and Arthur, we are assured, will return in another form. Lancelot, meanwhile, will also die a holy man. The picture is not so dark as it is usually supposed, for, although Arthur goes to the last great battle in the west, though the soul must pass to death, there is the promise of fulfilment beyond the grave, and the poem closes with signs of the new sun rising that might bring in the voice to cry "Rejoice!" once more.

So, while throughout the *Idylls*, parts of the design elaborate themselves or the whole is enacted in miniature, as with Dagonet or Edyrn, in the complete poem the design may also be seen in operation. I do not mean to contradict Tennyson's own image of the poem as "the dream of man coming into practical life and ruined by one sin," for the poem ends with the failure of the Order and the death of Arthur.[30] Tennyson was not attempting, in the *Idylls*, simply to reproduce old legends. His aim was to transform an appealing narrative into a beneficial parable. Like *Maud*, it was designed to transcend its own time and offer a moral lesson for all men and all times. Though Tennyson necessarily drew upon early accounts of the Arthurian legend, like other of his contemporaries he fashioned them to suit his purpose.[31] Having Lancelot arrive at Astolat by way of his fancy and alone was not a part of Malory's account, for example; nor was Gawain the mean figure there that he becomes in "Lancelot and Elaine." That Tennyson could follow the general pattern of the legend and yet inform it with his own purpose is as much a triumph as the technical skill exercised in the composition.

Beyond the simple allegory, if we may call it that, there is another ordering concept in the *Idylls of the King* and that is the pattern of faith triumphing over pride-engendered doubt through humility, love, and selflessness; and, although Arthur may die and the order may pass away, and the dream of man may be ruined by that one sin, still the moral assumptions reflected in Arthur's recognition of God's purpose in the changing order of things, and the hopeful indications in the salvation of Guinevere in this life, and Arthur in the next, belie the melancholy appearances of the tale itself and suggest rather the mood and spirit which conclude *In Memoriam*, a poem about another ideal man who passed away and whose passing occasioned the review of the same moral design that I have described here; a man who provided a glimpse of the potential man yet to come through the gradual process of self-fulfilment and self-improvement that the race and all individuals are hopefully engaged upon:

> Whereof the man, that with me trod
> This planet, was a noble type
> Appearing ere the times were ripe,
> That friend of mine who lives in God,
>
> That God, which ever lives and loves,
> One God, one law, one element,
> And one far-off divine event,
> To which the whole creation moves. (p. 988)

THREE

IDYLLS OF THE KING
Themes

Introduction

"To live in the Idea," said Goethe, "means treating the impossible as though it were possible."[1] This is both a justification and an explanation of Tennyson's *Idylls of the King*. Arthur's vows, we are told early in the poem, are not such as men can keep, yet any man should be ashamed not to take them. In short, man's way should be to commit himself to ideals that are unattainable. There is more here than an echo of Browning's "A man's reach should exceed his grasp / Or what's a heaven for?"[2] It is an idea which was current enough in Tennyson's time, and which was presented even by the unreligious Meredith in "The Woods of Westermain." Man approaches his divinity, which for Meredith is Nature, with humility, in order that he may fulfil himself in the necessary and inclusive progress from blood, to brain, to spirit. Spirit, of course, is never to be fully commanded. Even for Swinburne, it is ultimately spirit that is important, encompassing the substantial world and contributing value to human performance only insofar as it aspires to the spiritual.

With Tennyson, as with other poets and writers of his time, the ascent to spirit was not considered a finality, it was a process.

What was more, that process, for the religious and unreligious alike, was a part of some greater design, which, though constant in itself, occasioned the continual flux of material existence. One of the greatest lessons to be learned is submission to that design—that change is toward some end, as for Meredith "Change is on the wing to bud / Rose in brain from rose in blood."[3] Although Tennyson's view of man's necessary projection of a destiny resembled the views of his contemporaries, his insights were particularized in his works—and especially in the *Idylls*—in an excitingly individual manner.

Hallam Tennyson's account of what his father meant in the *Idylls*, along with his quotations of Tennyson's comments upon the poem, admirably specify the purpose and general method of the poem. Yet submerged in the statements of the *Memoir* are implications and suggestions too seductive to ignore.

Thus far, I have attempted to show that there is an overarching moral design that emerges from the *Idylls*. My presentation of this design is more involved than Hallam Tennyson's. For him, the poem pictures, basically, "the world-wide war of Sense and Soul, typified in individuals, with the subtle interaction of character upon character."[4] By no means do I dispute this summary of the poem. I simply wish to indicate that the design is more subtle—and more precisely elucidated in the poem itself. Hallam's comments on the poem suggest as much, for he explains the sequence of the *Idylls* in terms of man's capacity or incapacity to escape the self, and, through belief and hope, to offer humble service to a high ideal. But what it *means* to serve or live in the ideal is an important part of Tennyson's poem. Nor is it an easy subject to examine, since, as Goethe's remark indicates, it often depends upon a splendid illusion. Yet to have splendid illusions, to treat the impossible as though it were possible, need not be the practice of a fool. The American idealist, Henry David Thoreau, was among the most practical of men, and he remarked of dreams, "If you have built castles in the air, your work need not be lost; that is where they should be. Now put the foundations under them."[5] Tennyson's aim was similar. Though ideals be nothing more than splendid illusions, it may transpire that those illusions are more substantial than men suppose, if they are capable of transforming our lives. Meredith remarked, "Your prayers have been answered if you rise from them a better man."[6] What is most important is that men have ideals; for without such ideals to turn our eyes and natures upward, Tennyson felt, we have a tendency to wallow.

The importance that Tennyson placed on the function of ideals requires small verification outside his poems; still, his son's condensation of his sentiments, particularly in regard to the *Idylls*, invites us to examine this complex and subtle work in another of its several aspects.

> My father felt strongly that only under the inspiration of ideals, and with his "sword bathed in heaven," can a man combat the cynical indifference, the intellectual selfishness, the sloth of will, the utilitarian materialism of a transition age. "Poetry is truer than fact" he would say. Guided by the voice within, the Ideal Soul looks out into the Infinite for the highest Ideal; and finds it nowhere realized so mightily as in the Word who "wrought With human hands the creed of creeds."[7]

Ludwig Feuerbach also defined God in terms of man's projected ideals.

> Such as are a man's thoughts and dispositions, such is his God; so much worth as a man has, so much and no more has his God. Consciousness of God is self-consciousness, knowledge of God is self-knowledge. By his God thou knowest the man, and by the man his God; the two are identical.[8]

In another place, Feuerbach remarks that "every being is in and by itself infinite—has its God, its highest conceivable being, in itself."[9]

But Tennyson's conception of the highest ideal, most ably

141

represented in Christ, differs in that it is bound up with the truth of poetry. Tennyson's acknowledgment of Christ, the Word, as the realization of the ideal is not unconnected with the predicative approbation that Christ "wrought with human hands the creed of creeds." In his early lyric, "The Poet," Tennyson represented the poet flinging "the wingèd shafts of truth," and thereby establishing a climate suitable to Freedom cloaked in Wisdom. (p. 223) This regard for the poet's moral duty never left him. In the poem, "To the Queen," which closes the *Idylls of the King*, Tennyson lists, among the possible "signs of storm" threatening England and civilization, Softness, Cowardice, querulous Labour, and "Art with poisonous honey stolen from France." (p. 1756) Valuing art as of the highest moral significance, and convinced of the dangers of self-indulgent estheticism—as "The Palace of Art" clearly shows—an apparently corruptive art ranked among the major indications of impending disaster for Tennyson. Art was not, in any event, inconsequential.

What is yet more intriguing in Tennyson's attitude toward articulated art is his precocious and acute awareness of the potential effects of language and fable. In "Timbuctoo," the poem refashioned from the earlier "Armageddon," for which he won the Chancellor's Prize on June 6, 1829, at Cambridge, Tennyson was already expressing attitudes that not only persisted in his beliefs, but which became manifest in his poetry. "Timbuctoo" opens with the poet standing upon a mountain, the heavens "blenched with faery light, / Uncertain whether faery light or cloud." (p. 172)

> And much I mused on legends quaint and old
> Which whilome won the hearts of all on Earth
> Toward their brightness, even as flame draws air;
> But had their being in the heart of Man
> As air is the life of flame: and thou wert then
> A centred glory-circled Memory,

Divinest Atalantis, whom the waves
Have buried deep, and thou of later name,
Imperial Eldorado, roofed with gold:
Shadows to which, despite all shocks of Change,
All on-set of capricious Accident,
Men clung with yearning Hope which would not die. (p. 173)

The poet's meditations are interrupted by a glorious "Seraph"
who tells him

> 'Thy sense is clogged with dull mortality;
> Thy spirit fettered with the bond of clay:
> Open thine eyes and see.' (p. 175)

And in a moment the poet is endowed with the simultaneous
powers of panoramic and microscopic vision which free the
power of his thoughts as "dusky worms" breaking from sub-
aqueous and subterranean depths might "pass from gloom to
glory." (p. 177) The splendid Seraph identifies himself.

> 'I am the Spirit,
> The permeating life which courseth through
> All the intricate and labyrinthine veins
> Of the great vine of *Fable*, which, outspread
> With growth of shadowing leaf and clusters rare,
> Reacheth to every corner under Heaven,
> Deep-rooted in the living soil of truth.' (p. 180)

Of his powers he says:

> 'There is no mightier Spirit than I to sway
> The heart of man: and teach him to attain
> By shadowing forth the Unattainable;
> And step by step to scale that mighty stair
> Whose landing-place is wrapt about with clouds
> Of glory' of Heaven. (p. 179)

The Spirit has this beneficial potency for men because "few

there be / So gross of heart who have not felt and known / A higher than they see: They with dim eyes / Behold me darkling." (p. 179) Man's inborn craving for an ideal is what makes possible the leading power of poetry, of Fable, of Art.[10] Fabular art offers to man's famished imagination material images of his unuttered desire. Through these images—these stories or legends—it cloaks with circumstantiality for a time, in a new legend, a new creed, men's high ideals; and, for a time, men are led a step higher toward the Unattainable. Man does not, of course attain the Unattainable, as the Round Table does not fulfil Arthur's dream; but he does learn the *process* of attainment, and it is, as always with Tennyson, this process, the struggle toward the ideal, that is of conclusive importance.

In "Timbuctoo," as later in the *Idylls*, what begins in mystery ends in mystery, for, the Spirit having departed "Heaven-ward on the wing," the poet finds himself alone on his visionary mountain where first he had observed "a faery light," and where now "all was dark!" (p. 181) Man does not easily attain ideals. He possesses them only so long as he can express or enact them; thereafter, they resume their habitation in unattainable heaven. Vision is a fleeting gift.

This early poem, "Timbuctoo," specifically about the powers of constructive articulation, contains in it several motifs important in Tennyson's poetry—especially, as far as this present study is concerned, the *Idylls of the King*. The moral power of Fable is evident, but associated with this idea are related images and allusions concerning obscurity and clarity, authority and obedience, freedom and constraint. In "Timbuctoo" the poet's imagination is fired by a legend, or, more accurately, a meditation upon legends generically. From this region of "faery light or cloud" he advances to a state of intense visual clarity. Acute vision subsiding, he lapses once more into darkness. From mystery, as I have said, to mystery; yet all-importantly, with an intervening period of precise and mystical vision.

Inseparable from this alternation of obscurity and clarity is the poet's submission to the Spirit's authority. It is because he obeys the Spirit's commands, to which he is previously inclined by his elementary meditations on legend, that he attains his temporary vision. The Spirit's command involves yet another complex image of liberation, for it is because the poet's spirit is "fettered with the bond of clay" that he is unable to see. When he escapes provisionally from the bond of clay, his mind achieves a liberty imaged in the escape of a larval creature into winged existence; a wakening to the "Higher Laws" as Thoreau expressed it, employing similar images of spiritual enfranchisement.

As in the *Idylls*, it is man's physical nature, his confinement in the world of sense, that induces the obscurity and mystery of the true world of spiritual perception. Man's senses are the bog from which obscuring clouds arise, obliterating the heavens. Only at times is this mist blown away and a vision of the stars secured. Man's duty thereafter is to act as though the stars were permanently visible to him; perhaps even embodied, as real terrestrial guides.[11] In short, his duty is to behave as though the impossible were possible; the unattainable attainable.

In the *Idylls* the interwoven themes of articulation and silence, command and obedience, freedom and constraint, clarity and obscurity, are so important as to require serious examination. Elusive as they are themselves, they provide, nonetheless, a material fabric from which the over-all moral design is composed; they particularize our experience of the poem as an impelling moral declaration expressed in a deftly complex method. And *method* is of the greatest consequence, since the *message*, as Tennyson so often suggested, remained the same. All religions attempt the same fable. Tennyson remarked, in approving one of F.D. Maurice's views, "all religions seemed to him to be imperfect manifestations of the true Christianity."[12] Hence the articulating of the creed in a suitable legend assumes equal importance with the legend itself, for without it man's vision will not escape the fetters of clay. The ideal remains the same, but the Word changes; the creed of creeds does not alter, but it finds manifold expression in its changing parables and legends. The *Idylls of the King* is Tennyson's legend for the "yearning Hope" that will not die. Hallam Tennyson's paraphrase of Dean Alford's estimate of the *Idylls* shows that the poet's contemporaries appreciated its fabular significance.

> Yet in spite of the ebbs and flows in the tide of human affairs, in spite of the temporary bearing down of the pure and lofty purpose, the author has carefully shadowed forth the spiritual progress and advance of the world, and has enshrined man's highest hopes in this new-old legend, crowning with a poet's prophetic vision the vague and disjointed dreams of a bygone age.[13]

Language

The uses of language in the *Idylls of the King* are both numerous and complex, and to consolidate them into a unified and credible theme requires a paradoxical fragmentation. It is useless to demonstrate that various forms of utterance or transcription produce either good or evil without signifying the difference between silences and inarticulate utterances, between these and speech, and between speech and other modes of expression and formulation. Moreover, the many forms of speech may act in many ways: to inform, command, or confuse; to inspirit, create, or betray. Beyond illustrations of the manner in which language functions, it is necessary to consider its effectiveness or futility, since often in the *Idylls* language disarmed by apathy is useless or worse. Declarative or narrative language is also subtly distinguished from language as signification; notably in the practice of naming. Furthermore, Tennyson's own articulation must not be confused, intimately related as it obviously is, with his use of language as a theme. It is evident, then, that there are numerous pitfalls in an examination of this kind, though the profits are, I feel, well worth the risk.

It is, at any rate, reassuring to know that Tennyson's close friend, to whom he addressed "The Palace of Art," had published *On the Study of Words* only a few years before Tennyson returned to his Arthurian material. Although it offers no concrete evidence that Tennyson thought about language in the same terms as his friend, Richard Chenevix Trench's book does prove that a man who shared his thoughts with Tennyson held a view of language that placed it among the spiritual utilities.[14]

Man acquired his personality, or identity, Tennyson felt, in the same divisive act of creation that separated him from the purity of spirit. In assuming humanity, each man re-enacts God's incarnation in Christ. He also encounters the dilemma of converting sensations which participate in his spiritual existence into useful manifestations in an alien, material being. Language is the imperfect agent of this desire. Because language itself is a blending of the abstract and the material—the idea and the articulation—it is the proper metaphor and means for the communication of experiences neither wholly human nor entirely divine. The word is to the idea as substance is to spirit, and just as phenomena can either cloak or reveal the spiritual reality, so words are ambiguous and may distort or clarify abstract notions that they are meant to embody.[15] Language is a kind of magic, which, energized by man's imagination, sanctifies the world of substance and cloaks it with the glory of the spirit.[16] Throughout the *Idylls* Tennyson utilizies the parallel between man's spirit becoming flesh as God's spirit was made manifest in Christ; a familiar idea to Victorian thinkers. But Tennyson drew a further, less common parallel between the reduction of spirit to flesh and the reduction of idea to word. Arthur Symons, approaching the thought from a literary point of view, offers a clear exposition of the parallel, explaining that "Just as a soul, born out of eternity into time, takes on itself the impress of earth and the manners of human life, so a dramatic creation, pure essence in the shaping imagination of the poet, takes on itself, in its passage into life something of the impress of its abode."[17] But, miraculous as language may be, it is still an imperfect magic and may serve evil purposes with the good, for men are not divine, and some are hardly human.

The ur-text of all magic that Merlin describes to Vivien is "Writ in a language that has long gone by." (p. 1613) So obscure and cryptic is this source of enchantment, which preceded the arising of mountains and the building of cities, that no one, not even Merlin can read the original text. The unknowable text, however, is surrounded "With comment, densest condensation, hard / To mind and eye," and, Merlin explains, "none can read the comment but myself." (p. 1613) The inscrutable book of enchantments could have for author only the Unnameable, and the ur-text itself is the unresolvable signification of the mystery of existence, preceding mountains and cities. The numerous "scribbled, crost, and crammed" comments represent man's intellectual struggle to interpret a mystery never thoroughly decipherable. Only Merlin, the wizard of the imaginative intellect, can read the glosses because man's imaginative reason, not scientific evidence, is what Tennyson believed would lead man's mind to truth and wisdom. Merlin's book of enchantments is a fitting emblem of the Word as Mystery to complement the traditional idea of the Word as Divinity. Not through dry inquiry will man deal with the authentic mystery of human existence, but through the magic of intuition and imagination.

If the Word is mystery, however, it remains an unreadable symbol, or, more accurately, collection of symbols. Man can read only his own language, which is no more than his attempt to provide an order and form for existence. His comments can only approximate the authentic text, his ideals only approach the truth as extensions of his own being. Man's language is a sophisticated pattern superimposed upon the world whereby he finds an organization and system resembling himself as much as it resembles what is Real—that is, what is beyond himself and beyond the circumstantial world. In creating a language, man creates himself.

According to his fellow magician, Bleys, when Merlin discovered the "naked babe" upon the shore, he cried, " 'The King!' " (p. 1480) Thereby a king was made. It was the word that made it so. The babe, naked of all significance or meaning, was instantly clothed with the glorious garment of a materializing word. The ideal expressed became a fact, just as Camelot, believed, became the incarnate music of Merlin's harmonious scheme. And yet, Bleys' account of Merlin's royal discovery was not necessarily actual, though it might be the Truth. Merlin, when interrogated, answers with riddles that imitate the mystery of his power.

> And truth is this to me, and that to thee;
> And truth or clothed or naked let it be. (p. 1480)

The Truth revealed directly, or obscurely in a riddle, is nonetheless the Truth, though men may find convenient and disparate truths according to their fancies. Arthur, whether real heir or even real man or not, is still corporealization of the ideal.

Merlin's cryptic response indicates, at the same time, the glory and the danger of expression. If language can clothe the ideal or bedizen truth with a fable, then a lie may wear a garment of language, transforming unsubstanced slander to consequence. It was Merlin who fashioned The Siege Perilous, "carven with strange figures . . . and letters in a tongue no man could read." What Merlin's power of enchantment conceived is "Perilous for good and ill," (p. 1666) and Merlin himself was lost through forgetfulness of his own powers, though Galahad, in a similar posture, was saved.

Arthur, "in low deep tones, / And simple words of great authority," was able to bind the knights of the newly established Order to his vows. This was the highest function of language, deriving power from more than mere language.

> 'But when he spake and cheered his Table Round
> With large, divine, and comfortable words,
> Beyond my tongue to tell thee—I beheld
> From eye to eye through all their Order flash
> A momentary likeness of the King.' (p. 1477)

Through language, man is able to order existence. But he imposes this order not only on inanimate existence gripped in his mind, but on his fellow men as well, through their own imaging powers. Their vows are the *recreation* of the ideal vision, which they actually behold within themselves, through their *own* imaginative powers. Arthur's vision is not imposed upon his followers' minds, it is born in them. It is their own creative act, sparked by the King's.[18] That the vows may fail without being false, we have already seen in our examination of "The Last Tournament" and will have occasion to reconsider later. That they do fail is the inescapable converse of their potential success. They depend upon the embodying imagination. Like music, the power of the vows demands shaping attention and harmonious fulfilment. A man, as Thoreau might say, must not only listen to his own drummer, but never cease to follow the beat.

Balin, coming to court at a time when Arthur's music is not so mighty as it once has been, feels himself moving "in music with his Order, and the King." But the defect in his nature, as in the nature of all men, appears in the remark that "The nightingale, full-toned in middle May," may seem to have "another voice in other groves." So, for Balin, "after some quick burst of sudden wrath, / The music in him seemed to change, and grow / Faint and far-off." (p. 1582) Man hears in the nightingale as much music as his imaginative grove will permit. The nightingale renders, but the mind creates, as Keats had earlier concluded. Music requires the conjunction of independently progressing parts. To be a part of Arthur's music, it is inadequate merely to attend, one must also eagerly perform. The music within the heart hums sympathetically to Arthur's dominant tone.

The ur-text of the observable world, written in an undecipherable script, but before us always as a puzzle and a mystery, can be read by no man, nor can most men interpret even the comments upon that text. Yet all men have the power to view the text and the comment, and all men have the power to create from the text irresponsible or admirable tales: desponding prophecies or glorious fictions. Though a Balin may lose his faith in the vows he has taken, and a Tristram pervert them; though men may revive a doubt in the history of their King or the achievements of the very legend they themselves have witnessed; the power to read in existence what it is most worthy in man to read persists. Gareth, when first described, is rendering the natural world about him into incidents of a heroic conquest of evil; to him a falling pine becomes a false knight overthrown. What is more, he is aware of his own imaginative act, for he complains that while the cataract does God's will "and not knowest," he, knowing, is not permitted to act. (p. 1484) Later in his adventures, Gareth again displays an able tendency to interpret nature in terms of worthy action defending the good. For the innocent imagination, untainted by despair or self-indulgence, the world, though a cryptic manuscript, nonetheless is a book of emblems prompting the mind to high imaginings. If man will look for the highest ideals in nature, he will find them there, long engraved, awaiting his consort and consent to produce a superb harmony.

The pure and eager Gareth's reading of nature resembles Elaine's virtuous meditations upon Lancelot's shield. The marks upon the shield are not symbolic like those of Achilles'; they are no more than tokens of numerous conflicts. But to the pure imagination of Elaine, they become an animated history of Lancelot's greatness. Elaine "guessed a hidden meaning in his arms, / Now made a pretty history to herself," creating thereby a noble world in which "she lived in fantasy." (p. 1621) As Elaine's imagination has power to create a noble ideal from a naked shield, so Gareth has power to compose images of virtue from nature and read the world in virtuous terms. And so, in a like manner, Merlin has the power to say of a naked babe, ungarmented with absolute testimonials, "this is the King."

From the pure and constructive imagination ideals arise; through expression they are communicated; enactment makes them real. Gareth, clearly a representative servant of virtue, not only conceives the ideal, but enacts it; moreover, he is conscious of the force of language, especially in the form of narrative. When Gareth's associates in the kitchen of Arthur's castle fall to foul talk, his response is to "whistle rapid as any lark, / Or carol some old roundelay," and when telling his own tales he confines himself to exemplary stories wherein events present worthy models. This noble practice of the incipient artist is rewarded by reverence in his fellows. (p. 1498) Perhaps it seems like wishful thinking on Tennyson's part. But it is worth remembering that Tennyson had evidence that his own moral and uplifting narratives served exactly the purposes he championed. Moreover, he was more than casually aware of a certain reverence in his audience.

As the Spirit of Fable in "Timbuctoo" asserted, tales have great power to lead to truth. And for those who have glimpsed the truth, there is an obligation to go further: to venture expression of the truth in the plastic form of language and symbol or the assertive form of action. It was Merlin's rendering of Arthur's ideality into narrative that made possible the responsive audience of knights who accepted the obligations of Arthur's vows. Tristram, when soured, recalls that "that weird legend of his birth, / With Merlin's mystic babble about his end / Amazed me." (p. 1722)

152

A fable or narrative, by obliquely articulating an inexpressible hope in man's nature, touches emotions that fire the imagination, which struggle to condense its mysterious feelings of faith into material realities. When Percivale's sister, though sequestered in an anchoritic cell, hears the scandals of Arthur's Court, she craves some means to combat this pernicious fabulation. Learning of "the Holy Grail, / A legend handed down through five or six, / And each of these a hundred winters old, / From our Lord's time," she yearns to recall the Grail by her prayers and fasting. Before long, she does have a vision of the Grail which she is able to communicate to others. Most especially it is Galahad, purportedly "Begotten by enchantment," who "believed in her belief." (pp. 1665-66)

Ambrosius, surprised by Percivale's account of the Holy Grail, says that the old books he knows are "Mute of this miracle." (p. 1663) It is not through mere historical accounts that the questing spirit is animated, but more through legends that give breath to high ideals. Through the power of her belief, the holy nun transmits the legend of the Holy Grail and becomes one of the "five or six" whose imaginative faith is powerful enough to spark the holy flame in men. The nun supplements her visionary account with another esthetic resource for fixing the ideal in her disciple's imagination. She gives to Galahad an emblematic sword belt, signifying the need for conflict in the pursuit of truth, on which there is woven "a strange device, / A crimson grail within a silver beam." (p. 1666)

Only Galahad, mysteriously associated with enchantment already, is capable of fulfilling the quest, and he alone bears the nun's sacred device. It is Galahad alone who has been worthy of the quest, for all men see according to their sight, as Arthur later explains, and only Galahad had the visionary power to range beyond concerns of the flesh; only he could see before the quest began the achievable holy city. Others, who followed not because they had seen, but precisely because they had not seen, travelled only so far as their vision propelled them: into wilderness, captivity, or madness. Each man serves in his own way, and he who has not seen the vision would do best to serve humbly. Ambrosius has not seen the vision, yet he is not unworthy. His endeavours and accomplishments are as valuable as any, for they are moved by humility and love. Grand visions are only grandly conceived when the mind conceiving them is humble. If one has not first lost the self, the self is certain to be itself lost in the quest. The noble and inspiriting Fable, though comprehensible to all men of good faith, is only to be fulfilled by one to whom the impossible is possible. He alone lives in the ideal. He has made the vision his own, and accordingly, for him it is real. The others, fettered in individual bonds of clay, never discover the substance of the fleshless ideal.

Tennyson, in altering the "Morte d'Arthur" to "The Passing of Arthur," opened the later version with Sir Bedivere telling the "story" of the end of the Order, when he "was no more than a voice," and thereby pointed out more directly the function of his own narrative. The fading voice of a lost time, among "new faces, other minds," does not promise a noble era to follow as a consequence of the legend. Yet the legend is worthily preserved. (p. 1742) There is no expectation that Bedivere's auditors—represented both by the generations following Arthur's departure and the readers of Tennyson's fable—will rise to noble action, moved by more than a dry chronicle. In making Bedivere "no more than a voice," Tennyson may even be implying that he, too, is no more than a voice and that his task is to utilize language to express an ideal and keep the ideal alive in legend. Like the holy nun, he will not go forth to do actual battle, bearing a talismanic emblem or Excalibur. The poem is his gesture, his deed, and it signifies his faith in the positive though dangerous value of language.

If it is not always possible to act, it is at least possible to learn the proper respect for whatever powers we do possess to aid the doers. Though Lynette leads Gareth, her lead is ironically unsuitable, for she is the less equipped of the two in the combat with evil. Her tongue, though not leased to evil as Vivien's is, is nonetheless careless. Through pride, she is moved to speak improperly to her champion. At one point he ventures to correct her by suggesting, "Fair words were best for him who fights for thee," though he promptly utilizes her vilifications as pricks to sterner action. (p. 1511) Obliged to plead for Morning Star's life, Lynette begins to perceive the proper use of language. Gareth, when reviled by Morning Star, can retort "Dog, thou liest," (p. 1512) as he could not to Lynette, who was guilty of an identical offense. What is more, Gareth materially proves himself by defeating Morning Star. And, although the case is longer in being settled, he is able to prove himself with Lynette as well, for, when he battles with Star of Evening, she cheers him on, and he, armed with her support, fights more fervently. Geraint was similarly empowered by the supporting exclamation of Enid to overcome Edyrn. Those who only stand and wait may nonetheless call to those in the midst of battle, and their reminders of the goal foreseen, may prove a welcome auxiliary in the harsh combat.

Still, it is better if the reminding cries come from within, and that is the purpose of Arthur's vows. They are verbal emblems to keep the endeavor's aim before the mind of the knight of faith. The assembled vows are the individual's order, just as the Round Table is designed, on a larger scale "To serve as model for the mighty world, / And be the fair beginning of a time." (p. 1736) The vows, as we have seen in our examination of "The Last Tournament," can fail. And when they fail, they fail mightily. It is essential that the vows be as much the imaginative act of the individual who makes them as that the magician should believe in his magic.

Though the vows failed for Pelleas, there is evidence that it was Pelleas who failed first. An indication of Pelleas' fault is in

the nature of his seeing. When the young knight first sees Ettarre and her company, it is a sight "Strange as to some old
prophet might have seemed / A vision hovering on a sea of fire."
(p. 1689) But some old prophet's vision would not have been
confined to the superficial likeness of a simile, nor would his attention have been trapped in detail. The prophets who appear
in the *Idylls* do not see things of this earth in fanciful form, but
present in fanciful forms of this earth the unseen truths beyond.
Though Merlin, who riddled in truths, is undone by a sly slanderer and his own morose vision, it is not a surface illusion that
quells him. But Pelleas' false vision is its own best warning, for
in it Pelleas sees damsels who "talked confusedly . . . Because the
way was lost." (p. 1689) With hints like these, it is not difficult
for the reader, no matter how inept Pelleas may have been, to
understand that it is Pelleas' own 'vision' that blinds him. Unlike Gareth, who saw in the sights of nature emblems of his
anticipated conflict with evil, Pelleas sees in lovely women,
garbed with similes, nothing more than beautiful bewilderment.
Ironically, it is this youth, unsupported by an authentic vision
of his own and defended only by good nature, that the corrupt
associates of Ettarre select as their "pilot-star."

When Ettarre, having accomplished her selfish aim, came to
discard Pelleas, she "mocked his vows and the great King," and
the astonished young knight was "stricken mute" by her railing.
Overwrought with annoyance at Pelleas' innocence, she ex-
claimed of Arthur, "I never heard his voice / but longed to break
away.'" (p. 1694) It is the voice of truth that Ettarre does not
wish to hear, and so, unlike the more courageous narrator of
"The Two Voices," she listens only to her favorite voice. It is
much later, when all opportunity for practical redemption seems
lost, that she realizes which voice had deceived her.

When Pelleas, thoroughly disenchanted by Gawain's behavior, raves, "the King / Hath made us fools and liars. O noble
vows!" (p. 1701) he does not realize that the vows had altered

men from a "simple race of brutes," and offered them an opportunity to be more than fools and liars. Arthur gave the opportunity; only the individual can fulfil the idea presented to him. If the ideal was his own, the vows were his own, and only he can make himself a fool and liar. Pelleas' dream "that Gawain fired / The hall of Merlin, and the morning star / Reeled in the smoke, brake into flame, and fell," (p. 1702) is a true prophetic dream, unlike his earlier vision, which was an ocular and moral illusion. Both are products of his imagination. But the dream, born from Pelleas' mind, lives only there. Merlin's hall still stands, the morning star has not fallen. Only in the mystic city of his own spirit has there been holocaust, just as Merlin's prophetic dream involved mainly his own demise.

Sir Bedivere was "First made and latest left of all the knights," (p. 1742) perhaps because "bold in heart and act and word was he, / Whenever slander breathed against the King." (p. 1474) He is one model that persists throughout the *Idylls*. But the ammunition of evil is abundant. And he who wishes to combat it must be certain of his own defenses. Balin, for example, is eager to war for the good; he even acquires what he takes to be a talismanic emblem—the "crown-royal upon [his]shield." (p. 1582) Arthur, permitting the symbol, remarks that it is only a "shadow's shadow." In Balin's view, however, it is light, not shadow, and "golden earnest of a gentler life!" (p. 1582) But Balin's imagination is too easily inflamed by the sinister and scornful, and, though he distrusts the inclination in himself, he is its victim. Whereas Balin, overhearing an ambiguous conversation between Lancelot and Guinevere, contains his dark suspicions, he is not proof against the soiling hint cast in the form of an idle tale that Vivien provides.

Balin learns—or we learn through his unlucky career—that the sinister demon in the self, the "evil spirit" that eventually overcomes Balin, can assume a substantial being. If legends, vows, and other forms of worthy speech may make dreams and ideals manifest, so can less worthy forms of articulation. The Demon of the Woods is nothing more than an incarnation of the demon in the breast—man's susceptibility to the leering word. If the Word can be Divine, or Mysterious, it can be Demonic as well. The Demon of the Woods

> Was once a man, who driven by evil tongues
> From all his fellows, lived alone, and came
> To learn black magic, and to hate his kind
> With such a hate, that when he died, his soul
> Became a Fiend, which, as the man in life
> Was wounded by blind tongues he saw not whence,
> Strikes from behind. (p. 1580)

The black magic of the demon is the same power of the imagination that constituted Merlin's better magic, only it is evil and destructive.

The demon we may suppose to be ugly and repulsive, but just as Arthur wished to clothe his ideal with the finest visible form, Queen Guinevere, so man's lower nature may also find a lovely incorporation. Vivien, though "She lied with ease," (p. 1590) was beautiful. So was Ettarre. Vivien's flatteries and deceits are not limited to words, but take the form of sighs and looks and caresses as well. But, lovely as she may be, men would be shielded from her "dark sweet hints" (p. 1600) as Arthur is, if those same hints did not find amplifying answer in the hearer's heart. When Vivien "whispered" through the court, the others "heard and let her be." (p. 1600) An idle laxness leads to the yielding sin, as the entire idyll of "Merlin and Vivien" demonstrates. Before long, Modred's "silent smiles of slow disparagement" (p. 1726) would also go uncorrected, assisting Vivien's whispers, until that time when Gawain started a rumor and "All ears were pricked at once, all tongues were loosed." (p. 1641) It more became the members of the court to behave in Elaine's manner responding to her father who voiced the slanders against Lancelot only to spare his daughter a wounding disappointment. Elaine, whose vision encompasses the highest ideals —though she is powerless to do more than offer her service to one who performs—does not hesitate to condemn: "these are slanders: never yet / Was noble man but made ignoble talk." (p. 1650)

Appropriately enough, it is the slanderer and sinner who is ordinarily most susceptible to the slandering tongue. Vivien, so quick to traduce another, is, as we have seen, uncommonly sensitive to hints against herself. Merlin tells her that she "dreams" that others "babble" of her (p. 1613) and concludes: "She cloaks the scar of some repulse with lies." (p. 1617) Language, which Merlin has just used to correct Vivien's blackening tales by applying straightforward questions and offering forthright accounts, is, for Vivien, no means to uncover the truth, but a disguise to mask a personal deformity. The lovely lies cloaking her scar are comparable to her lovely form masking a disfigured soul.

The vermin-voiced are among the first to learn that "the vermin voices . . . sting." (p. 1625) But the sting is most significantly felt by one initially most scornful of the world's babble. Guinevere was not so sensitive to scandal, not so careful of her fame, when she and Lancelot first learned to sin.

> 'Then of the crowd ye took no more account
> Than of the myraid cricket of the mead,
> When its own voice clings to each blade of grass,
> And every voice is nothing.' (p. 1624)

But though Lancelot may thus chide his queen, he too is concerned about the world's tongue on Elaine's behalf. Few, aside from Arthur, are free from the worry of the world's tongue, and the world's tongue is decidedly unlike the clear voice of its King transforming inspired knights, garbing them with his grandeur.

The world at large is a place of unappealing noise. Sir Per-

159

civale, seeking peace and salvation, passed from "noiseful arms
and acts of prowess" to a "silent life." (pp. 1661-62) The world
he abnegates is peopled with tale-tellers, "chatterers they, / Like
birds of passage piping up and down, / That gape for flies."
(pp. 1665-66) Percivale's own passage from the world of noise
to that of silent and secluded life condenses a general pattern in
the *Idylls*. The greater figure consists of an endless periphery of
noise through which the individual consciousness confusedly
struggles, approaching gradually, or breaking suddenly, into a
silence that may be favorable or malign, and where a lonely
sound, usually a voice, signifies largely by the fierce contrast.

In Percivale's case, the process is gradual. Having left Camelot with the other seekers after the Holy Grail to the sound of
the Queen's grief as she "wailed and shrieked aloud," (p. 1672)
Percivale advances into a wilderness wherein there are few
voices to be heard beyond his own and where he encounters an
old man who has "Scarce any voice," and who, having spoken,
falls into dust. (p. 1674) Name and fame, approval and condemnation, desert Percivale equally, and he takes refuge in a
chapel, where for the first time he experiences profitable dialogue. It is the preface to his dialogue with Ambrosius in his
"silent life" at the monastery. Percivale has escaped the chattering, noisy world, passed through a region of grisly silences,
and found another "silent life" where voices provide, if not the
means to high ideals, a mode of accepting the ordinary. In this
confined and silent world, Percivale meets Ambrosius, for
whom the general world is filled not with noise, but with amiable babble, "Chafferings and chatterings at the market-cross."
(p. 1677) Even the world's noise may be agreeable to an agree-
ing ear.

For the most part, however, the larger world remains an un-
pleasantly cacophonous region. It was the "brute world howl-
ing" that forced the innocent Sir Sagramore and a maid to marriage. (p. 1615) There is a "roar of riot" at the Red Knight's

tower, where enemies of Arthur's Order have convened. (p. 1716) Moreover, the roar of these brutes, who shout their contempt for Arthur's once orderly court, is answered by the enraged howls of Arthur's knights, who, massacring, "slimed themselves: Nor heard the King for their own cries." (p. 1717) Meanwhile, at the tournament, Arthur's court displays an uncommon clamour with "revels, and with mirth so loud / Beyond all use, that, half-amazed, the Queen" broke up the sports. (p. 1711) Like Vivien, an apt representative, the world at large in "blind and naked Ignorance" delivers its "brawling judgments," (p. 1613) and in its crude and violent conduct, scurries like Garlon's knights pursuing Balin in "blindfold rummage." (p. 1587)

Amid such dinning random noise, even Arthur—last to judge, last to lose heart— says, "I seem as he / Of whom was written, 'A sound is in his ears.' " (p. 1708) The pity is that the dinning world infects the central region of reticence and decorum, for, as Merlin observes, the finest things can be transformed to foulness in the "mouths of base interpreters." (p. 1616) Balin, an "unmelodious" figure by his own admission, accuses the "hissing" scandalmonger, Garlon of "mouth[ing] . . . a foulness," (p. 1586) though he is to mouth far worse himself when Vivien, who has hushed the "wholesome music of the wood," (p. 1588) brings his contagion to the surface. Then Balin "cursed the tale, the told-of, and the teller." It is now, self-cursed and cursing, that his demon jumps upon him, identifiable by its "weird yell." (p. 1590) The noises of the unwholesome, chattering world have infected him fatally. There is no harmony where every noise is a personal reverberation. Whereas high praise and noble tales encourage a harmonious society; scandal, curses, and lies rebound in mocking echoes upon the speaker. Vivien, sensitive to the world's words, succeeds in entrapping her magician

> And shrieking out 'O fool!' the harlot leapt
> Adown the forest, and the thicket closed
> Behind her, and the forest echoed 'fool.' (p. 1620)

It would seem that gentle and simple speech would be an antidote to the world of vermin-voices stinging Guinevere and her lover, but Elaine, who is characterized by a "simple face," that employs no disguises, and who makes "full simple" answers to all of Gawain's shifty "eloquence" and "adulation," is no success. Though her declaration of love is candid, she is not valued. Straightforward speech and behavior are unappreciated. Only in the simple directness of her posthumous letter, and in the yet more noble address of her lifeless body, will her story have effect.

> There surely I shall speak for mine own self,
> And none of you can speak for me so well. (p. 1652)

The consequence of Elaine's pathetic honesty and candor is a sad comment on the decline of the power of fable to prompt noble ideals and noble actions. Arthur commands that "the story of her dolorous voyage / For all true hearts be blazoned on her tomb." (p. 1658) But a legend become epitaph is not the high fable beckoning to action that once brought spiritual animation to Arthur's court. Here is another story of Dead Innocence. A story with a futile conclusion; a life craving noble service in a good cause, wasted and lost because the offer is foregone. Amid the confused, futile and noisy world of the "Lancelot and Elaine" idyll, Elaine is the noble ideal of Innocence, and the diamonds are her emblems. As the diamonds should be valued not for themselves but for their significance, so Elaine should be valued for what she represents. But Lancelot seeks the emblems of Innocence to crown a sinful queen and refuses Elaine's purity for the soured pleasures of Guinevere. His ideals have been confused. His honor is rooted in dishonor; his noble character is noble yet, but set in a cracked foundation. The ideal will not be wedded to the act, and the legend that might have been a love story of the highest kind merely recapitulates in another form the failure of Arthur's own marriage of ideal and material. Innocence dies, its lovely song stiffening to words blazoned on a tomb.

A good part of the world's noise, which deafens men to the harmonious voice of honesty, is little more than animal outcry, but some is, because more purposeful, more pernicious. Dagonet remarks to Tristram that once Arthur had freed the land, people set themselves "To babble about him, all to show [their] wit." (p. 1713) So insolent did they become that they "played at ducks and drakes / With Arthur's vows on the great lake of fire." (p. 1714)

A uniform purpose requires a uniform language, and a melodious order cannot endure false notes. But with the gradual transformation of Arthur's Order from courteous to courtly society, another language arises. When the innocent Pelleas first encounters Ettarre, he is so amazed that he can only stammer; he is, after all, a man of action, not discourse. Ettarre then asks of him, " 'O wild and of the woods, / Knowest thou not the fashion of our speech?' " (p. 1690) And, indeed, Pelleas does not know the fashion of their speech, for theirs is a language of lies, broken vows, slander, and deceit. Until he met Ettarre, the King's "lightest whisper moved him more / Than all the ranged reasons of the world." (p. 1691) But when Pelleas has learned the language of Ettarre and Gawain, he is no longer able to attend direct speech, and his own utterance collapses into disordered ravings and shrieks, and finally a hiss and silence.

Like the anti-vows that Pelleas as the Red Knight establishes to oppose the high vows of Arthur's Round Table, there is an undeclared anti-speech within Arthur's realm that corruptively supplants the original language of Arthur's ideal. This is a language of blunt and brutish speech, of flattery and deceit, or cynical punning, like that of mockers at the Tournament of Dead Innocence. Like the comments in Merlin's book of enchantments, Arthur's language gradually becomes unintelligible, until only a few can still piece out a meaning from his words.

If language can thus be so treasonous, silence would seem to be the wiser way. Merlin instructs the chattering Vivien, " 'Who are wise in love / Love most, say least,' " though she pertly responds, " 'you are wise who say it; let me think / Silence is wisdom.' " (p. 1602) But silence, without the evidence of worthy action, is no more wise nor good than utterance. Elaine's wordless servant is silent by force, since, because he warned his lord against the heathens' "fierce design . . . they caught and reft him of his tongue." (p. 1628) His subsequent silence is no cowardly refusal to meet the contending voices nor a retreat into silence; his wordlessness becomes the insignia of service. So well does he serve, so unquestionable are his acts, that no language is needed. And yet, his grim and silent service may speak more openly than words, for his task is to guide the boat that carries dead Elaine to Camelot. There, the amazed audience observing his haggard face, "As hard and still as is the face that men / Shape to their fancy's eye from broken rocks / On some cliffside," conclude: " 'He is enchanted, cannot speak.' " (p. 1655) In fact, it is they who are enchanted and cannot read. Their inadequate fancies have left them powerless to divine the simple meaning of a living emblem, not a figure carved in stone. The silent servant is, if enchanted, then enchanted to silence by the impercipience of those who witness. His action is the language they cannot read: the noble, enduring service of one who serves through love and respect. It is the language of Elaine's career; a language that few at Arthur's court still comprehend. The "dumb old servitor" is, like the legend to be blazoned on Elaine's tomb, a silent, uncomprehended monument, meant to inspire admiration, inspiring only wonder. Silence, too, is a language and must be challenged, as Gareth challenges the silent knight, Sir Mors, whose silence, once explained, is cause for joy, not terror. If the many could read the meaning of the mutely loyal servitor, there would be cause for joy and hope.

Silence, like language, can lose its favorable form. Reticence

164

may become crafty deceit. Ironically it is Vivien who reveals the nature of this pernicious silence; a silence of stilled music, not an anticipating pause.

> ' "It is the little rift within the lute,
> That by and by will make the music mute,
> And ever widening slowly silence all." ' (p. 1606)

The ruined lute, the failing music, is well forecast in Merlin's faltering speech, for "He spoke in words part heard, in whispers part, / Half-suffocated." (p. 1617) This is the dangerous silence of lost command, not the silence of wisdom. It is the silence of a Balin, overpowered by rage, who "spake not word," but rushed madly against his own brother. (p. 1590) And it prepares the way for King Mark, a creature who "spake not any word, / But bode his hour, devising wretchedness." (p. 1715)

The ever widening rift in the lute—the broken music of Tristram, Gawain, and the other uncourteous knights and ladies—ruining the frame of Arthur's Order by extending its original fault, advances a spreading silence. Pelleas, whose tongue Guinevere kindly wishes to "loose," hisses " 'I have no sword,' " and rushes away into darkness. The silent deed of service, the bold stroke against evil, now would be against Arthur's Queen. The symbol of justice under which the Order arose now would be directed against the source of that Order itself. As in the aged metaphor, the scorpion, entrapped and maddened by a ring of fire, aims its poisoned tail at its own most vulnerable point. Pelleas, however, does not act, choosing darkness instead.

> And all talk died, as in a grove all song
> Beneath the shadow of some bird of prey;
> Then a long silence came upon the hall
> And Modred thought, 'The time is hard at hand.' (p. 1704)

The Geraint and Enid idylls best display the manner in which the various modes of sound and silence operate in the

Idylls. At the beginning of the adventure that brings him to Enid, Geraint comes to a town from which there arises a noise "like a clamour of the rooks," yet the people of the town, noisy as they are, are not communicative, and Geraint is obliged to ask more than once that the individuals he interrogates "Speak!" Geraint is annoyed by the uncooperative folk and exclaims: "Ye think the rustic cackle of your bourg / The murmur of the world!" (p. 1534) Later, he has occasion to repeat the charge in slightly different terms.

> They take the rustic murmur of their bourg
> For the great wave that echoes round the world;
> They would not hear me speak. (p. 1539)

But Geraint's later behavior suggests that the bourg's rustic murmur does indeed share kinship with the greater world. He himself falls into sullen silence and unreasonable uncommunicativeness with his own wife, Enid. Moreover, just as Enid's first suffering is due to a slander spread by Edyrn, so her later unhappiness is caused by a slander that finds root in Geraint's mind. Geraint himself, then, is not so free of the rustic's cackle, the rustic's murmur. Again, when Geraint first hears Enid's voice in song, he says: " 'Here, by God's grace, is the one voice for me.' " (p. 1536) Yet it is this same voice, later, that he commands to silence. What is more, he unjustly claims that Enid's enforced silence is willful when he tells Limours, " 'Get her to speak: she doth not speak to me.' " (p. 1559)

Geraint, in his ignorance, silences the voice that can lead him best to a joyful music. In so doing, he makes language the test of Enid's obedience, while he, himself, can hardly sustain utterance because "his passion masters him." (p. 1552) As with Merlin or Balin, when self-command wanes, utterance also fails as a worthy adjunct. Geraint, not comprehending his lapsing authority, stiffens to silence; but, in a foolish inversion of his own state, he utilizes a hollow authority to impose mimic silence on Enid, saying "I charge thee, on thy duty as a wife, / Whatever happens, not to speak to me." (p. 1551) Enid, conversely, yearns for directness of speech, since she has nothing to fear from honesty and candor. She is quite willing to hear her fault in order that she may correct it "If he would only speak and tell me of it." (p. 1552) In the wilderness of Geraint's wayward mutterings and brutish commands, Enid's only utterances are loyal alarms against danger. Whereas the wordless servant of Astolat was appreciated for the warning that saved his master, Enid's service is answered with reproach. " 'Did I wish / Your warning or your silence?' " Geraint asks roughly. (p. 1553) The silence imposed by Geraint is a foolish and dangerous silence. When we have found the only voice for us, we should have the wisdom to permit it to sing. Geraint's reason for muffling this trustworthy voice is mistrust. But the rumour that occasions distrust is but another perversion of language, an expression of the growing anti-language of Arthur's court.

Geraint is "Suspicious that [Enid's] nature had a taint," (p. 1528) but it is his own nature that is tainted, for "though yet there lived no proof" of the rumour against the Queen, "Not less Geraint believed it." (p. 1526) Geraint, waking from sleep to Enid's sad self-estimate "heard but fragments of her later words;" (p. 1529) it is his tainted nature that composes these fragments into a vile story. Poor "tongue-tied" Geraint finds it impossible to make a direct charge against his lovely wife, preferring the easier way of maintaining his unfortunate mistake, and is only annoyed the more that Enid can speak. (p. 1554) He makes no attempt, of course, to investigate that other aspect of communication which is audition. So vain is he, so certain that his own perceptions are correct, that he describes himself to Enid as one "With eyes to find you out however far, / And ears to hear you even in his dreams." (p. 1562) And surely the irony is that Geraint is still wrapped in a dream, for he has misunderstood and through his tainted fancy created a sinful fiction.

And so the rent lyre of Geraint's love spreads slowly to a silence. Eventually, the couple find themselves "Apart by all the chamber's width, and mute / As creatures voiceless through the fault of birth," (p. 1558) when Limours' riotiously noisy crowd breaks on them. The contrast of this mute pair and the "rout of roisterers" is all the sharper because both clamor and silence are manifestations of the same failure of utterance, the same absence of high purpose to give speech fair form.

Limours himself is an arch representative of the false forms of language, for he

> jested with all ease, and told
> Free tales, and took the word and played upon it,
> And made it of two colours. (p. 1559)

And like many another foolish vagrant of speech, with no high purpose in his talk, he who would deceive by language, is most easily himself deceived—even by himself.

> At this the tender sound of his own voice
> And sweet self-pity, or the fancy of it,
> Made his eye moist. (p. 1560)

And again, like so many adeptly unprincipled speakers, he "babbled to his men," a set of lies. (p. 1561) Yet even Limours is able to see something that Geraint in his tendentious blindness cannot see, though he claims acute percipience. Limours tells Enid " 'your wretched dress, / A wretched insult on you, dumbly speaks / Your story.' " (p. 1560) Even if Limours misreads the story through his own tainted fancy, the fact remains that there are other signs than the symbolic sounds of speech that "speak" the truth, and if men are deaf to honest speech, let them fear a compounding blindness to what is emblematically clear.

The encounter with Limours does not cure Geraint of his folly, and from courtly perversion of language he and Enid lapse to the brutishly inarticulate utterance of Doorm's domain. Doorm's men, having deposited Enid and the wounded Geraint at the castle because they have been detained in pillage, depart

growling as before
And cursing their lost time, and the dead man,
And their own Earl, and their own souls, and her. (p. 1566)

Likewise, at Doorm's table, "none spake word, but all sat down at once, / And ate with tumult in the naked hall." (p. 1567) Enid, however, remains deaf to any speech but Geraint's and scarcely makes a sound when answering Doorm's proposals. And Doorm, characteristically, makes no attempt to hear her answer, assuming that she concurs in his wish.

Appropriately, it is in this condition, where rational argument and reasonable discourse are valueless, that Geraint is awakened to his wife's value, for it is an *act* that first moves him and leads him to say to his own heart, " 'She weeps for me.' " (p. 1566) And it is Enid's "sudden sharp and bitter cry," that rouses Geraint to action by her side. (p. 1570) Where no discourse could persuade, Geraint's true heart is touched by a simple cry. He is, after all, a man of action. Though he may be unsettled by language and the slippery turnings of his own tainted imagination upon unsteady facts, or, in better times, perceptive of the grand and noble in worthy legends and the vows, his deeds always remain direct. He is slow to realize that there is the same need for directness and faith in abstract perceptions. The point at which the utterance and purpose meet for Geraint is in "his terrible war-cry." (p. 1555) What he must learn is to attend Enid's "low firm voice and tender government," which imitates the manner of the King. (p. 1556)

After his adventures in the wilderness, Geraint does learn, and he recovers respect for the "fine reserve and noble reticence" that Edyrn has learned to value in Arthur's court. (p. 1573) Geraint and Enid advance to a proportioned life, and "the spiteful whisper died," replaced by the joyful "cry of children, Enids and Geraints / Of times to be." (pp. 1575-76)

But not all will hear the inarticulate cries of children, which in their imprecision permit the hopeful fancy to read superb tales of what is to be. Some, who have not provided for the

169

future, will hear other voices. Guinevere, fleeing from Camelot, her name finally condemned to ugliness,

> heard the Spirits of the waste and weald
> Moan as she fled, or thought she heard them moan:
> And in herself she moaned 'Too late, too late!' (p. 1728)

It is the voice of interior wilderness she hears, a voice she has long ignored. As "The Two Voices" and other poems indicate, it was Tennyson's conviction that the internal dialogue was an essential step to proper self-command, and achievement of actions to support ideals. Especially those who stand exposed before the world and have a special purpose must come to terms with the internal voices, for as the little novice explains, "howsoever much they may desire / Silence, they cannot weep behind a cloud." (p. 1730)

Nor are the guilty the only ones who will hear no happy voices. Arthur had felt, before the Tournament of Dead Innocence, an ominous sound was in his ears; and when he returned to Camelot after the tournament, there awaited him

> A voice [that] clung sobbing till he questioned it,
> 'What art thou?' and the voice about his feet
> Sent up an answer, sobbing, 'I am thy fool,
> And I shall never make thee smile again.' (p. 1724)

This is not the last disembodied voice that Arthur will hear. Before the last battle in which he will be wounded, he hears Gawain's voice lamenting, and in the battle hears "Moans of the dying, and voices of the dead," unseen in the obscuring mist. (p. 1745)

The wave that, in the legend, had brought Arthur to Camelot was "full of voices," (p. 1480) and the Lady of the Lake had "A voice as of the waters." (p. 1477) These were the untranslatable voices of a mysterious nature from which Arthur derived his being and his power. Now, at the last battle in the

West, he has returned to "The phantom circle of a moaning sea." (p. 1745) As Arthur is borne away, Bedivere hears a shrill cry of lament.

> Then from the dawn it seemed there came, but faint
> As from beyond the limit of the world,
> Like the last echo born of a great cry,
> Sounds, as if some fair city were one voice
> Around a king returning from his wars. (p. 1754)

In Leodogran's dream when Arthur's career was yet new, a "phantom king /Sent out at times a voice; and here or there / Stood one who pointed toward the voice, the rest / Slew on and burnt." (p. 1481)

In this world, the phantom king's voice is understood by too few. The anti-language of deceit, of lies, false wit, and brutal command drowns the music that so few can hear. Perhaps it is only those who are fools to this world who will hear it. Tristram is blind and deaf to the star that Dagonet sees.

> It makes a silent music up in heaven,
> And I, and Arthur and the angels hear,
> And then we skip. (p. 1714)

It is only the self-deceived, those trapped in their own fantasies—distortions of the imagination as their language is distortion of the word—who will hear the forests echo after them 'O fool!' Eventually those who have undeceived themselves of the false language of this world, and who have heard the music of Dagonet's star, will pass, like Guinevere redeemed, "To where beyond these voices there is peace." (p. 1742)

Even when the voices of this world are not misleading, they are not, by themselves, sufficient. The achievement of moral proportion requires that ideals be manifest in deeds. The imagination may conceive highly, but there must follow the physical incorporation of the highly conceived. If Merlin's powers, the forces of human imagination, are perilous for good or ill, as the Siege Perilous suggests, there is no hint that Excalibur, the gift of the Lady of the Lake, "who knows a subtler magic" than Merlin's, will be misused. (p. 1477) For Excalibur is offered only to one who is worthy to wield it. Its significance is not reducible to a single term, but it may accurately enough be said to represent the power of the truth. Excalibur's first command, "Graven in the oldest tongue of all this world," is ever appropriate, since the struggle to free men to the truth is perpetually required; the second command is known specifically to the inheritor and is "written in the speech ye speak yourself." (p. 1478) Each age understands the need to take up its Excalibur; only the individual knows when he must relinquish it. Each age, too, pursues the same high ideals, enacts the same overarching pattern; but the enactment is in terms proper to that age.

Deeds are not unlike narratives in their relationship to ideals. As the narrative records a sequence of actions—tells a story—to make clear the nature of the ideal and clothe it with emotion, so the deed makes attractive the otherwise abstract ideal. Noble acts, besides achieving an immediate good, have the added effect of providing noble models. And it is from such deeds that the noblest narratives are composed. Enid, herself willing to perform what deeds and services she can, according to her position in life, takes great delight in Geraint's tales of Arthur's Order.

> So grateful is the noise of noble deeds
> To noble hearts who see but acts of wrong. (p. 1539)

Whereas speech may serve to define the nature of man or his ideals in ambigous terms, deeds may be somewhat clearer, though not absolutely so. Gareth, as yet unproved but simply fortified with the noblest ideals, prefers to achieve definition not by expressions, but by acts.

> 'Let be my name until I make my name!
> My deeds will speak: it is but for a day.' (p. 1500)

Knowledge of antecedent qualities is not required to judge a noble act. As Gareth says, "The knave that doth thee service as full knight / Is all as good, meseems, as any knight." (p. 1514) Although Gareth has his particular quest in mind, and although he himself has no fear of being discovered a knave by origin, his sentiment is in harmony with his behavior. One fashions identity through acts, which are, if noble, the necessary manifestation of ideals. This does not mean that all worthy acts are prompted by ideals, for Geraint, when his ideals are shaken, does not lose his power of action; only his purpose is diseased. An excess of action is Balin's failing. Arthur says to him, " 'Thou hast ever spoken truth; / Thy too fierce manhood would not let thee lie.' " (p. 1579) But that fierce manhood in action overflows to irresponsibility. The thrall who spoke evil of Balin was the smaller man because he could slander, but the man who, like the Demon of the Woods, is transformed by a tale into a beast, is the more dangerous—to himself and others. Action verifies ideals, but while an authentic passion is required to perform the deeds, a comparable discipline is required to insure that the deeds remain serviceable to the ideal. Balin's is not a hand to hold Excalibur. Though he may wish to serve the high cause, his power is not sufficiently harnassed to reason. Man must not be moved by his passions or superficial emblems of his own desire, but by an objective, if intuitive, perception of the truth.

In "Akbar's Dream," Tennyson summarized the relationship of imagined ideal and performed deed.

> To pray, to do—
> To pray, to do according to the prayer,
> Are, both, to worship Alla, but the prayers,
> That have no successor in deed, are faint
> And pale in Alla's eyes, fair mothers they
> Dying in childbirth of dead sons. (p. 1442)

The "deedless dreamer" described in "St. Telemachus" is neither

173

admirable nor worthy of his beliefs. When Arthur's order, which was raised "By noble deeds at one with noble vows," (p. 1708) began to fail, it was through the gradual disjunction of vows and deeds. When knights "sware but by the shell," (p. 1712) the worthiness of deeds correspondingly waned. Tristram triumphed in his cynical power over the feckless knights left at Arthur's tournament; while Lancelot, the noblest in all deeds but that which violated most ignobly the ideal he maintained, "saw the laws that ruled the tournament / Broken, but spake not." (p. 1709) As Geraint's speech failed him when passion conquered, as Balin's utterance was reduced to a selfish, bestial howl, so Lancelot, burdened with one guilty act, subsides into grim silence and morbid langour. Though chafing to join combat himself, he is obliged to sit in Arthur's seat, judging.

The inverted world of pernicious utterance opposing Arthur's Order finally explodes into overt contrary action, prompted ironically by anti-vows in desperate harmony with their belief. That belief, however, is based solely upon opposition to Arthur's hypocritical community. The sinew torn from the nerve no longer wields a terrible weapon. The inept tool swings wildly, injuring everything. Perdition is a spreading silence where the noise of noble deeds no longer sounds, and all noble action becomes a tale: stories of fame to hand on the high ideal to another, fresher generation.

The great names of past times serve men as models, as the great tales of the past preserve man's deathless aspirations. But just as tales may be fictions that yet embody a truth, so names are but terms to clothe an ideal. Arthur was not King by name alone, but by his powers. Despite the doubters in his wake, Arthur was King so long as Arthur's schemes remained. Naming is an inadequate but useful means for defining ideas, it is likewise a useful means of defining the self.[19] Like all other language, though, names may have a double effect, and fame's darkling twin is infamy. One of the first consolations occurring to Bedivere, when Arthur expresses his dismay at the collapse of his grand Order, is that Arthur's accomplishments will, at any rate, illumine ideals hereafter.

> 'O me, my King, let pass whatever will,
> Elves, and the harmless glamour of the field;
> But in their stead thy name and glory cling
> To all high places like a golden cloud
> For ever. (p. 1744)

Merlin's fear of being "lost to life and use and name and fame" signifies more than vanity. (p. 1601) To live authentically is to be useful. Our use establishes our name; our name will constitute our fame. Gareth will achieve his name through the performance of high deeds. His name will emerge brilliantly from disguise as he emerges from the smoky mystery of the kitchen, breaking like a winged creature to higher life. To achieve a name is to consolidate one's purpose and one's deeds; if these are united harmoniously, fame follows and lifts the individual to a higher use, to an intenser life. So life and use and name and fame are almost cognate, from particular deed to particular designation and thence to general definition and general service.

Although Arthur's name and fame are not in jeopardy—for his was a flawless life—any other name is. Moreover, the very function of fame is doubtful. As Vivien says, "And what is Fame in life but half-disfame, / And counterchanged with darkness?" (p. 1608) Man's vision leaps not far beyond his own attributes. Feeling the beam in his own eye, he supposes the speck in another and is grateful if that speck be large enough to balance his own blemish. The crowd more easily sees the stain than any glory in great names.

Nonetheless, a great name commands attention. When Guinevere advises Lancelot to take part in the diamond jousts, she says, "your great name, / This conquers: hide it therefore." (p. 1625) Thus, inadvertently, Lancelot has the opportunity to test his nature against his fame; his adventure in disguise provides him with a test of his use and name and fame. It is "A fiery family passion for the name / Of Lancelot," (p. 1634) that drives Lancelot's kinsmen viciously against him in his disguise. This is the first mighty signal that fame may injure the famous.

Just as the passion for Lancelot's fame turns his kinsmen against him in his disguise, indicating that it is not his deeds, but his name that they value, so Lancelot's fame draws on him the viciousness of slander, where, as an unknown man, he would have been unassailed and harmless as well. Fame is a magnet, and when it does not draw the mace of violence, it attracts arrow-heads of spiteful slander. What Lancelot learns about himself, by escaping his formal identity, is that he is both more and less of a man than his name permits. He is a great warrior, but not unconquerable; he is vulnerable, like all men. He is something more than a famous warrior; he is a man. It has been necessary for Lancelot to experience physical infirmity that he might discover his moral strength.

Unlike those who know Lancelot's name and who value the name perhaps more highly than the man, Elaine loves Lancelot before she learns his name, because she loves him for his qualities. Once more Elaine is the representative of all that Lancelot has lost. This was the love for him, a love that transcended fame, a love that wished to serve and by serving, lead to higher accomplishments. Lancelot has abrogated all such high love. Still, the recognition of his loss means much. At the conclusion of his adventure, Lancelot has been made aware of the ambiguity of his fame. "Why did the King dwell on my name to me?" (p. 1659) he asks himself, then discerns that his great name may be an easy route to sin for others, and its continuing "use" more vile than Merlin's suspended utility. Lancelot's great name, so clear a cause for pride, leaves its bearer ashamed and desperate.

What is, perhaps, more melancholy than the evil ends to which Lancelot's fame may be employed, is the irony of Arthur's

concern for his great knight's posterity. Saddened by the death
of Elaine, the King laments the pure, fair maiden

> 'Who might have brought thee, now a lonely man
> Wifeless and heirless, noble issue, sons
> Born to the glory of thy name and fame,
> My knight, the great Sir Lancelot of the Lake.' (p. 1659)

But there will be no heirs to Lancelot's name; and his name,
like Arthur's, will be resolved into a tale. No acts will follow
from his history of great accomplishments; only the fable precariously preserving his ambiguous reputation remains: the tale
of a knight who, sinning greatly, also served well.

Lancelot's fear that his name might ease others into sin is
justified, for Tristram uses his history of sin to seduce Isolt, and
others after these draw "foul ensample from fair names." (p.
1737) If Lancelot fears the contagion of his fame for the sake of
others, some are not so nobly wretched, for Guinevere fears that
her name "will ever be a name of scorn." (p. 1740) Her immediate dread is a personal one, though her symbolic dream, in which
her sin spreads like a mephitic shade over the entire realm, indicates the greater scope of her infected name.

Once names were valued in Arthur's court by achievements.
The knight who had not done great deeds bore no device upon
his shield, nor was his name of consequence. Name and emblem
were signs of service to the ideal. Men strove to acquire a name,
as Gareth did, through deeds. But in the later times of Arthur's
court, the ambition to achievement of a name through the glory
of high service is replaced by the fear of losing name and fame.
The debased concern for titles is represented in Ettarre whose
"mind was bent / On hearing, after trumpet blown, her name
/ And title, 'Queen of Beauty,' in the lists / Cried." (p. 1690)

So confused and unreliable do names and titles become that
Tristram can scarcely distinguish between his two loves, neither
of which constitutes a high and loyal affection in him. Having

been separated from Isolt of Tintagil, who was not pure like her "namesake" in Brittany, Tristram fled overseas.

> But then what folly had sent him overseas
> After she left him lonely here? a name? (p. 1715)

Later, Tristram insists to his first Isolt that he only followed a name. "Did I love her? the name at least I loved." (p. 1720) Tristram's careless indifference to his own motives and emotions in this instance is a splendid indication of how little he comprehends the nature of reality. Like a rat in a laboratory experiment, he is easily excited by a mere signal or name, which replaces for him the meaning that should be the central concern in human response. Just as Balin replaced the spiritual reality with a mere physical emblem, Tristram replaces the reality of humanity with an empty cipher.

Tristram's own name has subtly altered, not as a sign, but in its signification. His fame as a knight was attained by physical power, but his moral nature has been sapped by self-indulgent sin. His name remains the same, but the man is altered. It is a discouraging parallel to Lancelot's alteration. His name, too, remained the same, the man gaining self-awareness through a temporary revocation of identity. For Tristram, there is no self-awareness. Isolt herself remarks the slide toward bestiality in Tristram and exclaims, "Far other was the Tristram, Arthur's knight!" (p. 1721) The transformation, necessarily involving the once knightly name, is aptly embodied in an incident that Isolt relates. She explains that one day she was musing on a light song she had heard Tristram sing

> "And once or twice I spake thy name aloud.
> Then flashed a levin-brand; and near me stood,
> In fuming sulphur blue and green, a fiend—
> Mark's way to steal behind one in the dark." (pp. 1720-21)

Tristram's name no longer is the invocation of a noble knight, but of a fiend. The magic name becomes an evil conjuration. To say Lancelot was still to image nobility, but to say Tristram is invitation to a fiend. As Balin is transformed into a raging demon by slander, so Tristram is transformed into a fiend by adopting fiendish morality, for his way approximates Mark's way. The man he despises is ironically his mentor in immorality, and, in the end, he is extinguished utterly by the incorporation of his sin. Tristram is the victim of the way that he has chosen; Mark, the fiend who answered Isolt's involuntary call to Tristram, again appears as Tristram places the jewels of Dead Innocence upon Isolt, saying, " 'Thine Order, O my Queen!' " and strikes Tristram dead with the shriek, " 'Mark's way.' " (p. 1724)

While some names remain untainted, and others lose their power for good or become positive aids to evil, yet others disappear entirely. Thus Pelleas, answering Lancelot's request for his name, shouts:

'No name, no name,' he shouted, 'a scourge am I
To lash the treasons of the Table Round.'
'Yea but thy name?' 'I have many names,' he cried:
'I am wrath and shame and hate and evil fame,
And like a poisonous wind I pass to blast
And blaze the crime of Lancelot and the Queen.' (pp. 1703-4)

Pelleas' name is effaced by his frictive encounter with a debased world. It can be so easily marred and scoured off because it was, in fact, superficial; as superficial as the beauty of Ettarre that Pelleas so fondly admired. Lancelot, too, is marked by his experiences in the world, but none of these experiences has touched his true nature; he is scarred, but not effaced. Pelleas' entire nature being superficial, it is lost in the first rough surgery and he resolves himself into abstractions, desiring to become a deed incarnate, for names and words have proved such false things. So, later, as the nameless Red Knight, he sets out to be a scourge to Arthur's court, championing all that contradicts Arthur's rules, and Arthur, meeting him, "knew his voice [but] the name / Went wandering somewhere darkling in his mind." (p. 1716) While Arthur's court hoped to raise great names up as models of noble action, the Red Knight wishes only to present the anonymous performance of infamy, and, appropriately his identity is lost forever, reduced to an indistinguishable slime.

Though language may diliquesce eventually into nothing and names become confusing signs or blank emblems, there is a form of utterance in the *Idylls* that seems never to lose its function, even in the mouths of the most evil. Though Vivien may still the music of the woods, her false song reveals a true thing. Though she sings of the "old sun-worship," her song has another valuable lesson, which is to acknowledge the "fire of Heaven," the natural inclinations of man, and use them, not struggle to suppress them privately. (p. 1588) "Far other was the song that once I heard," says Merlin of the song that had "such fire for fame, / Such trumpet-blowings in it," that it roused all men to action. (p. 1606) And different again is the song, "Late, so late," that the babbling novice sings to Guinevere. It is an innocent song, but its significance is stern for Guinevere.

It was Enid's voice in song that awakened Geraint's love, and Lancelot recalled that in his confused pursuit of the Grail

> always in the quiet house I heard,
> Clear as a lark, high o'er me as a lark,
> A sweet voice singing in the topmost tower. (p. 1684)

There is a truth inherent in song, for song embodies in it a mystery of utterance. Song, produced by the same powers that make for speech is yet different. Music is the spirit of words in song, and the intangible quality of their harmonious combination suggests the proper union of spirit and soul in man. Yet all men do not know the music of the spirit; as Dagonet says, only he and

Arthur and the angels seem to hear the music of the guiding stars. Not all can see the truth in the mystery. As Arthur says, "one hath sung and all the dumb will sing," (p. 1671) when criticizing all those knights who, lacking the power to see the Grail, are yet anxious to pursue it. Many may try to sing, but few will know the song they voice.[20]

Voices and names as they contend in the world may lead to merciless confusion. At times it may become almost impossible to distinguish the true name from the false, the good voice from the bad. In such a world, it is not easy to determine upon the rightful deeds and men may flounder in purposelessness, with no high ideals. But names and words are only emblems that the mind fashions. Man commands the world through his imagination; he gives form to substance as much through the acts of his mind as by the shaping of material objects. It is imagination that must be disciplined and brought to service, and from that inner world other names and other voices will emerge. We turn from the confusions of outward sound, the periphery of our experience, to the central silence within, where a more significant dialogue may begin. Unbodied voices, unpronounced words, replace the broken formulas of uttered language.

The entire dialogue of "The Two Voices" is a monologue in the narrator's mind. The suggestion in that poem is that an honest encounter in the self will open the gates to a rich and purposeful world. These views are more precisely stated by the Ancient Sage.

> If thou wouldst hear the Nameless, and wilt dive
> Into the Temple-cave of thine own self,
> There, brooding by the central altar, thou
> Mayst haply learn the Nameless hath a voice,
> By which thou wilt abide, if thou be wise,
> As if thou knewest, though thou canst not know. (p. 1351)

The Nameless is so because it is *all* names. It is man who gives names, thus the ultimate extent of man's imagination, the furthest capacity of his ability to give names, remains undefined. It is in this world that names are a convenience, but they are not essential to redemptive vision.

> And when thou sendest thy free soul through heaven,
> Nor understandest bound nor boundlessness,
> Thou seest the Nameless of the hundred names.
>   And if the Nameless should withdraw from all
> Thy frailty counts most real, all thy world
> Might vanish like thy shadow in the dark. (p. 1351)

What words are to the inexpressible vision, substance is to spirit. But it is possible to escape the bondage of words, of language and names,

> As when we dwell upon a word we know,
> Repeating, till the word we know so well
> Becomes a wonder, and we know not why. (p. 1649)

And when we escape the bondage of language and its tricks and deceits, we shed with that bondage the word that defines our self. Our own name is, in a way, a trap to our nature, just as the body is a bond of clay to our spirit. Names provide us with particularity suited to the substance that constitutes mortality but, like that substance, divides us from the Infinite. Consciousness of self is both gift and incarceration. The Ancient Sage describes the method of escape.

> And more, my son! for more than once when I
> Sat all alone, revolving in myself
> The word that is the symbol of myself,
> The mortal limit of the Self was loosed,
> And past into the Nameless, as a cloud
> Melts into Heaven. I touch'd my limbs, the limbs
> Were strange not mine—and yet no shade of doubt,
> But utter clearness, and through loss of Self
> The gain of such large life as matched with ours

Were Sun to spark—*unshadowable in words,*
Themselves but shadows of a shadow-world. (p. 1356; italics mine)

In the *Idylls of the King*, voices, language, names, words, all are an ambiguous feature of the veil that separates the spirit from the substance of life. Deeds remain in the realm of matter, but words are only shadows of those deeds. They are, however, shadows of another world as well, since through man's imagination the words that inadequately express an unutterable vision are partially communicated. In a way it is possible to conceive of one of Tennyson's purposes in the *Idylls* as an attempt to establish the subject and predicate of existence. In the ideal is the subject, the predicate is the act, and utterances the multiform modifiers. Signification is not an achievement, but a process that must forever be incomplete, for in the ever-changing circumstantial world the hundred names of the Nameless must be constantly renamed. The attributes which are at once the highest qualities in man and the attributes of the Nameless undergo a continuous transformation. Man can never fully define the material world in which he exists because he defines it in terms of himself, and he is not wholly of the material world. But the language he uses to make arbitrary definition of his world will not serve to designate an existence beyond the shadow world of substance and its shadowing words. Though words are useful tools, as fame may be of use to men of high purpose, words are dangerous, too, like fame. After all, utterance will not serve to communicate the ideal; the vision is beheld within, in the temple-cave of the self. Each man sees the Grail according to his nature. Only Galahad sees Galahad's Grail.

Such a view of language may seem peculiar in a poem which is itself an attempt, through language, to celebrate a moral conviction. But as one theme of *In Memoriam* reveals, Tennyson conceived of poetry as an action. It was his mode of defeating Morning-Star, Noon-Sun, and Evening-Star, and brought him hopefully to face the dreadfully silent Night. Poetry is not simple language, but a controlled imitation of a divine creation of which "all, as in some piece of art, / Is toil cöoperant to an end." (cxxviii, p. 978) Poetry resembles Arthur's music; or the song of the hopeful young knight, in the tale of the hart with the golden horns, that prompted men to action. The *Idylls*, like *In Memoriam*, as the imagery in both poems suggests, was, for Tennyson, such a purposeful song of celebration, and is, in its own way, a fulfilment of Arthur's desires, embodying the ideal in a form of earthly loveliness.

Identity

Disguise, in the *Idylls*, is not always associated with deviously malign characters, nor is confused or obscure identity an inconsequential romantic device.[21] Much of the disguise described in the *Idylls* is related to deceit. Vivien, for example, assumes a rôle of innocence when she visits Arthur's court; and she goes convinced of "The monkish manhood, and the mask of pure / Worn by this court." (p. 1597) And, at the court, Vivien finds others like her who verify her opinions. But the true purpose for going to Arthur's court should have a positive value. Hopeful men like Gareth or Balin come to Camelot "To learn what Arthur meant by courtesy, / Manhood, and knighthood." (p. 1581)

Earlier in this study, I have drawn a distinction between courtesy and courtliness, and it is this distinction that discriminates between the worthy and the worthless, or worse, of Arthur's court. Courtesy is an accomplishment; courtliness an acquisition. Courtesy is the external manifestation in gesture and manner of an inner nobility, while courtliness is the superficial mastery of socially ritualistic gestures that may disguise the moral nature just as courtesy reveals it. Courtesy and courtliness may easily resemble one another, as Gawain's manner

suggests; but to the informed there is always the critical difference of authenticity. "For manners are not idle, but the fruit /
Of loyal nature, and of noble mind," Guinevere says. (p. 1733)
For some, courtesy has become so thoroughly a part of them, in
their emulation of Arthur, that it is readily evident. With Percivale, for example, "a courtesy / Spake through the limbs and
in the voice." (p. 1662) When, however, the individual loses
inner integrity, courtesies seem pointless if not foolish, as
Tristram bluntly remarks. Guinevere, more and more conscious
of her guilt, found that "the guileless King, / And trustful courtesies of household life, / Became her bane." (p. 1727) The
King, it is worth noting, is associated with guilelessness, trust-
fulness and courtesy. Lancelot, too, almost merits approval on
each of these attributes, except as they pertain to his one sin.
Only when he has employed a form of guile, his disguise, does he
realize how distant his courtesies are—noble as they yet may be
—from the absolute virtues of the King.

Balin, unable to establish harmony in himself, frustrated by
his own high ambitions, laments, " 'Too high this mount of
Camelot for me: / These high-set courtesies are not for me."
(p. 1582) And the next moment he finds himself witness to a
private conversation between Guinevere, and Lancelot, whom
the Queen terms, "the king of courtesy." (p. 1583) What Balin overhears is, in effect, the betrayal of that high ideal of
courtesy, that Lancelot truly values but violates, and which
Balin truly covets but does not fully understand. In courtesy
there can be no disjunction between manner and morality. However, although Lancelot's courtesy is qualified by his sin, he
does not descend to courtliness, and "the one discourtesy that
he used," upon request, was a discourtesy of omission; he neg-
lected to bid Elaine farewell. (p. 1648)

Arthur, in establishing his order, had intended, among other
things, to teach "high thought, and amiable words / And courtliness." (p. 1737) Still, in a description of Lancelot it is neces-

sary to remark that he behaves "full courtly, yet not falsely." (p. 1627) Since to be courtly implies some delinquence, a qualification is required when the term is meant in approbation. And it is not hard to understand why this might be so, when we consider the reputation of Gawain "surnamed The Courteous," (p. 1636) whose manner was "Courtesy with a touch of traitor in it." (p. 1639) Arthur's "courtliness" is all too quickly transformed into a hollow term. It is a short step from Gawain to Tristram, whose behavior at the Tournament of Dead Innocence occasions the remark, "All courtesy is dead," (p. 1710) and to the cynical messenger to the Queen who snickers maliciously in his "courtly heart." (p. 1653)

"The greater man, the greater courtesy," Isolt says, and as she says it, implies that the greater men are far fewer in number than once was true. Courtesy is the noble made manifest; courtliness a mask to the ignoble. The former is to the individual with a high purpose, at one in mind and heart, what Arthur's Round Table is to a community, undivided in the support of its leader. Courtesy is the individual's unselfconscious materialized ritual of his own high ideals, but courtliness is a thing to be learned and practiced. The opposition is that of the eloquently simple Elaine and the crudely eloquent Gawain. There is no disguise in Elaine, no practiced behavior; therefore, she may feel melancholy, but no guilt and no fear. Her death, like her life, is open and generous. Few in Camelot are worthy to bear her to her tomb. To the court, the dead Elaine is a figure in a romantic story. To the few who still understand the proper nature of courtesy, from which innocence can hardly be separated, she is an arrested emblem, a gracious gesture frozen in a world of sub rosa hints and signs. Once inanimate symbols took life from the stimulating deeds that begot them; now active beings are immobilized to stony emblems, like stained-glass windows in a cave.

It is not surprising that human behavior can be a form, or even a formal mask, for we have already observed that human utterance is also open to misuse and distortion. Once again, in the material world, though forms may be unavoidable, they must not be trusted above the undefinable but more certain realm of spirit.

> And what are forms?
> Fair garments, plain or rich, and fitting close
> Or flying looselier, warmed but by the heart
> Within them, moved but by the living limb,
> And cast aside, when old, for newer,—Forms!
> The Spiritual in Nature's market-place—
> The silent Alphabet-of-heaven-in-man
> Made vocal. (p. 1447)[22]

It is at the fair beginning of a time that Arthur hopes to clothe his high ideal in the lovely garments of beauty, to give physical comeliness of form to the spiritual in Nature's market-place. To the audience at Arthur's wedding, "The Sun of May descended on their King, / They gazed on all earth's beauty in their Queen." (p. 1482) The spiritually beautiful is to assume a beautiful form; Arthur weds Guinevere.

It was the purpose of "The Palace of Art" to show that beauty alone was an insufficient ideal, that "Beauty, Good, and Knowledge, are three sisters / That doat upon each other, friends to man." (p. 399) Although Arthur knows this, he cannot make these separate desirable abstractions meet for long. Nor does the failure of his attempt lead him to disvalue Beauty, for betrayed as he is by the flesh, he can still say to Guinevere, "My love through flesh hath wrought into my life / So far, that my doom is, I love thee still." Even so, he is aware that Guinevere's beauty has been only an eloquent form as far as he is concerned.

> O imperial-moulded form,
> And beauty such as never woman wore,
> Until it came a kingdom's curse with thee. (p. 1738)

As Akbar observed, forms are only garments, and Guinevere has only *worn* her beauty. So Guinevere might wear beauty and stun the world, yet there are better garments and more fitting that men might wear, and thus follow the model of Christ. So Percivale learns from the holy hermit he encounters on his adventures.

> " ' "O son, thou hast not true humility,
> The highest virtue, mother of them all;
> For when the Lord of all things made Himself
> Naked of glory for His mortal change,
> 'Take thou my robe,' she said, 'for all is thine,'
> And all her form shone forth with sudden light
> So that the angels were amazed, and she
> Followed Him down, and like a flying star
> Led on the gray-haired wisdom of the east." ' " (pp. 1674-75)

A true garb in a true form, though simple; and it is this garment of humility that Guinevere lacks, so that her exposed beauty, a lovely but dangerous form, fails to conform with the spiritual heart that has raised her from the realm of beasts. The true confluence of spiritual and material beauty is rare, as Arthur discovers. In his late dismayed moments of frustrated ambition he exclaims:

> O me! for why is all around us here
> As if some lesser god had made the world,
> But had not force to shape it as he would,
> Till the High God behold it from beyond,
> And enter it, and make it beautiful?
> *Or else as if the world were wholly fair,*
> *But that these eyes of men are dense and dim,*
> And have not power to see it as it is:
> Perchance, because we see not to the close.
> (pp. 1742-43; italics mine)

Arthur, in his thwarted desire to fashion an order of incomparable beauty, has touched upon a truth. Perhaps the world is beautiful, if man could see it rightly. But to see it rightly, he must escape the bonds of flesh which confine his vision. Although it is necessary to dive into the temple-cave of the self to hear the voice that we must trust, it is also necessary to re-emerge from that temple-cave to a broader and clearer world beyond the self. Man's imagination can conceive the orderly and beautiful; he cannot always embody it, though it is noble to try. Only when the High God enters it, does it become beautiful.

But if men cannot mold the material world to their desires, they can mold the material world to emblems of their desires.[23] And these symbols serve, as does Fable, to picture to men's imaginations, the ultimately unutterable ideal. Although Arthur when active in the zone of deeds "neither wore on helm or shield / The golden symbol of his kinglihood, / But rode a simple knight among his knights," (p. 1471) in official regality he was "Robed in red samite, easily to be known." (p. 1633)

It is not in garments and crowns, though, that the King's ideal is exhibited, but in "many a mystic symbol" fashioned by Merlin. One of these symbols is a "statue in the mould / Of Arthur, made by Merlin, with a crown, / And peaked wings pointed to the Northern Star." (p. 1669) That the emblems of Arthur's idea participate in its success or failure is notably demonstrated when the knights, returning from the unwise quest that has damaged Arthur's purpose, discover that a storm has "Half-wrenched a golden wing," from the statue. (p. 1681) Arthur's plan will not reach the Northern Star with but one wing to rise on. In Arthur's hall, "twelve great windows blazon Arthur's wars," (p. 1669) serving the same moral purpose as the mystic symbols sculpted on the walls. The mystic symbols in Arthur's hall embody in material form a paradigm of Arthur's purpose; and when that purpose is marred, so is the symbol. In these symbols, which are of course a form of art, human aspirations are fittingly presented; and this is the highest use of art.

So emblems may serve a high purpose. But it is always necessary to recall that they are emblems; that they do not replace the ideal, but merely signify. King Pellam's desperate idolatry is a false utilization of emblems. Similarly, Balin's superstitious hope that the Queen's insignia upon his shield will help him to achieve self-control represents a misconceived notion of the function of emblems. For it is through the human imagination that fashioned symbols take life. The symbols, like legends, are meant to arouse the inner life. It is, again, a correspondence of tangible and intangible, a kind of harmony of spirit and flesh—Arthur's music of successfully wedded spirit and sense where sense is persuaded to serve the spirit through the agency of the imagination.[24]

When Gareth and his attendants come to Camelot, among the first amazements they experience is the wonderfully crafted gate depicting events from the legend of Arthur's career. As the servants gaze upon the gate, "The dragon-boughts and elvish emblemings / [Begin] to move, seethe, twine and curl." They seem to move, as well, for Gareth as he gazes long upon them. Just then "Out of the city a blast of music" peals and Merlin appears. (p. 1490) Merlin's art having pinched the imaginations of the new arrivals to excited attention, they are ready to face the ward of useful imagination himself. Appropriately enough, Merlin's appearance is heralded by music. The riddling Seer makes evident to Gareth that there is a purpose to illusions for the mind that can contain them. So there is a reason for the illusion of the gate, which signifies the transformation of the ideal into the real, the symbol to fact, through the power of the imagination both in the creator who has this way made incarnate the materials of his vision, and the observer whose imagination catches the sacred contagion of the ideal.

The incarnation of Christ is perhaps the finest example of ideality transmuted to fact. That this incarnation was, in fact, identical, in some minds, with the notion Tennyson presents of an embodied ideal, may be confirmed with a quotation from

Tennyson's friend, F. D. Maurice. Maurice is speaking of the Will of God.

> This Will demands that which the Necessity excludes. It must speak, it must utter itself. A Will cannot be without a *Word*. A Will that is, and lives, must utter itself by a living Word. This is what St. John, in his divine theology, declares to us. But if he speaks in one sentence of a Word, he speaks in the next of a Son. Then names are used interchangeably; but we should, I believe, lose more than we know, if either had been used exclusively. Experience has shown that those who determinately prefer the first, soon fall into that notion of a mere emanation from some mysterious abyss of Divinity, which haunted the oriental mystics and the early heretics, or else into the notion of a mere principle indwelling in man. The Word becomes impersonal: the Will becomes impersonal: very soon the man forgets that he is a person himself, and becomes a mere dreamer or speculator. The blessed name of Son, which connects itself with all human sympathies and relationships, is the deliverance from this phantom region. While we cleave to it, we can never forget that only a Person can express the Will of the Absolute Being; that only in a Person He can see His own image. But the Son of God will soon be merged for us in the Son of Man,—we shall refer His relationship to ours, not ours to His,—if we do not recur to that other name, if we do not, by meditating upon it, save ourselves from the unspeakable dangers into which those fall who think of the Son only as their Saviour, and not as the brightness of His Father's glory.[25]

Should we fail to maintain in our mind the proportionate view of Christ as human Son but embodied Word, Arthur's music falters, and men yield to selfish superstition.

As Arthur lies dying, and the end of his order seems surely imminent, Sir Bedivere, the loyal knight, blunders into a superstition. He cannot bear to cast away forever the beautiful brand, Excalibur. " 'What record, or what relic of my lord / Should be to aftertime, but empty breath / And rumours of a doubt?' " (p. 1749) Bedivere would like to preserve the sword in a treasure-house as evidence of Arthur's existence; a material proof of the ideal that once had lived incarnate among men. If the sword were preserved as a relic, it might serve as the basis for a recital of the times past.

> 'So might some old man speak in the aftertime
> To all the people, winning reverence.
> But now much honour and much fame were lost.' (p. 1749)[26]

But Arthur realizes that there is no place for relics in true faith. Symbols serve so long as they fire the believing imagination; but they serve mainly those who see the Grail, not those who suppose it. Galahad believes in the nun's belief, he does not merely crave to believe. Arthur realizes that " 'The old order changeth, yielding place to new,' " (p. 1752) and that the new time will require new forms to clothe the ideal. The old accoutrements no longer serve; they would become as courtly manners to the true courtesy. Relics are mere objects, the identity of which depends upon an essence long lost. Like men who have not found themselves, relics are disguises to the truth, not aids to vision.

We have already, in other parts of this study, touched upon the ways in which disguise operates. It is our own imaginative fabrications that may disguise others to us, or ourselves to ourselves. Galahad is a mystery, supposed by some "a son of Lancelot," by others "Begotten by enchantment." (p. 1665) This example displays the ambiguity of identity as well as the dubious service of language. In fact, Galahad *is*, in his nobleness, a son of Lancelot whether he is his offspring or not. Likewise, he is indeed the product of enchantment insofar as he is the representative of those high ideals conceived by the imagination, which enchants existence and lends the possibility of exaltation to human life. Yet Galahad's "real" origin remains a mystery, as much as Arthur's does, while his functioning identity, like Arthur's, is unmistakeable. He is one of the few personages in the *Idylls*, about whom there can be small doubt.

Like Arthur, his purpose is clear; unlike his King, he accomplishes it fully. The implication here is perhaps clearer than elsewhere in the *Idylls*, but no different. What Tennyson is saying in the poem is that we are what we are, despite external trappings. We are defined by our ideals and our enactment of them.[27]

In *The Princess*, Tennyson had already been aware of the esthetic utility of thematic disguise.[28] The Prince, in order to win for himself the companion of his dreams, disguises himself as a woman in order that he may pass unnoticed among women who have appropriated the behavior of men. But if Princess Ida, in her craving for power, and the prince, in his devious method of winning her, are both mistaken, both, when they shed their assumed identities, shed them only partially. The Prince's disguise as a woman has bestowed upon him female attributes that men are better for having. Similarly, Princess Ida's masculine impersonation has alerted her to her authentic identity and, though relinquishing the male rôle, she maintains certain worthwhile qualities.

In the *Idylls*, Gareth is one who sacrifices identity to achieve an identity. He will create his identity by fulfilling the ideals that spark his imagination. If yielding an apparent identity proves Gareth's purpose; it is Arthur's purpose that proves his identity. He is the embodiment of the principles he expresses; Gareth is their faultless enactment. Lynette may be romantically disappointed when she discovers Gareth's material identity because "The marvel dies," (p. 1520) but her disappointment is evidence of immaturity. She values not the man and his acts, but the label denoting him. His real identity becomes, in effect, a disguise once more, masking his true qualities. Fortunately, Lynette is quick to correct her temporary disenchantment and substitutes a genuine for a sentimental response.

Gareth's achievement of identity culminates with his unmasking of Death. Death's disguise is half the product of the perceiving imagination, since a good part of his terror is in the interpretation of his silence. When directly challenged, Death proves "a blooming boy." The conventional terror gives way, upon redefinition, to a hopeful joy. Abstracts, like men, may have misleading identities, which, if not always planned disguises, are misapplied interpretations of their authentic natures.

Not every attempt at identification is successful in the manner of Gareth's career, for Lancelot, as we have seen, while stripping himself of his conventional identity to accidentally discover a new and more perplexing one, gradually reshapes his nature. In wearing Elaine's favor, for example, he does as he has never done. And Elaine's words are true, that those who know Lancelot will be deceived because of this uncharacteristic act. But what is more important is the fact that Lancelot *does* a thing that he has never done before, and this act—the acknowledgment of the favor—is, in a way, a step towards things as they really are. Elaine is an attainable ideal, and, according to Arthur's estimate, was the woman designed for Lancelot, the woman whose favor Lancelot should willingly have worn.

But Lancelot has not taken the path to a new identity, and proper identity, voluntarily. In fact, his entire adventure begins with deceit—an attribute that should be most foreign to the noblest of Arthur's knights. Thereafter, Lancelot sheds other familiar properties, including his shield, and almost his physical being, for he appears "the skeleton of himself," when Elaine comes to nurse him in the hermit's cave. (p. 1642) But Lancelot is incapable of the surgery that Gareth performs upon himself—shedding a former identity like the cocoon of an insect and rising bright and remarkable. Lancelot's sin is in the bone itself. His noblest, most genuine qualities, are thoroughly intertwined with his sins, leaving him with a false identity and incapable of shaping a true one.

When Gawain wonders of Lancelot, "Must our true man change like a leaf at last?" (p. 1640) he overlooks the possibility that change may be for the best. Change is inescapable, as Lancelot is soon to learn in his own romantic entanglement. The secret is to turn the mutability of existence to moral advantage. Now is Lancelot's opportunity for self-redemption; he learns only self-awareness. Yet self-awareness is no mean achievement. There are many pains and punishments awaiting those who deceive, but there are worse offenses than fooling your fellows.

> 'Ay well—ay well—for worse than being fooled
> Of others, is to fool one's self. (p. 1521)[29]

What Lancelot achieves is only a partially redemptive act, characterized mainly by his aspirations and his self-awareness. His mistake is to suppose that he can sever the sin from the virtue in himself without a preliminary redefinition.

> And in my madness to myself I said,
> 'I will embark and I will lose myself,
> And in the great sea wash away my sin.' (p. 1683)

In his madness he had this hope. In his melancholy, after the death of Elaine, he desired oblivion. Neither remedy is adequate or right. To struggle and contend is the only solution. Percivale is one who chose to abdicate command in favor of a secluded, nameless anchorite's life. Though he was offered a kingdom and the moral leadership of a populace, he renounced both, along with the love of a noble lady, in favor of his own idealistic pursuit, for which he already doubted his suitability. In consequence, he terminates his career in obscurity, renouncing all significant identity. His withdrawal is not disguise, but it is, nonetheless, a form of veiling.

If men are unable to judge their own identities adequately, how then can they contend with the appearances of things around them? Yniol's clothing belies his real merit; likewise, through a suit of scraggy old armor "Princelike [Geraint's] bearing shone." (p. 1542) Geraint's entire career, we have already seen, is the gradual discovery that attributes are neither to be discovered nor imposed in externals. At first, Geraint feels compelled to clothe Enid in beauty, "so loved Geraint / To make her beauty vary day by day, / In crimsons and in purples and in gems." (p. 1526) But when he leads her into the wilderness of his own dismay, Geraint obliges Enid to wear the colors of his spirit. Enid, unconcerned with the externals of her nature, determined only to act in harmony with the righteousness within her, refuses to alter her appearance.

> And this poor gown I will not cast aside
> Until himself [Geraint] arise a living man,
> And bid me cast it. (p. 1569)

In effect, what Geraint has done, is to disguise not himself, but his own wife to himself. Enid's mother correctly says, "Let never maiden think, however fair, / She is not fairer in new clothes than old." (p. 1547) But the new clothes that she wears must be the garb of her true nature. Enid is already apparelled in the noblest kind of beauty; it is Geraint's ignorance that requires first the superficial raiment of splendor and then shabby insignia of shame.

Geraint does not realize that identity is not to be so easily determined. It is the harvest of a prolonged, sincere investigation; the reward of an ordeal or endeavor. Just as our own identity comes to us through the enactment of our ideals, so the identities of others emerge to us through an honest examination of their acts and ideals. But Geraint, refusing to acknowledge the subtle necessity, simplifies his perceptions to falseness by substituting a caricature of his own manufacture for the genuine being he has espoused. If Enid is Geraint's better self, it is only after the ceremony of the marriage and the ordeal of the withdrawal into the self, that Geraint hears clearly, and not in fragments, the voice by which he will abide if he is wise.

A suitable paradigm of the functioning of identity throughout the *Idylls* as a whole is the character of Edyrn. Geraint's attempt to discover Edyrn's identity is provoked by an act of rudeness. Subsequently, Geraint's quest becomes a search to disclose the secret of disorder, violence, and incivility in man. It is not long before he isolates the fount of these human weaknesses in the excesses of passion and pride. Up to this point, Edyrn is characterized by his behavior, which is predation. Accordingly, he is known as the sparrowhawk. Through Geraint's noble actions, Edyrn is overthrown, and only then is his identity suitably established. Geraint demands: " 'Thy name?' To whom the fallen man / Made answer, groaning, 'Edyrn, son of Nudd! / Ashamed am I that I should tell it thee.' " (p. 1543)

Ashamed Edyrn may be, redeemed he certainly is. His predatory nature, unharmonious with the highest human potentials, is more suited to beasts, and hence, while a slave to acquisitive passions, his identity is that of an animal. But once the potentiality of his nature is made clear to him through the rude liberation from pride that Geraint performs, Edyrn is on the way to salvation. It is in his naming of himself that he expresses his own identity and becomes aware of what that identity, truly, should be. He resumes his humanity. It is worth pointing out, I believe, that this achievement does involve a *resumption*. Human he was, until his passions mastered him; human he can be again. Having acknowledged his proper identity, Edyrn proceeds to shape it and "slowly drew himself / Bright from his old dark life." (p. 1544) This is a more painful and a slower process than Gareth's sudden spring from smoky knave to gleaming knight, but essentially it is the same event.

The disguises that men use are, for the most part, of small use. They can deceive only in a world of shadows, the world of materiality. The circumstantial world, characterized by flux and change, will not surprise wise men by its capricious mutations, for they see beyond the substance to the intangible truths and values. Men may disguise themselves to others, others to themselves, or themselves to themselves. Their identities remain largely unaltered, though some insight may be gained by the temporary transformation. Men are what they may do; and true identity is achieved in the harmony of ideal and act. In the *Idylls of the King*, those most mysterious of men, Arthur and Galahad, are those of clearest identity. An emblem or symbol without meaning is dead matter; only the emblem that embodies a truth moves with the vitality of an incarnate being. At times it is necessary for men to ask

> Earth, these solid stars, this weight of body and limb,
> Are they not sign and symbol of thy division from Him?
> ("Higher Pantheism," p. 1205)

Though Tennyson addressed his son, in "De Profundis," "O dear Spirit half-lost / In thine own shadow and this fleshly sign / That thou art thou," (p. 1282-83) he did not intend to be discouraging. Though man assumes the necessary disguise of flesh for his spirit, that disguise is not a frozen symbol, but malleable to the spirit, for the "main-miracle" of existence is "that thou art thou, / With power on thine own act and on the world." (p. 1283) Identity will be, not of the flesh, which is an ambiguous sign, but of the spirit that gives that sign meaning.

Authority

As difficult as the perceiving of true identities may be, obscured by the shadows of this-worldness, such perception is, nevertheless, imperative. For men to act righteously, they must be certain of the right, and, although each man has an inner voice of righteousness ready to inform him should he condescend to listen, there are other modes and representations of authority that must be acknowledged. In the end, of course, what Tennyson is concerned with is not the agencies of authority known as institutions, but the forms of authority within the self. Societal establishments of authority are only valid insofar as they imitate the moral dominion within the individual. Hence, Tennyson may approve Queen Victoria, his sovereign, because he recognizes in her an admission of the higher authorities. "O loyal to the royal in thyself," he begins his dedication "To the Queen" that concludes the *Idylls*. (p. 1755) And this is the meaning of Tennyson's epic, for what he wishes to show in "this old imperfect tale, /New-old, and shadowing Sense at war with Soul/ Ideal manhood closed in real man," (p. 1756) is what it is that is royal in ourselves in order that we may follow it. If we acknowledge the highest in ourselves; we find ourselves in the region of the divine. In this same concluding dedication, Tennyson objurgates evidences of weakness, among them "that which knows, but careful for itself, / And that which knows not, ruling that which knows / To its own harm." (p. 1756) Tennyson's poem is an appeal to men to recognize the royal in themselves and thereby lead themselves as well as others from harm.

Only disaster can result when we misread the rules of authority within us. Balin, "whose anger was his lord," became a savage thereby. (p. 1589) Pelleas, seduced by the surface of existence, not only misconstrues Ettarre's nature and accepts her as his moral authority, but, in a piece of harsh irony, is himself mocked as a "pilot-star." However, he knows no more of proper authority than those he leads, for his ideal is a King, not a morality. Gareth can say to Lynette, "Lead, and I follow," because he already has a spiritual guide within him. Wherever Lynette may direct him in the world of sense, he follows the truer guide within. And it is fortunate that he does, since, at the very outset of their expedition, Lynette admits " 'I have missed the only way.' " (p. 1506) Pelleas, on the other hand, though he may lament in maudlin dismay the "sweet star, / Pure on the virgin forehead of the dawn," (p. 1702) which no longer operates symbolically for him, never truly attends the moral royalty within him, for his vision is fixed on earth.

Gawain tells Pelleas that he will "tame thy jailing princess to thine hand." (p. 1696) But that Pelleas can even consider such dominion by proxy, and in such terms, suggests that he does not comprehend the rightful nature of authority. Authority should be assumed by representatives of Wisdom, and representatives of Sense should willingly serve. However, admirable as devoted service is, it may be both abject and misconceived, like Pelleas' stubborn subordination, or like the foolish young squire's unwise attendance upon Vivien. In both cases, sense serves only sense.

Authority and obedience may be misunderstood—and therefore wrong. Far worse is the offense of witting refusal of obedience to an acknowledged authority. Gawain, told by his King not to cease in his quest, relinquishes it before it is fulfilled. Consequently, upon Gawain's return to court, Arthur is obliged to judge him severely:

> 'Too courteous truly! ye shall go no more
> On quest of mine, seeing that ye forget
> Obedience is the courtesy due to kings.' (p. 1641)

Gawain, a good physical being, but slave to his passions and appetites rather than servant unto his King, is indifferent to the worthy but unknown and intangible. Half-submerged in circumstantiality, he mistakes it for true and solid reality. Ultimately, he discovers the insubstantiality of that supposed reality, and, blown along in the wind, no longer a significant substance himself, but only an insubstantial voice, he wails "Hollow, hollow all delight!'" (p. 1743) Rejecting all self-command, he forfeits control eternally.

If Gawain is one clear indication of the inability to perceive the true object for man's obedience, Elaine is once more his contrast. Acknowledging Lancelot as the lord she wishes to serve because of the nobleness she finds in him, Elaine desires no more than to serve him and be his squire. Moreover, when she learns of Lancelot's illness, she declares to her father that the gentle-born maiden is bound "to be sweet and serviceable / To noble knights in sickness." (p. 1642) Elaine entertains a dual concept of service. She accepts her position as a well-born woman as one involving certain offices and obligations, and far more importantly, she desires to serve that one individual who has evoked in her the sentiment of admiration and love. Both forms of service deserve applause, and, conjoined, are of the highest merit.

> And never woman yet, since man's first fall,
> Did kindlier unto man, but her deep love
> Upbore her; till the hermit, skilled in all
> The simples and the science of that time,
> Told [Lancelot] that her fine care had saved his life. (p. 1644)

But for this service Elaine desires no applause and no other reward than to continue her service. She asks Lancelot only that she be allowed "To serve you, and to follow you through the world." (p. 1647) This is the motive animating Arthur's true knights, who, accepting the King's authority, wish to serve him and follow him through the world. It is, likewise, a service roughly imposed upon the obedient Enid. In the two latter instances, obedience is offered or at least not refused, and the pattern of authority and service is maintained; with Elaine, the pattern is broken, because her noble offer is rejected. It is authority rejecting service. Elaine has been the agent of salvation for Lancelot's physical being; permitted further service, we are led to believe that she could save his soul as well. But Lancelot has lost proportion, and though he may still serve his ideal in a fragmentary way, he is incapable of leading others. It is his awareness of this fact, brought about largely by the death of Elaine, that makes him doubt the moral utility of his name and fame.

At the critical moment, when the jealous Guinevere casts the diamonds that Lancelot has won for her into the water, Lancelot himself reaches a crisis, and he leans from the window, watching the lost gems fall "in half disdain / At love, life, all things." (p. 1654) But at that moment the barge bearing Elaine's corpse passes, and Lancelot sees her lying "like a star in blackest night." (p. 1655) Elaine's service is not ended; even in death she has the power to save Lancelot from a bitter melancholy. Lancelot, throughout the poem, has suffered a divided internal kingdom, metaphorically resembling the realm destroyed by the warring brother kings whose lost crown provided the jewels Lancelot forcefully claimed for his queen.

If Lancelot failed in the test of his loyalty, Bedivere survived a similar ordeal of faith and trust. When Arthur, at the last battle, tells Bedivere that he no longer sees anything clearly, not even his own authority, Bedivere responds: " 'My King, / King everywhere! and so the dead have kings, / There also will I worship thee as King.' " (p. 1746) However, he later hesitates in his obedience when he fails to throw Excalibur away, and Arthur corrects him, saying, " 'Thou hast betrayed thy nature and thy name.' " (p. 1748) And Bedivere, who admits that it is "Deep harm to disobey, / Seeing obedience is the bond of rule," (p. 1749) ultimately does obey.

But it is not obedience to Arthur as a King that is important; just as it is not a lover that Enid or Elaine serves. Were that so, any lover, even a misguided lover such as Pelleas, or a misguided subject like Balin, might prove noble. Noble truth is the authority that the true servants acknowledge. We revert to Pallas' scheme for a worthy life.

> ' "Self-reverence, self-knowledge, self-control,
> These three alone lead life to sovereign power.
> Yet not for power (power of herself
> Would come uncalled for) but to live by law,
> Acting the law we live by without fear;
> And, because right is right, to follow right
> Were wisdom in the scorn of consequence." ' (pp. 392-93)

Pallas further promises that her vigor wedded to Paris' blood will grow "Sinewed with action, and the full-grown will, / Circled through all experiences, pure law, / Commeasure perfect freedom." (p. 394) Tennyson had suggested in *In Memoriam* and the *Idylls* that both doubt and fame should be made "vassal" to the larger love. Love is the spiritual authority; and as the narrator of *Maud* discovered, it is a spiritual authority within the self that brings proportion and the power of action, just as a leader of a nation consolidates a people's will. The internal spirit, having assumed control over disciplined senses, is capable next of submitting itself to a yet higher authority, which is the changeless ideal beyond the self. Discovering the proper authority is no more than determining the true and the just, and Tennyson seems to say that all men may achieve this knowledge to varying degrees. This achievement is the purpose of Guinevere's ordeal. Though she may disregard Arthur's authority to indulge her passions, saying that her King is " 'A moral child without the craft to rule,' " (p. 1625) she later admits that she had always felt that Arthur was more noble than Lancelot, who, in turn, asserts "there lives / No greater leader." (p. 1629)

In "Faith," Tennyson declared, "Doubt no longer that the Highest is the wisest and the best," (p. 1455) and what Guinevere has known, but not admitted until too late, is that Arthur *is* "the highest and most human too." (p. 1741) Nor is there a contradiction in this expression, for, to be most human in this sense is to express the highest potential of man's humanity. It is the Feuerbachian equation again: that man's God, his Ideal, is the consolidation into symbol or fable of his own limitless imaginative potential. Guinevere admits, having acknowledged Arthur's excellence, "We needs must love the highest when we see it;" (p. 1741) and might have added that seeing it and loving it, we make it so. It is thus that the Ideal may survive in the world. Had she, the representative of material beauty, been truly wedded to her King, Arthur's dominion would never have been sundered. Pallas would have been wedded to Paris, divinity and humanity joined, high laws ruled passions.

Although many sentimental readers of Tennyson may object to Arthur's apparent implacability with his Queen, they overlook the necessity of Arthur's nature. He is authority and cannot vary a law to pardon what would destroy all. It is the law that demarcates his nature, not he who proposes the laws. Although he establishes the laws that govern his order, to be the true King he could not compose other laws than these. Arthur has said, "the King must guard / That which he rules," (p. 1687) and just as he cannot irresponsibly pursue a vague vision when his dominion is circumstantial, so he cannot yield to a beloved detail, when his duty is to an Order. Guinevere's submission is useless, where her obedience would have saved.

Authority and obedience are not social activities in the *Idylls*, but essentials of a harmonious order; most accurately, they apply to the individual. It is the ideal, the highest value conceivable by man, to which the conceiving man of flesh owes obedience. Recognizing the sublime potential, he commits self-treason if he will not bind himself to it by vows, though it be unattainable in the illusory world of the flesh. But in takng the highest, the most royal in himself as that to which his loyal service is most deeply committed, he makes that royalty live, and thereby frees himself from his fetters of clay. Using imagery similar to that of Tennyson's *Idylls*, F. D. Maurice expressed a similar view in his *Theological Essays*, which were, of course, dedicated to Tennyson.

> "That *righteous King of your heart* whom you have felt to be so near you, so one with yourself, even while you confessed that you were so evil, He is the Redeemer as well as the Lord of you and of man. Believe that He is so. Ask to understand the way in which He has proved Himself so. You will find that God, not we, has been teaching you of Him, that He has been talking with you in the whirlwind, while we were darkening counsel with words without

knowledge; leading you, to the sight of His glory, that He might make you willing to confess your own baseness. He has taught you that you have been in chains, but that you have been a willing wearer of the chains. To break them He must set you free. *Self is your great prison-house.* The strong man armed, who keeps that prison in safety, must be bound. *The rod of the enchanter, who holds your will in bondage, must be broken by some diviner spell before the arms can be loosed, and the captive rise and move again.*"[30]

Confinement / Freedom

For Pallas, in "Oenone," self-control and the proper use of man's powers led to freedom. Throughout Tennyson's poetry, freedom is associated with moral achievement, and unbelief is constraint.

> Let blow the trumpet strongly while I pray,
> Till this embattled wall of unbelief
> My prison, not my fortress, fall away!
> ("Doubt and Prayer," p. 1455)

True freedom, for Tennyson, was putting the self in harmony with God's intent, as "The Two Voices" so clearly suggests. Accordingly, the characteristic action of Arthur is liberation, and the *Idylls* opens with his supplying freedom from oppression to a land overrun by selfish and brutal lords. But the set toward liberation involves acknowledgment of law, and hence Arthur's vows. To be free is to select voluntarily those rules worth following.

There are many forms of constraint in the *Idylls*, but few are noble in the manner of Arthur's vows, and those who refuse to be bound by the vows, like Tristram find liberty a dubious acquisition. Tristram claims he is "not bounded save by love." (p. 1723) But his love is a love of the flesh, and not long after he has declared this bondage, he feels the truest bondage of the flesh in death. Conversely, Lancelot, who *wishes* to be bound only by Arthur's vows, and who can appreciate the pure love that Elaine represents, though reduced to the skeleton of himself, still feels "The shackles of an old love." (p. 1645) The worldling, completely divorced from noble discipline, is abruptly engulfed by mortality; while the partially noble, though he reach the limits of mortality, cannot unfasten his shackling love. It is, perhaps, because that love is not solely of the flesh and cannot be shed as the flesh is shed. Lancelot's is an honor rooted in dishonor, a faith unfaithful that keeps him falsely true. The bondage, however, is none the weaker for all that.

But, as the passage quoted from F. D. Maurice declares, wearers of such chains are willing prisoners. No better example of this conscious entrapment is necessary than Pelleas. Pelleas, who claims to follow Arthur's vows, can yet declare to Ettarre, "Behold me, Lady, / A prisoner, and the vassal of thy will," (p. 1694) though that Lady is the incarnate contradiction of all that the vows signify. Pelleas cannot serve two such masters, and his submission to physical fetters for love of Ettarre intimates his real choice.

The irony of Arthur's vows is the mystery of Arthur's music. Discipline contributes purpose to existence as measure orders sound to music. Man has a will; that will is his identity to shape as he can. But an undisciplined will can shape nothing, for it has not the habit of form. Since random existence remains ungoverned, the libertine or worldling is most entrapped. Freedom is will and will is order.[31] Arthur's vows free men and send them out to perform deeds of honor in the broad land; but Pelleas "alone in open field," meanly craves to assume confinement in Ettarre's castle. He has refused the open field of directed, purposeful aspiration for the cooped sphere of self-indulgence. When he finally penetrates the fortress, Pelleas discovers no ennobling structure, but the "nest" of the sinful Gawain and Ettarre. The discovery leads Pelleas to covet the destruction of "her towers that, larger than themselves / In their own darkness, thronged into the moon." (pp. 1700-1) The towers he once hungered to enter, he now enlarges darkly in his imagination, for his whole world has been darkened by them. His bondage has been amplified infinitely, for it has entrapped his imagination, and the small, vile nest that he has discovered amidst Ettarre's towers now extends itself even to the noblest structures, for when he sees

> High up in heaven the hall that Merlin built,
> Blackening against the dead-green stripes of even,
> 'Black nest of rats,' he groaned, 'ye build too high.' (p. 1703)

The reason for this infectuous bondage, which spreads from physical to spiritual dimensions in Pelleas, is supplied by Ettarre's response to Guinevere's rebuke, in terms appropriate to the larger, inclusive scheme of constraint.

> 'Had ye not held your Lancelot in your bower,
> My Queen, he[Pelleas] had not won.' (p. 1692)

Lancelot is too frequently embowered, and though his corresponding confinement in a hermit's cave comes after all, serving as a partial antidote, his descent into the temple cave of his own self, the true danger in his constraint is the model it sets for others far more willing to be thus interned.

It is the familiar bondage of a court inclining to corruption that Pelleas experiences. Nor are the wisest exempt from this constraint, as Merlin's downfall clearly reveals. Merlin's yielding to the weary passions of the flesh entraps him through the binding enchantment of his own betrayed imagination. It is his own charm that seals his limbs. And though Vivien may call Merlin her "Master," and appear a simple "cageling" letting herself be conquered, it is she who will do the caging because her victim half-willingly embraces the bars.

The *Idylls* abounds with images and conditions of confinement and constraint, though not all of them signify the same moral conditions. Nevertheless, through the poem as a whole, there is an accumulating sense of constraint, which achieves its finest release in the transportation of Arthur from his worldly kingdom to that enchanted isle, which was already so much a part of the poetic mythography of the nineteenth century, and which was, if anything, to become more significant as a symbol of release and spiritual freedom as the century progressed. After the first 'open' idylls, a sense of huddling captivity oppressively increases through the poem, broken only by occasional forecasts of freedom—as in Galahad's easy flight to the heavenly city— until, in the last idyll, Arthur moves to freedom paradoxically in a coffin-like barge, and Bedivere alone but beyond the mists is left on an eminence, "the highest he could climb," facing the new dawn and new year. (p. 1754) The *Idylls* begins with the offer of freedom and concludes with its promise. But between the offer and the promise are the many circumscribing rejections.

As in *Maud*, images of confinement in the *Idylls* are equatable with submergence in self; but as we have already seen, though retreat into self may be an attempted burial, as it is in *Maud*, it may also be an approach to the sacerdotal antrum, described by the Ancient Sage. There are dangerous confinements, such as the Demon's cave or Pellam's castle in "Balin and Balan." The latter is described as "low-built but strong," and a "home of bats." It has a "low dark hall of banquet," and a "glimmering gallery" along which Balin is obliged to flee. (pp. 1585-87) Furthermore, the castle is overgrown with ivy and "cankered boughs" which bring to mind the setting in which Balin's fierce passion for strange adventure was aroused: the "dark bower" wherein he overheard the questionable conversation of Lancelot and Guinevere. (p. 1590) The fruits of that sinful "dark bower" are the "cankered boughs" of Pellam's castle, and ultimately the "dark bower" will spread and increase, becoming the "lone wood" in which Vivien and the Demon dwell. That "lone wood" in turn becomes the "wild woods of Broceliande" which finally contains Merlin and the high dream in invisible confinement.

"The Last Tournament" begins with an account of the Nestling, saved from a perilous nest, and continues to fix its points of degradation in confined locales, from the "low lodge" where Tristram and Isolt had stayed together in the early days of their adultery to Isolt's tower where the crime is terminated, and beyond to the brutal revelry and massacre at the Red Knight's tower. The Red Knight's tower is established as a conscious antiposition to Arthur's noble hall, which is, of course, "Broader and higher than any in all the lands." This "mighty hall" is evidence that not all containment is evil. (pp. 1668-69) A hermit's chapel-cave may signify aid and peace for Lancelot; and Elaine, alone in her tower, communing with the many-voiced shield that she, through the power of her own imagination, duplicates and animates, is a type of worthiness. It is in this solitude that she consolidates her high aspirations. Confinement, then, can serve a useful and positive purpose by leading the self into secluded converse with itself. This trial is, however, only one possible phase of the general movement toward spiritual restoration and must proceed from the state of private compression, to a public benevolence and outward expression of love in deeds.[32]

I have described only a few of the more evident examples of confinement, but they are, perhaps, sufficient to indicate the manner in which similar examples, when considered in the aggregate, effect an atmosphere of constraint or circumscription. That confinement and constraint in the realm of the spirit is a voluntary wearing of chains, we have already seen, but one adventure summarizes the case. Sir Bors, though genuine in his quest of the Grail, is unable to repulse the pagan sun-worshippers who "Seized him, and bound and plunged him into a cell / Of great piled stones." (p. 1680) Here, Bors is left in darkness to meditate alone, until a stone falls away and he sees the stars

called "Arthur's Table Round," and across the constellation
passes the vision of the Grail.

> 'Afterwards, a maid,
> Who kept our holy faith among her kin
> In secret, entering, loosed and let him go.' (p. 1681)

Surrounded by a hostile belief, Bors is forced into the solitude of
his own spirit; there, because his faith is strong, his vision is disclosed to him, and, having seen the vision clearly at last, he is
free once more. It is, significantly, the keeping of "our holy faith"
that leads to his manumission.

Though Bors was forced into his confinement, there to experience the redeeming vision in what amounted to the "Temple
cave" of his own self, others pursue a similar burial not for salvation's sake, but to escape the pain of another, more earthly
awareness. Both of the capital offenders in the poem ultimately
feel the lust for obliteration. Lancelot, afflicted by the death of
Elaine and the Queen's changed manner, cries:

> 'I pray him, send a sudden Angel down
> To seize me by the hair and bear me far,
> And fling me deep in that forgotten mere,
> Among the tumbled fragments of the hills.' (p. 1660)

It is guilt that prompts this desire, like that of the narrator of
Maud, who wishes to bury himself in himself, and finally succeeds in doing so; though he, like Bors, is resurrected from his
cave through the vision of a star. Lancelot, we are told, will also
achieve redemption, as will Guinevere, who, parting from Lancelot says, "Would God that thou couldst hide me from myself!"
(p. 1728)

Lancelot will shut himself up in his kingdom, but Guinevere's
is a more striking confinement, for she finds sanctuary at the convent in Almesbury. Here, in the natural humility of the setting,
the Queen for the first time puts off her identity, as Lancelot had

done earlier. A parallel self-awareness follows the shedding of her customary self-definition. Her disguise is a forced step outside (or inside) herself, for she sees herself through the eyes of innocence once more, the eyes of the naive and garrulous novice. It is the child's "innocent talk" that directs Guinevere's thoughts to the opposition of her experience of the world and the child's. She asks the novice:

> "O closed about by narrowing nunnery-walls,
> What knowest thou of the world, and all its lights
> And shadows, all the wealth and all the woe? (p. 1733)

But, as we have already seen, the great world is honeycombed with subtle immurements. What is more, the wisdom that the Queen has gained from her sojourn in the world sadly resembles the "wisdom" of Vivien or Tristram, confessed worldlings. She herself realizes that what she has learned is the projection of her own lurid failings upon those around her. A strange freedom that extends the prison of the self endlessly into the surrounding world! Suspecting the novice of treachery, the Queen is forced to admit:

> 'The simple, fearful child
> Meant nothing, but my own too-fearful guilt,
> Simpler than any child, betrays itself.' (p. 1734)

After all, Guinevere elects to stay in the convent, where she can offer the service in which she has so long been deficient. The consequence is that she achieves mastery of the small compass over which her good powers have been exercised.

The obvious parallel to Guinevere's elected confinement is Percivale's, though his is not a compelled election of place. Once more confinement, though a secondary achievement, is yet a means to grace and neither a simple escape nor a moral failure. Ambrosius, resembling Guinevere's novice, serves to establish a contrast between the wide world that Percivale has known and

211

rejected and the narrow world of the cloister and its environs. Ambrosius says that he has "never strayed beyond the cell, / But [lives] like an old badger in his earth." (p. 1679) Yet he has the wisdom of innocence and announces that he can "Rejoice, small man in this small world of mine," and in all the trivia of that world. (p. 1677) It is worth remembering that the vision of the Grail appeared to Percivale's sister, a nun self-confined to a cell for prayer's sake. Moreover, in Percivale's own adventures, it is the "hermitage" in the "lowly vale" to which he must turn from the "ruinous city" on the "mighty hill." (p. 1674)

"The Holy Grail," of course, is primarily about humility, and therefore an approval of humble withdrawal for purposes of self-examination is more pronounced in it than in other idylls. But illustrations of the proper uses of solitude and confinement are not lacking elsewhere, not only in the *Idylls*, but in Tennyson's poetry generally. Disregarding such obvious examples of the selfish uses of spiritual constraint as in "St. Simeon Stylites," we may still find suitable examples. There is, of course, the "lordly pleasure-house" of "The Palace of Art." (p. 401) There, all the powers of the imagination and the spirit were to be devoted to the gratification of the self. Coming to an awareness of her mistake in dwelling thus selfishly in the Palace, the Soul makes a significant request.

> 'Make me a cottage in the vale,' she said,
> 'Where I may mourn and pray.' (p. 418)

And Ida, another image of the Soul, also withdraws from a disillusioning world to devote herself exclusively to the fulfilment of her private desires, though they wear the mask of benevolence. To be a true Princess is to rule a kingdom wisely, but it is not wise to exclude from that kingdom half of what Nature has signified as necessary. Recognition of her mistake introduces Ida to sensations of emptiness resembling those experienced by the narrator of the "Supposed Confessions." Selfishness and despair are empty citadels, whereas love is overbrimming freedom. God's "house," as "The Two Voices" suggests, is the vast world.

Although these familiar examples may be of some purpose, it is just as well to return to the *Idylls* itself for a more satisfying account. Merlin, in explaining the origin of the charm that is ultimately to rob him of his use, tells Vivien the tale of the King, who, having obtained his Queen from a pirate who had in turn carried her off from two warring cities, finds the woman to be so beautiful that she is endangering the stability of his kingdom. Jealously he wishes "To find a wizard who might teach the King / Some charm, which being wrought upon the Queen / Might keep her all his own." (p. 1611) An old wizard is found who does, indeed, have the powers that the King requires.

> And then he taught the King to charm the Queen
> In such-wise, that no man could see her more,
> Nor saw she save the King, who wrought the charm,
> Coming and going, and she lay as dead,
> And lost all use of life. (p. 1612)

The King, consumed by a passion to possess the beautiful for his own gratification, discovers that in complete possession that beauty loses "all use of life." It is the tale of "The Palace of Art" retold in a less direct manner, but with greater incisiveness, for it is, we must recall, a tale of a fleshly passion that must forever be frustrated to find its captive beauty without the "use of life." Moreover, the story is told by a weakening sage who is, inversely, about to relinquish his own use of life by yielding to a fleshly passion. The King and Merlin draw their selfish charms around themselves. It is, after all, the same charm. Men cannot enjoy an entirely appropriated desire. Love, like music, requires response and accord. Whereas the King loses the enjoyment of his dream, Merlin himself is rapt in the dream.

The self, filled with pride and indulgence, discovers that these ingredients are deceptively vacuous. The gleaming internal cornucopia becomes a wasteland where all values and pleasures fall to dust, until humility and the escape from the self returns joy to the inner kingdom. This is precisely what Percivale learns, but the lesson is by no means limited to him. Gareth began with no false pride and was open to the many joyful images that the highly inspired imagination can provide. There was no vanity to usurp his imagination. Pride stuffs the self with airy volume that proves an emptiness at last, as "The Two Voices" proves. The same poem demonstrates, as do many of the idylls, that virtue can fill the imagination with true objects if humility cleanse it and make it worthy. Fill the imagination with the self, and an infection spreads to the external world; but the humble imagination is free to read in that world untainted lessons and hear the music of a harmonious order. And virtue is liable to assume command in those uncertain moments when the self is in jeopardy, when it is cast low by disease, or when its very identity is in doubt. If Gareth grows to self-fulfilment by gradually acquiring the valued trappings of his soul, a figure such as Edyrn abruptly discovers an inner vacuum and tediously must refurnish that valuable temple cave. To one, virtue is an unalienable friend; to the other, a fortunate guest of confusion.

The entire theme of constraint and freedom refers, fundamentally, to the duality of Sense and Soul, for it is the bondage of the flesh that establishes the metaphor of man's struggle to liberate the enchained soul.[33] But Tennyson enlarges the complex of image and incident to make confinement something more subtle and intriguing in the *Idylls*. Tennyson was evidently aware of the contrary motion of man's nature which, instead of freeing the soul through selflessness, seeks to contain the world through futile acquisition. In the *Idylls*, he hinted the folly of this misleading appetite.

Since it is impossible to contain the world, it is necessary to set limits in the self. We may establish our angry towers, from which to rage against false virtue with a true vileness, or creep into nests of self-indulgence. We may bury ourselves beneath the earth to avoid the terrors of retribution, or suffer confinement only to find liberation a matter of vision. Or we may voluntarily withdraw to that holy antrum to work out, through careful study, our possible salvation. It is this kind of communing with the self that leads the narrator of "The Two Voices" finally to decide that though there may be an unmanacling "from bonds of flesh" in death, this is not the kind of liberation that he is seeking. Instead, he throws open the casement and admits the influence of the world around him. Himself expunged, he is open to unperverted impressions, and he sees that it is not into the grave that he must descend in order to be free; elsewhere he should direct his aspirations.

> On to God's house the people prest:
> Passing the place where each must rest,
> Each entered like a welcome guest. (p. 540)

This does not, in my reading, mean that the narrator intends to depart immediately for Sunday morning services, but that he has passed outside of himself to the greater realm suggested by the phrase "God's house," and represented by his going forth into the fields where he too could enter "like a welcome guest." Only those who have labored to keep their kingdom orderly in this world will, at the waste and wild land on the edge of death, have any hope of an island home where they will enter, not like a convict, but like a king returning from his wars.

Obscurity / Clarity

Explaining, in "To the Queen," that his story of Arthur is not the old tale, but one "shadowing Sense at war with Soul," Tennyson used an apt image when he referred to the legendary Arthur as "that gray king, whose name, a ghost, / Streams like a cloud,

215

man-shaped, from mountain peak, / And cleaves to cairn and cromlech still." (p. 1756) Arthur is another of those subjects that men, through their imaginations, translate from cloudy mystery to animate incident. The legend is a cloud, but it is, ambiguously, a cloud "man-shaped." The grand legends at the beginning of "Timbuctoo" are described also as shadows to which mankind hopefully clings, like a faithful Priestess who clasps the "marble knees" of her deity's likeness "and gazeth on / Those eyes which wear no light but that wherewith / Her phantasy informs them." (p. 174) The mystery is forever a mystery, and "Timbuctoo" opens and closes in forms of obscurity, though between these mysteries is the clarity that the imagination may temporarily provide. For in this world, the only clarity is that which the believing imagination provides. Tennyson would have said, with Wordsworth,

> And conquering Reason, if self-glorified,
> Can nowhere move uncrossed by some new wall
> Or gulf of mystery, which thou alone,
> Imaginative Faith! canst overleap,
> In progress toward the fount of Love.[34]

The obscurity-to-clarity trajectory of visionary perception has a complex expression in section xcv of *In Memoriam*. In this poem, the movement is from apparent clarity to real clarity, and then back.[35] The poem opens with the poet enjoying sensuous details of a genially warm summer evening. He hears the cricket, the brook, the "fluttering urn," sees the bats in "fragrant skies," and notes minutely the "ermine capes / And woolly breasts and beaded eyes" of night creatures. The summary of this evening scene has the poet and his companions singing old songs

> that pealed
> From knoll to knoll, where, couched at ease,
> The white kine glimmered, and the trees
> Laid their dark arms about the field.

216

As though the word "glimmered" is a signal, the poet's companions are now removed and the poet is absorbed in thoughts of his dead friend, who was

> bold to dwell
> On doubts that drive the coward back,
> And keen through wordy snares to track
> Suggestion to her inmost cell.

Gradually the material world fades away entirely, erased by language which teases toward the spiritual, though it remains untrustworthy, as later it will prove inadequate to describe the poet's experience. The circumstantial world obliterated, the poet's soul whirls "About empyreal heights of thought," encountering "Aeonian music measuring out / The steps of Time—the shocks of Chance— / The blows of Death." But with the word "Death," doubt revives, the vision fades, and now

> the doubtful dusk revealed
> The knolls once more where, couched at ease,
> The white kine glimmered, and the trees
> Laid their dark arms about the field.

We have returned through the glimmering midworld between the spheres of sense and spirit to precisely the same material world from which we recently departed—as the identical lines indicate—where a breeze rustles the leaves and fluctuates "all the still perfume." The senses have recaptured the self. To the recaptured mind, the increasing breeze says, 'The dawn the dawn," and then dies away,

> And East and West without a breath,
> Mixt their dim lights, like life and death,
> To broaden into boundless day.

The world of sense, so seemingly secure, can glimmer and fade, and man may pass into another, higher sight, a profounder clarity. But that vision does not last. Back through the twilight where Sense and Soul join, the spirit returns. But it brings with it a trace of hope regarding the larger mystery that this experience distantly recapitulates, like those various disguisers in the *Idylls* and elsewhere in Tennyson's poetry who never completely discard the fortunate identities they briefly assume. As man, when spirit, passes temporarily into material existence; so man, while flesh, temporarily rises to spiritual experience. East and West, life and death, are "dim lights," mysteries obscuring our perceptions in between. When these mysteries are not limits to our hope, but the frontier of a vaster, freer realm, when they are mixed in the common mystery of our real being, the dim light they provide broadens "into boundless day" and we may understand that man is spirit only held for a time in bonds of clay.

The material world is inevitably a world of mystery, for it is severed from the world of reality, which is the world of the spirit. The poem "De Profundis" makes Tennyson's opinion on this subject amply evident. The infant, who has come "out of the deep," "From that true world within the world we see, / Whereof our world is but the bounding shore," receives the poet's condolences.

> O dear Spirit half-lost
> In thine own shadow and this fleshly sign
> That thou art thou—who wailest being born
> And banished into mystery. (pp. 1282-83)

In the same way, Merlin says of Arthur, "From the great deep to the great deep he goes," (p. 1480) and he dies on the bounding shore of his kingdom amidst the confusions of death, for a "blind haze" obscures everything in the King's mortal moment. (p. 1744) But though the end of Arthur's Order, and Arthur's physical presence as well, may understandably be shrouded in obscuring mists, it requires a more careful examination to explain the frequent appearance of mists, clouds, mysteries and dreams that occur throughout the *Idylls*, for, although consistently indicating that the world of substance is a shadowy mystery, references to various forms of mystery and obscurity require a more elaborate explanation than Dagonet's simple judgment that "the world / Is flesh and shadow." (p. 1713)

The difficulty of the explanation is displayed in one of the several ironically applicable songs of the *Idylls*. It is Tristram, the arch-worldling, who sings this song.

> 'Ay, ay, O ay—the winds that bend the brier!
> A star in heaven, a star within the mere!
> Ay, ay, O ay—a star was my desire,
> And one was far apart, and one was near:
> Ay, ay, O ay—the winds that bow the grass!
> And one was water and one star was fire,
> And one will ever shine and one will pass.
> Ay, ay, O ay—the winds that move the mere.' (pp. 1723-24)[36]

Indeed, the song is a summary of Tristram's misunderstanding. Once he followed the true star that he can no longer see because the dubious daylight of this world has obscured it. Instead, he sees only the reflected image of that star in the earthly mere—the physical reflection of spiritual beauty, which is, for him, Isolt. But the mere can be troubled by the capricious winds of this world, and Tristram may be impelled not by reason, but by his wayward passions. Furthermore, as an earlier image indicates, the waters reflecting the heavenly star also reflect the image of the gazer and mix the self with the mimic ideal. Not long after Dagonet has disclosed Tristram's blindness to the spiritual star in an unreflecting heaven, Tristram muses on its earthly transmutation.

> Before him fled the face of Queen Isolt
> With ruby-circled neck, but evermore
> Past, as a rustle or twitter in the wood
> Made dull his inner, keen his outer eye

> For all that walked, or crept, or perched, or flew.
> Anon the face, as, when a gust hath blown,
> Unruffling waters re-collect the shape
> Of one that in them sees himself, returned;
> But at the slot or fewmets of a deer,
> Or even a fallen feather, vanished again. (p. 1714)

So the light winds of capricious fancy and an unanchored will ruffle and settle the broken image in the waters of the imagination reflecting the gazer's fragmentary self.

It is not by following a star in a mere that we will arrive at the heavenly city. The holy nun of the Holy Grail, through fast and prayer, acquires a supersensual vision, and she recommends the same course to others.

> "So now the Holy Thing is here again
> Among us, brother, fast thou too and pray,
> And tell thy brother knights to fast and pray,
> That so perchance the vision may be seen
> By thee and those, and all the world be healed." (p. 1665)

But the knights hope to leap to vision without putting aside the obscuring circumstantiality of this world, and for them the Grail is like a cloud. Only Galahad sees the Grail clearly because his spirit stands partly in another world and therefore deals with this world as though it were a troublesome shadow. Nor is it sufficient merely to forego the pleasures of this world. A more thorough negation is required; one that accepts the things of the world while seeing a greater reality beyond them. Pellam, in his asceticism, claims, " 'I have quite foregone / All matters of this world,' " (p. 1580) but, in fact, he is enmeshed in the world through his dependence upon the material evidences of faith, his relics and other holy *things*.

He only will be able to command the world of substance who first acknowledges its shadowy nature; thereafter, the power of the imagination is free, and the world is open to its healthy enchantments. It is the old unsensual wizard of Merlin's recounting who is the true Seer; owning no sensual wishes, "to him the wall / That sunders ghosts and shadow-casting men / Became a crystal." (p. 1612) So little is this old wizard lumbered with self that he has almost extinguished his physical being; but spiritually he has nourished himself with the secrets of the superhuman world and through his liberated imagination has come to terms with the world of substance. Like Arthur, he has put ideal before material concerns and, like him, wishes to influence the material by the ideal.

The difficulty in this high purpose is that, too often, to men still constrained by their bonds of flesh, it is not the material world but the ideal which seems the less real, the cloudier and more mysterious. Even Lancelot suffers this pernicious confusion. During his convalescence he makes "Full many a holy vow and pure resolve." But his vows do not last, because, "Full often the bright image of one face, / Making a treacherous quiet in his heart, / Dispersed his resolution like a cloud." (p. 1645) Because, noble as he is, he is yet straitened by fleshly wishes, Lancelot will only be capable of seeing the Holy Grail veiled, never clearly and unquestionably.

Our allegiances bind us or make us free and determine the colors of our dreams. Men chained in the flesh will suppose the world of flesh true and the heavens cloudy, while men whose spirits ascend, will see substance as no more than a dream. But all dreams are tenuous. And dreams of the flesh are among the most easily overturned. Excited by the picture of Lancelot and Guinevere's love, Vivien exclaims:

> ride, and dream
> The mortal dream that never yet was mine—
> Ride, ride and dream until ye wake—to me! (p. 1599)

Not believing the genuineness of the dream, it is to her nothing more than a dream; nor is Arthur's great vision more than a

221

dream. That which we do not credit becomes for us a dream, no matter what it may be to others. Unfortunate Pelleas undergoes a harrowing sequence of dreams. Upon first seeing Ettarre, who appears to him as a "vision," the stunned Pelleas explains " 'I woke from dreams.' " (p. 1690) But the dreams that he has wakened from were dreams of high ideals and innocent romance. One would suppose that, now he has been awakened from his dreams, he will be at ease in his sensual alertness. But Pelleas has waked from one dream into another, "for he dreamed / His lady loved him." (p. 1691) He has passed from vague but worthy dreams into a more material but equally unreal dream, and he finds himself at last in such utter confusion that Percivale must ask if he is "mazed with dreams." (p. 1702) Pelleas is indeed mazed with dreams, because each value that he discards promptly becomes a dream. What is no longer felt in faith no longer is real and becomes a dream. A dream, to be made real, must find expression in faith and action. For Lancelot, struggling in the slavery of his sensual guilt, the trumpets announcing the Tournament of Dead Innocence "sounded as in a dream / To ears but half awaked." (p. 1709) While the sinful Tristram "dreamed," "Arthur with a hundred spears / Rode far" to contend with the evil forces threatening his order, itself the manifestation of his high ideal. (p. 1715)

Firm faith is essential in the world of sense, because dreams, no matter how noble, are ambiguous, since they are products of the human imagination. That this is so is most sadly illustrated by Merlin's condition, for "the work by Merlin wrought, / Dream-like," (p. 1669) springs from the same power that later elicits his great melancholy and leads him to walk "with dreams and darkness." (p. 1601) While Merlin's troubling dream came to him "Dark in the glass of some presageful mood," even Vivien, the material presence, "seemed a lovely baleful star / Veiled in gray vapour." (p. 1603) Merlin, who has participated in raising the "dim rich city" of Camelot, (p. 1668) and who, before the

coming of Arthur's Order, hunted the hart with the golden horns
through a promising "dim land," (p. 1607) now finds himself
in a dark mood that prefigures the betrayal of that promise and
the ruin of the mystic city. Men may, it is clear, make real their
evil dreams as well as their nobler visions, and may, after flail-
ing wildly in a dream, find themselves in the sad situation of Balin
and Balan. Having contended confusedly in the world of misleading phantoms, near death "all at once they found the world,
/ Staring wild-wide." (p. 1592)

But the dreams that undo men are their own creations, and it
is a willed resistance that keeps the clouds about them, just as
their chains are voluntarily worn. Elaine, whose imaginative urge
is toward the noble and virtuous, and who is capable of prophetic dreams, demonstrates at least a rudimentary capacity to
dispel the "cloud / Of melancholy severe" that hovers over the
sinful Lancelot. (p. 1630) But Lancelot consciously discourages
the cloud-dispersing power of Elaine's devotion and returns instead to the already dissipating dream of his romance with Guinevere.

Man is consigned to mystery in this world, but mystery has
many attributes, and the individual spirit may design dreams that
it can itself make real. As Tennyson wrote in "The Higher Pantheism," "Dreams are true while they last, and do we not live in
dreams?" (p. 1204)[37] The world was full of signs and wonders
before the coming of Guinevere. The miracles that the novice
says her father saw could all be interpreted as imaginative readings of natural phenomena, but these readings were hopeful, and
"all the land was full of life," (p. 1731) because men were conscious of a new beginning. "Wildest dreams / Are but the need-
ful preludes of the truth," Tennyson said in *The Princess.* (p.
843) But there is that in man which cannot comfortably dwell in
mystery. The narrator of the "Supposed Confessions" demands
clarity from the first and is unwilling to devote himself to an
ideal obscured by cloudy mystery. He does not recognize that *we*

are the cloud that obscures our vision. To see clearly the individual must cleanse himself of himself. This is, we recall, the meaning of the Siege Perilous: Lose the sense of self and the vision becomes real.

But men can follow the dream only for a time. Gradually, after Guinevere has joined Arthur, after the ideal has taken to itself a physical manifestation, the wonder begins to fade. Faith is gradually reduced to a desire for physical proofs and rewards. The miracles that sprang from the exuberant imagination fade, and earthly visions supplant them. The hopeful animation of broad nature slowly becomes restricted to fleshly bowers, nests, and towers; men draw gradually back into themselves, consolidating their identities, either for good or for evil. Only a few still move unimpeded in their pursuit of their ideal, for they have realized that real things are seen in the imagination and that the world of substance is plastic to that truer vision.

The ideal is born in mystery and is necessarily vague. That it might be real, we attempt to implement the ideal in this other realm of mystery and shadow, the world of substance and of flesh. Here, between the mystery of its inception and the mystery of its passing, man seeks a certain clarity. It is the clarity that the narrator of "Timbuctoo" achieves between the two mysteries, and it is the clarity of Arthur as well. But the dangerous pursuit of clarity in the material world is represented not only in Guinevere, who is the incorporation of the ideal with physical beauty, but in the numerous instances of obscured perception. Although to be complete in this world the ideal must find embodiment, marrying the ideal to circumstantiality subjects it to the same forces of decay that operate upon all matter. It is, as well, subjected to the test of man's lower nature, the selfish and the savage. And man being a weak creature, sinful and flawed, it is true that the ideal will not persist for long in any specific form. Like all the world, it must observe the rules of change. The ideal itself remains unchanged, but in this world it must forever assume new forms.

Beneath the apparent level of a failing ideal is another layer of real achievement, for in each ideal that succeeds even for a time there is the promise of another. This the narrator of "The Two Voices" learns, when, in the temple cave of his own self, he has heard the true voice tell him to "Rejoice."

> 'A hidden hope,' the voice replied:
>
> So heavenly-toned, that in that hour
> From out my sullen heart a power
> Broke, like the rainbow from the shower,
>
> To feel, although no tongue can prove,
> That every cloud, that spreads above
> And veileth love, itself is love. (p. 541)

Man is his own prison, accepting the incarceration of the flesh; he is self-blinded, accepting the opacity of substance; he is self-defeated, crediting the apparent inutility of faith. But faith itself is the liberating force. It is not an argument that will save him; for arguments are composed of words, which, we have seen, are dubious adjuncts to belief. What is required is an incarnation of the private word, the transformation of the self, through emancipating the imagination. To believe in a hidden hope, is to exclaim within oneself, "Rejoice, Rejoice."[38]

Ultimately, no argument will persuade, yet language may preserve one of its highest powers and render in a tale what cannot be argued. We may remember, at this point, the words young Tennyson gave to the Spirit of Fable.

> 'There is no mightier Spirit than I to sway
> The heart of man: and teach him to attain
> By shadowing forth the Unattainable;
> And step by step to scale that mighty stair
> Whose landing-place is wrapt about with clouds
> Of glory' of Heaven. (p. 179)

And, in another place, Tennyson set forth clearly enough the model for his belief that a legend or a tale well told, with high intent, might be itself the manifestation of the ideal in the world of substance and lead men, like a symbolled king, beyond the mystery into which all men have been banish'd in birth.

> Though truths in manhood darkly join,
>   Deep-seated in our mystic frame,
>   We yield all blessing to the name
> Of Him that made them current coin;
>
> For Wisdom dealt with mortal powers,
>   *Where truth in closest words shall fail,*
>   *When truth embodied in a tale*
> *Shall enter in at lowly doors.*
>
> And so the Word had breath, and wrought
>   With human hands the creed of creeds
>   In loveliness of perfect deeds,
> More strong than all poetic thought.
>   (*In Memoriam*, xxxvi, p. 894; italics mine)

Conclusion

William Allingham records a conversation with Tennyson in 1884 in which the aged poet remarked, "I think Matter more mysterious than Spirit. I can conceive, in a way, what Spirit is, but not Matter."[1] This sentiment was fundamental to Tennyson's belief and was responsible for his conviction that it was necessary to entertain doubt in order to verify faith.[2] The ambiguity of material existence fascinated him; his remark upon looking through a microscope is characteristic: " 'Strange that these wonders should draw some men to God and repel others. No more reason in one than in the other.' "[3] And yet he found himself drawn toward the spiritual through observation of the wonders of nature, and he admired others who moved in the same direction.

Tennyson read and praised the popular scientist and philosopher, James Hinton,[4] who founded his beliefs in a distinction between the "phenomenal" and the "actual." For him the material world was deceptive until viewed in terms of spiritual truth. It was "higher meaning" that gave man the true power of perception.

> God's act in Nature appears to us under the form of physical or merely passive necessity, but that is our infirmity and defect of vision. It is necessary truly, every least fact and part of it, but necessary by a truer, deeper necessity than we perceive, the necessity that Love should do infinitely well and wisely.[5]

It is easy to see why Tennyson would find such sentiments agreeable, or to see that he might approve of Hinton's assumption that "the limitation, which causes man to perceive a spiritual action as matter and force [is] an absence of life."[6] Hinton held, moreover, "that matter and force, being mental hypotheses, substrata supplied by constitutive elements of mind, it is impossible to derive thought from these creations of its own."[7] Tennyson, too, felt that interpretations of the phenomenal world and attempts to understand the supernatural were fruitless since "man imputes himself" in his observations and "sows himself on every wind." What is more, he felt that the material world itself was entirely dependent upon the spiritual. Tennyson apparently agreed with Alfred R. Wallace when he declared " 'that all the Matter in existence might be immediately destroyed by the withdrawal of the sustaining Force.' "[8] For Tennyson that Force was divine, as he indicated in the Ancient Sage's comments to his young friend.

> And if the Nameless should withdraw from all
> Thy frailty counts most real, all thy world
> Might vanish like thy shadow in the dark. (p. 1351)

But despite his distrust of phenomenal existence, Tennyson never advocated contemplative or mystic withdrawal, though he often utilized the subject of withdrawal in his poetry. Instead, he urged participation in the world. The clearest instance of this attitude is in Arthur's famous statement at the close of "The Holy Grail," but there is another explicit presentation of it in *The Princess* when Ida instructs her charges about "the workman and his work."

> 'Let there be light and there was light: 'tis so:
> For was, and is, and will be, are but is;
> And all creation is one act at once,
> The birth of light: *but we that are not all,*
> *As parts, can see but parts,* now this, now that,
> And live perforce, from thought to thought, and make
> One act a phantom of succession: thus
> *Our weakness somehow shapes the shadow, Time;*
> *But in the shadow we will work.*' (p. 782; italics mine)

In *The Princess* and other poems, Tennyson persistently demonstrates that it is possible to live in the world of phenomena without forgetting the world of the spirit, and ultimately that is what the *Idylls of the King* is about. The war of Sense and Soul that Tennyson described in that poem would, even for the fortunate, end in a draw. But it was the ability to discover the proper balance that was important.[9]

Matthew Arnold once remarked that Tennyson's "reach of mind [was] petty,"[10] but at another time he credited him with an "extreme subtlety and curious elaboration of thought."[11] Dr. James Mann also saw "the one leading characteristic of Tennysonian poetry [as] *intellectual elaboration.*"[12] I have attempted to show that this is indeed an important characteristic of Tennyson's poetry, and that, although he is not an obtrusively philosophical poet, he is preoccupied with metaphysical questions regarding the relationship of the material and the spiritual world, the apparent and the actual, the nature and extent of man's capacity for accurate perception. Nor is it necessary to attribute Tennyson's thoughts along these lines to the great German philosophers of his time, for, as I have tried to show, there were writers in England who expressed similar views, such as James Hinton and the Hare brothers, in a manner more directly accessible to Tennyson.

For Tennyson the material world, though a shadowy part of the Infinite, was illusion and dream. This world was superficial, and the profound truths were only visible in ambiguous signs because man's nature was inferior. *If* one could understand the flower in the crannied wall, *then* one "should know what God and man is." (p. 1193) But men's perceptions were, to Tennyson, untrustworthy from a thoroughly earthly perspective. To perceive and comprehend this world most accurately, it was necessary to focus one's interests beyond phenomena and their lures to the senses. To see this world from the vantage of the Ideal was to see it as much unsullied by the senses and the self as was possible for man's fallen nature. But to so see it was to become aware of man's smallness, first as individual and then as race, and this awareness in turn could lead on to the gradual improvement of mankind. To be thus oriented toward the Ideal was to liberate the spirit from the chances of existence and free it to deal more successfully with the world of matter.[13] Enid, in her song addressed to Fortune, sings:

'Turn, turn thy wheel above the staring crowd;
Thy wheel and thou are shadows in the cloud;
Thy wheel and thee we neither love nor hate.'

Men who live in the spirit "go not up or down" with Fortune's wheel, "For man is man and master of his fate." (p. 1537) Tennyson urged his own new-born son to preserve in himself "that true world within the world we see—/ Whereof our world is but the bounding shore," from which the infant had so recently travelled, and to be ever conscious of that "infinite One" that had occasioned his existence. He prompted the child to strive

Nearer and ever nearer Him, who wrought
Not Matter, nor the finite-infinite,

> But this main-miracle, that thou art thou,
> *With power on thine own act and on the world.*
> (pp. 1282-83; italics mine)

I think it is sufficiently clear that Tennyson was a thoughtful and subtle poet, aware of the implications of his art, and moreover, that above all he was a moral poet.[14] His poems ordinarily follow recurrent patterns, and I have chosen to describe at length one such pattern which is, to my mind, evident in much of Tennyson's poetry, and is clearly redemptive.[15] This pattern describes man's progress from pride of self, through an essential humbling process which opens the pride-hardened heart to the influence of love, thereby revealing to it the potential fullness of life that love provides and leading the self to deny its own desires and appetites in the more rewarding experience of benevolent action toward others.

It is in the *Idylls of the King* that the implications of Tennyson's use of the design and its relationship to man's ability to perceive the truth are most thoroughly developed. This development is, however, in the nature of a subtle elaboration. It has for a foundation the primary assumption that Matter is mystery; this world is inescapably ambiguous and derives meaning from man's moral perceptions.[16]

According to Stanley J. Solomon, "rather than conveying ideas as a primarily 'reflective poet' (in T. S. Eliot's term), Tennyson in *Idylls of the King* presents paradoxes which are in themselves meaningful; that is, instead of imposing ideas on the poem in order to enrich the texture, he developes his paradoxes so that the significance of the Idylls inheres in the narrative structure itself."[17] Perhaps the willingness of readers to stop at the paradoxes and not proceed to the intuited resolutions of them has occasioned a misvaluing of Tennyson's most important work. I have tried to show that Tennyson does indeed indicate that manifestations of the ideal can be untrustworthy. Although Arthur's statue points "to the Northern Star," (p. 1669) and Enid, in her goodness is likened to "the white and glittering star of morn,"

(p. 1547) and Galahad, departing toward the spiritual city is "like a silver-star" over whom the Grail, from which "the veil had been withdrawn" glows, (p. 1676) there is also, at the periphery of this splendid sphere, a Vivien who seems "a lovely baleful star / Veiled in gray vapour." (p. 1603) It takes more than mortal eyesight to distinguish Arthur's star in the broad confusing daylight of this world. Once the ideal is perceived, however, all that was obscure becomes clear, all that was confining leads to forms of freedom, and the longed-for authority makes itself heard, thereby fixing the self's identity as part of a great design.[18] And the way most men must discover the ideal is by being humbled and painfully awakened to the truth. Arthur's advice to Balin is advice for all men. "Rise, my true knight. As children learn, be thou / Wiser for falling! walk with me, and move / To music with thine Order and the King." (p. 1579)

But even with this awareness, the truth is not easy. Though "Man's word is God in man," (p. 1473) and Arthur "honours his own word, / As if it were his God's," (p. 1625) not all men are capable of so rigorously dealing with the most slippery of human symbols. Language is the highest approach to understanding and correspondingly the most insidious threat to that approach as well. Only once "the Word had breath," (p. 894) when Christ became flesh, but for man all crucial choices are presented "in a tongue no man [can] read,"[19] and he may consider himself too often like an "infant crying in the night . . . with no language but a cry." (p. 909) Nonetheless, for those who are willing to listen, "the phantom king," as in Leodogran's dream, sends "out at times a voice." (p. 1481) And if one listens, then all the clamor of this world fades, and the voice becomes clear as it did for the narrator of "The Two Voices," or for the Prince in *The Princess*, meditating upon his idea, who found that

A wind arose and rushed upon the South,
And shook the songs, the whispers, and the shrieks

> Of the wild woods together; and a Voice
> Went with it, 'Follow, follow, thou shalt win.' (p. 754)

In the *Idylls*, Tennyson was asking men to heed that voice
and thereby free themselves from the illusions and entrapments
of material existence. Once this could be done, a new awareness
was available to man. And this new awareness would be a positive force for good. The *Idylls* is not concerned with declared
tragedy, but with incipient salvation. It is not a despairing but a
hopeful vision. Following its message, man could continue to
progress, first individually and subsequently as a race, as Browning also had hopefully forecast in *Paracelcus*.

> With apprehension of his passing worth,
> Desire to work his proper nature out,
> And ascertain his rank and final place,
> For these things tend still upward, progress is
> The law of life, man is not Man as yet.
>
> . . .
>
> When all mankind alike is perfected,
> Equal in full-blown powers—then, not till then,
> I say, begins man's general infancy.
>
> . . .
>
> When all the race is perfected alike
> As man, that is; all tended to mankind,
> And, man produced, all has its end thus far:
> But in completed man begins anew
> A tendency to God.[20]

Tennyson's own opinion is just as clearly stated in the late poem,
"The Making of Man."

> Where is one that, born of woman, altogether can escape
> From the lower world within him, moods of tiger, or of ape?
> Man as yet is being made, and ere the crowning Age of ages,
> Shall not aeon after aeon pass and touch him into shape?
>
> All about him shadow still, but, while the races flower and fade,
> Prophet-eyes may catch a glory slowly gaining on the shade,

Till the peoples all are one, and all their voices blend in choric
Hallelujah to the Maker 'It is finished. Man is made.' (p. 1454)[21]

If Tennyson was trying to indicate, for others, a correct mode
of apprehending reality, he was engaged as well with determining to what degree his art could facilitate this purpose.
Tennyson was convinced as early as "Timbuctoo" that the Spirit
of Fable empowered the artist to teach men aspiration toward the
Unattainable and to make them feel and know "a higher than
they see." (p. 179) However, he was also aware that there are
dangers to threaten the accomplishment of that aim. Two such
dangers are the self and the intellect. In "The Vision of Sin,"
the narrator describes his vision in which a youth "rode a horse
with wings, that would have flown, / But that his heavy rider
kept him down." (p. 718) I do not think it is a far stretch of the
imagination to suppose this youth is mounted on his Pegasus and
would soar in poetry if he were not entrapped and spoiled by
sensuous indulgence. Failing to interpret the divine presence in
nature—God's "awful rose of dawn" goes "unheeded"—the
would-be poet lapses into a grim parody of the celebration of life
that he should have sung. Finishing his bitter exhortation, this
fallen creature's "voice grew faint," while another "voice" on an
apocalyptic summit cried, " 'Is there no hope?' " and "an answer pealed from that high land, / *But in a tongue no man
could understand.*" The answer is: "God made Himself an awful
rose of dawn" once more. (pp. 724-25; italics mine)

This poem is a parable of the young poet who, instead of seeing the divine significance of nature, buried himself in his senses
and lost his soul. No man can understand the language of heaven,
but he can strive to interpret the emblems that surround him.
The poet's self, like any other, may constitute an entrapment. If it
was necessary for Lancelot to assume a disguise in order to discover his true identity, then, also for the poet it might have been
necessary to test himself in a new guise and become the voice of
the narrator of *Maud*. Such an artistic "disguise" could be as

233

much a means to self-awareness as Yeats' anti-self was meant to be. Unlike the individual personal poems, such works as the *Idylls*, *The Princess*, and "The Ancient Sage," among others, provide an opportunity to speak not with an individual voice, but with the voice of mankind.[22] It might even seem necessary to come before the world in genuine disguise as Tennyson did when he published *In Memoriam* anonymously. Like his own Lancelot, he had an opportunity to discover whether it was his deeds or his name and fame that had the greater force.

Martin Dodsworth says that the "contradiction within [Tennyson's] poems between the 'never-ending' nature of the states of mind represented and rhetorically conclusive endings finds a parallel in the opposition between Tennyson's sense of boundless being' during a trance and the fight for *mein liebes Ich* which follows it."[23] Just as the movement from consciousness of personal to universal identity may be traced in Tennyson's real and poetic trances, so the poems themselves frequently indicate Tennyson's sense of a boundary between the ordinary world described in the frame of a poem and the more universally representative world described in the fable. It is worth observing that the frame, the world in which use and name and fame are important, reasserts itself after the vision or the fable. The self, then, is not to be disregarded but is to discover its true place and identity through the medium of some universal experience that transcends the boundaries of self. Poetry, in short, is the poet's mode of escape from the confines of the self.

If one danger to the poet is entrapment in the sensuous self, another is confusion through intellection. Patricia M. Ball observes that, for Tennyson, "the mind alone with itself is and remains cause for panic, not creative joy."[24] This is true in that Tennyson obviously found the human intellect's amplifying powers awesome. The mind all too willingly accepts the logical concatenation of ideas that progresses infinitely to chaos. But Tennyson realized as well that love can make man trust apparent chaos.[25] It is egoism that constructs threatening designs, as the narrator of *Maud* reveals. Faith creates of the ambiguous world of matter a series of emblems and benevolent designs. These creations or discoveries are not mere stylistic necessities. For the artist, they are essential. "The Two Voices" dramatizes Tennyson's conviction that a highly charged emotional mood, an intuitive impulse, may convert a dead mechanistic or a savagely chaotic world into a stylized emblem of divine purpose.

For Tennyson, the poet's fundamental purpose was, as I have said, to provide men with an awareness of reality. He did this by interpreting the symbols of the world that were, for ordinary men, incomprehensible. "The marvel of the everlasting will, / An open scroll, / Before him lay" and eventually became the "poet's scroll" that "shook the world." ("The Poet," pp. 223-24) Charles Kingsley referred to this impulse in Tennyson as "his subjective and transcendental mysticism."

> It is the mystic, after all, who will describe Nature most simply, because he sees most in her; because he is most ready to believe that she will reveal to others the same message which she has revealed to him. Men like Boehme, Novalis, and Fourier.[26]

Like the mystic, the poet was an interpreter or translator whose qualifications were sympathy and love. Although he, like Merlin, could not fully decipher the mysterious ur-text, only he could make out the commentaries upon it. This notion of the function of the artist was common in Tennyson's time and frequently taken for granted. Elizabeth Barrett Browning declared that the artist in his "ecstasy" felt "the spiritual significance burn through / The hieroglyphic of material shows." She affirmed that "Art's the witness of what is / Behind this show." It is the artist's function to manifest the unity of the spiritual and material aspects of the world.

[He]
Holds firmly by the natural to reach

The spiritual beyond it, fixes still
The type with mortal vision to pierce through,
With eyes immortal to the antetype
Some call the ideal, better called the real,
And certain to be called so presently,
When things shall have their names.[27]

E. T. A. Hoffmann's remarkable *Märchen*, "The Golden Pot,"
is an ingenious presentation—half allegory, half psychological
drama, all fable—that develops these notions admirably. The
Student Anselmus is an efficient scribe, but only after he has
heard the supernatural voice and seen the enchanting eyes of
Serpentina, a spirit of nature, does he learn to employ his techniques properly. The Archivarius Lindhorst—in reality the
Prince of Spirits—gives him the task of transcribing a peculiar
manuscript, reminiscent of Merlin's strange text. The leaves of a
mystic palm tree are actually rolls of parchment with "strangely
intertwisted characters; and as [Anselmus] looked over the
many points, strokes, dashes, and twirls in the manuscript, he almost lost hope of ever copying it."[28] Failing temporarily in this
task, which is, after all, nothing more than interpreting the mystery of nature and "living in poesy,"[29] Anselmus is confined in a
crystal container. He is aware of his confinement, whereas
others who have never felt the yearning for the Spirit, though
similarly confined, remain unaware of their dilemma. Like the old
sage in Merlin's tale, for whom "the wall / That sunders ghosts
and shadow-casting men / Became a crystal," (p. 1612) Anselmus learns that all men are entrapped in life until they learn to
live in the Spirit. Realizing this, he is freed from his confinement.
Ultimately, Anselmus succeeds in copying the marvellous manuscript flawlessly. He becomes a true poet, thereby making available to others wisdom only the artist can provide.

Like other artists of his time, Tennyson felt a moral obligation
in his art. This did not mean that he felt obliged to compose only
poems like "The Higher Pantheism," "The Voice and the Peak,"

or "The Ancient Sage." Although poetry was not merely a maneuver or a strategy for his own self-discovery, it could serve such a purpose and still embody the truths—no matter how obliquely—of which Tennyson was convinced. Poetry, to serve its purpose, had first to command the imagination. Like Keats in this respect, Tennyson was capable of suppressing his own opinions and presenting dramatically views that he did not necessarily share in order that his poetry be an enactment and a rendering of experience, not a disquisition upon it. Beyond all of the apparent rage, despair, and doubt, however, there remains a fundamental pattern of belief in Tennyson's poetry. It is particularly dangerous to read Tennyson out of the context of his times. To ignore the designs that Tennyson himself never forgot is to misvalue a principal aim of his poetry and to turn deafly away from the heartfelt adjuration of Merlin to all voyagers in this world to imitate his example and go "after it, follow it, / Follow the Gleam." ("Merlin and the Gleam," p. 1417)

Footnotes

Preface

1. Jerome Hamilton Buckley, *The Victorian Temper: A Study in Literary Culture* (New York, 1964), p. 92.

2. St. Augustine initiates his *Confessions* with a modest denunciation of pride, and a parable such as that of the Prodigal Son exhibits the pattern of voluptuous pride leading to a saving degradation. So apt was this pattern, that the Prodigal Son emblem occurs frequently in Victorian literature.

3. Gladstone, in his essay on the *Idylls* and Tennyson's earlier works, recognizes the controlling shape or design behind Tennyson's long poem. He implies, further, that the noble designs of great narratives are as much the will of God as the choice of the poet. I would rather believe that Tennyson's utilization of the design, followed from esthetic control, not spiritual inspiration. Gladstone's remarks run as follows:

"Nature herself prompted the effort to bring the old patterns of worldly excellence and greatness—or rather the copies of those patterns still legible, though depraved, and still rich with living suggestion—into harmony with that higher Pattern, once seen by the eyes and handled by the hand of men, and faithfully delineated in the Gospels for the profit of all generations. The life of our Saviour, in its external aspect, was that of a teacher. It was in principle a model for all, but it left space and scope for adaptations to the lay life of Christians in general, such as those by whom the every-day business of the world is to be carried on. It remained for man to make his best endeavour to exhibit the great model on its terrestrial side, in its contact with the world. Here is the true source of that new and noble cycle which the middle ages have handed down to us in duality of form, but with a nearly identical substance, under the royal sceptres of Arthur in England and of Charlemagne in France." (Reprinted in *Tennyson: The Critical Heritage*, ed. John D. Jump (London, 1967), p. 250.)

4. W. Stacy Johnson, *The Voices of Matthew Arnold: An Essay in Criticism* (New Haven, 1961), p. 1.

5. It is difficult not to accuse Meredith of a superficial reading of Tennyson when he could say of a poem that incorporated ideas nearly related to his own:

"The 'Holy Grail' is wonderful, isn't it? The lines are satin lengths, the figures Sevres china. I have not the courage to offer to review it, I should say such things. To think!—it's in these days that the foremost poet of the country goes on fluting of creatures that have not a breath of vital humanity in them, and doles us out his regular five-feet with the old trick of the vowel endings—The Euphuist's tongue, the Exquisite's leg, the Curate's moral sentiments, the British matron and her daughter's purity of tone:—I repeat with my Grannam,—to think!—and to hear the chorus of praise too! Why, this stuff is not the Muse, it's Musery. The man has got hold of the Muses' clothes-line and hung it with jewelry." (*Letters*, Vol. 1 (New York, 1912), p. 197).

6. Jerome Hamilton Buckley, *Tennyson: The Growth of a Poet* (Boston, 1965), chapter six; and J. C. C. Mays, " 'In Memoriam': An Aspect of Form," *University of Toronto Quarterly* (Vol. XXXV, no. 1, (1965)), pp. 22-46. I am not in total agreement with either of these interpretations, but I feel no reason to part syllables when the general tendency is so similar.

7. John Killham, in *Tennyson and The Princess: Reflections of an Age* (London, 1958), has called attention to one such fabular device.

"We can see, then, that in 'Edwin Morris,' *Maud*, and to some extent "Locksley Hall,' a fairy-tale situation—which appears undisguised in 'The Day Dream' and *The Princess*—is used to illustrate a theme, the influence for good or evil of women." (p. 192).

8. All quotations from Tennyson's poetry are from *The Poems of Tennyson*, ed. Christopher Ricks (London, 1969).

9. Basil Willey, *More Nineteenth Century Studies* (New York, 1966), pp. 89-90.

10. William R. Brashear, in *The Living Will: A Study of Tennyson and Nineteenth-Century Subjectivism* (The Hague, 1969), shows some of the clear as well as probable connections between Tennyson's thought and the thought of certain nineteenth-century philosophers.

11. Hallam Tennyson, *Alfred Lord Tennyson: A Memoir*, 2 vols in 1 (New York, 1905), vol. 2, p. 424.

12. Matthew Arnold, *Literature and Dogma*: *An Essay Towards A Better Apprehension Of The Bible* (London, 1876), p. 44.

13. I have used Richard B. Brandt's *The Philosophy of Schleiermacher*: *The Development of His Theory of Scientifiic and Religious Knowledge* (New York, 1941) to buttress my estimate of this philosopher's views.

14. *Troilus and Cressida*, II. ii. 52.

15. Plato, "Apology," *The Dialogues of Plato*, trans. B. Jowett (Oxford, 1875), vol. 1, p. 371.

16. Patricia M. Ball, in *The Central Self*: *A Study in Romantic and Victorian Imagination* (London, 1968), while discussing Tennyson's "chameleon impulse," indicates that his ability to entertain contradictory views led to the risks of seeing all views as equally meaningless or valid, or of threatening individual integrity by dividing the will. (pp. 168-69)

One: Introduction

1. Valerie Pitt, in *Tennyson Laureate* (Toronto, 1963), while presenting a stimulating and useful examination of Tennyson's public art, unaccountably encourages a biographical reading of the "private" poetry that would tend to diminish the value of her own contributions. Similarly, Elton Edward Smith, while attempting to deal with Tennyson's poetry according to a firm theoretical pattern, frequently lapses into biographical readings which seem mere conveniences to avoid more formidable technical explanations (*The Two Voices*: *A Tennyson Study* (Lincoln, 1964)).

Some of the more sophisticated approaches to Tennyson's poetry include Joseph Sendry's excellent essay " 'The Palace of Art' Revisited," *Victorian Poetry*, Vol. IV, no. 3 (1966), pp. 149-62, in which he offers a description of that poem as "the Soul's progress towards self-awareness [becoming] a paradigm of universal moral experience;" (p. 151) and W. David Shaw's "The Idealist's Dilemma in *Idylls of the King*," *Victorian Poetry*, Vol. V, no. 1 (1967), pp. 41-53, which approaches the *Idylls* from a different point of view from my own; Clyde de L. Ryals' *From the Great Deep*: *Essays on Idylls of the King* (Athens, Ohio, 1967); and Lawrence Poston, III's, essays on the *Idylls*, which I shall have occasion to refer to later.

2. I prefer Patricia M. Ball's estimate of the poem. "*The Two Voices* provides a paradigm of [Tennyson's] imagination. *The Palace of Art, In Memorian*, and *Maud* all in their different ways follow the same movement from a self-concern which has become paralytic to a recognition of the value of losing the ego in order to find it." (*The Central Self*, p. 173) Obviously, this account resembles my description of Tennyson's "design."

3. *Memoir*, vol. 2, p. 402.

4. *Ibid.*, vol. 1, p. 278.

5. R. B. Wilkenfeld points out the pervasive application of this dialectical

approach in Tennyson's poetry in "The Shape of Two Voices," *Victorian Poetry*, Vol. IV (1966), pp. 163-73.

6. *Memoir*, vol. 1, p. 185.

7. Biographical interpretation is the traditional approach to Tennyson's poetry, and is, therefore, difficult to overcome. Of the "Supposed Confessions," for example, Sir Charles Tennyson says that Tennyson "gave direct expression to the mental anguish he had endured during the last few years at Somersby." *Poems of Alfred Lord Tennyson*, ed. Sir Charles Tennyson (London, 1954), p. 21. The words "direct expression" are, to me, the disturbing feature of this view, for they discourage, not to say obviate, a careful technical analysis of the poem. In the later part of this chapter, I make reference to a biographical study by Ralph Wilson Rader, which, though both interesting and worthwhile, arrives at esthetically dangerous conclusions about Tennyson's poetry.

8. For a developed discussion of Tennyson's attitude toward love, see Gerhard Joseph's *Tennysonian Love: The Strange Diagonal* (Minneapolis, 1969). Joseph notes that Tennyson's later sentiments reinforced "his early belief that love is a thing of pure spirit." (p. 185)

9. To say that Tennyson is merely using the supposed narrator as a mask for his own sentiments in this poem, or that the narrator of "The Two Voices" is a mouthpiece for Tennyson, is to oversimplify the biographical equation. Tennyson was capable of imagining the arguments in both poems without accepting or believing them. That he should have said: "When I wrote 'The Two Voices' I was so utterly miserable, a burden to myself and to my family, that I said, 'Is life worth anything?' " (*Memoir*, vol. 1, p. 193n) does not necessarily mean that he was therefore on the point of suicide, but that he reviewed the attitudes expressed in the poem. There is no need to suppose that the poem was occasioned by the death of Arthur Henry Hallam, since Ricks provides evidence that the poem was probably begun before Hallam's death. (Ricks, p. 522). Nor does the joyful conclusion of the poem indicate that Tennyson himself found final consolation in the sentiments there described. As I indicate in my comments above, the poem is a dramatic design of moods, not a thorough intellectual exercise.

10. I quote the version of the poem in *Memoir*, vol. 1, p. 60. This poem describes, in little, the design with which I am concerned; it also, interestingly enough, presents certain motifs later to appear in *In Memoriam*, such as the progress from spiritual darkness to spiritual light and the achievement of calm through an acceptance of divine purpose operating through a world of change. Needless to say, the same ideas appear in the *Idylls*. Ricks speculates that the poem may have been addressed to Hallam, but more likely to R. S. Tennant. (Ricks, p. 282)

11. *Memoir*, vol. 1, p. 81.

12. Sir Charles Tennyson mentions the resemblance in *Poems of Alfred Lord Tennyson*, p. 179; and Buckley repeats the observation (*Tennyson: The Growth of a Poet*, p. 65).

13. Buckley states this view (*Tennyson*, p. 63), but it is shared by others, among them E. D. H. Johnson (*The Alien Vision in Victorian Poetry* (Prince-

ton, 1952), p. 7). Aside from the tendency to make biographical material more important than technique, Buckley's book seems to me to suggest the views that I wish to promote, and, understandably, I find it quite sound.

14. *Memoir*, vol. 1, pp. 304-5.

15. *Ibid.*, p. 396.

16. Though Wordsworth was not exactly a dramatic poet, as Tennyson himself remarked, he did make a statement about poetry with a purpose that bears some relationship to the conception of poetry behind poems like *Maud*. Of poetry with purpose, Wordsworth said a "circumstance must be mentioned which distinguishes these Poems from the popular Poetry of the day; it is this, that the feeling therein developed gives importance to the action and situation, and not the action and situation to the feeling." ("Preface to the Second Edition," *The Poetical Works of Wordsworth* (London, 1939), p. 935.)

17. Compare with the lines from "Locksley Hall":

> I had been content to perish, falling on the
> foeman's ground,
> When the ranks are rolled in vapour, and the
> winds are laid with sound. (p. 694)

18. Ball, *The Central Self*, p. 170. This notion is summarized later: "In Tennyson's poetry, the isolation indicated by Pater's phrase 'the thick wall of personality' becomes an experience. It is explored through a spectrum of implications, from neurotic panic at such incarceration, to triumph over fear in the conviction that the 'solitary prisoner' can establish vital contacts and so construct his 'own dream of a world,' not desperately, but in creative fulfilment." (p. 185)

19. E. D. H. Johnson, in *The Alien Vision in Victorian Poetry*, is unfair in stating that the narrator's vacillating state of mind is settled by an outside influence. This attitude devastates the neat subtlety of the poem. The point is that the narrator has felt a change of heart, resulting from the inadequacy of his own discontent, and the family emblem which appears before him is merely a convenient focus for and reagent of the new mood. In his dark mood, the family group might have been the object of solemn commination. Compare the narrator's rediscovery of early emotional and moral enthusiasm with these lines from "Locksley Hall":

> O, I see the crescent promise of my spirit
> hath not set.
> Ancient founts of inspiration well through all
> my fancy yet. (p. 699)

20. A similar escape from the self is achieved by the Ancient Mariner through the blessing of the world outside himself. Similarly, the implication of that poem, as I am suggesting about Tennyson's redemptively designed poems, is that the need to face the question of guilt and salvation recurs. The Mariner is not forever freed because he came once to self-awareness.

21. Arthur Hugh Clough, *Poems of Arthur Hugh Clough* (London, 1890), pp. 46-47.

22. Joseph, in *Tennysonian Love*, views the action of *The Princess* as "a barely disguised psychomachy." (p. 89) This struggle manifests itself in various motifs and images throughout the poem.

"The polarity of East-West, North-South, lily-rose thus all point to a sexual dislocation or a character imbalance that must somehow be set in order." (p. 98)

23. Compare Charles Dickens', *Nicholas Nickleby* (London, 1960) p. 122. Emblematic presentations of this kind were, of course, not uncommon in the period. See, for example, Agnes in Dickens' *David Copperfield*, who serves David as his "Good Angel."

24. The Prince's feeling for Ida seems to be more than mere romantic affection in lines such as the following:

> my nurse would tell me of you;
> I babbled for you, as babies for the moon,
> Vague brightness; when a boy, you stooped to me
> From all high places, lived in all fair lights,
> Came in long breezes rapt from inmost south
> And blown to inmost north; at eve and dawn
> With Ida, Ida, Ida, rang the woods;
> The leader wildswan in among the stars
> Would clang it, and lapt in wreaths of glowworm light
> The mellow breaker murmured Ida. Now
> Because I would have reached you, had you been
> Sphered up with Cassiopëia, or the enthroned
> Persephonè in Hades, now at length,
> Those winters of abeyance all worn out,
> A man I came to see you. (pp. 796-97)

25. The Prince's seizures were, like the songs, added to the poem later; probably to increase the contrast between substantial and ideal and make the Prince's need for substance more evident.

26. Lionel Stevenson, *The Ordeal of George Meredith: A Biography* (New York, 1953), pp. 103-4.

27. See Buckley's *The Victorian Temper*: especially the chapter entitled "The Pattern of Conversion" (pp. 87ff). Professor Buckley describes the intellectual pattern in *In Memoriam* and other writings of the Victorian period, but the scope of his study prevents detailed technical analysis. My own arguments are not for the existence of this pattern of thought, which I assume, but for the technical utilization in Tennyson's poetry.

28. James Benziger, in *Images of Eternity: Studies in the Poetry of Religious Vision from Wordsworth to T. S. Eliot* (Carbondale, 1962), concludes that "Tennyson's encounter between hope and despair is something of a mock battle. He was, as he says, fix'd in truth.' (*sic*)" (p. 156)

29. Clough, pp. 51-52.

30. Ralph Wilson Rader, *Tennyson's Maud: The Biographical Genesis* (Berkeley, 1963), pp. 115ff.

Valerie Pitt, in her *Tennyson Laureate*, sees *Maud* as a political poem. (pp. 179ff) Although there are obvious political overtones, the poem, I feel, is overwhelmingly a moral statement. Professor Buckley, in *Tennyson*, presents one of the sanest views of the poem, though open to certain modifications. (pp. 140ff) Again the emphasis upon personal elements is disturbing. For Tennyson's comments upon *In Memoriam*, see the *Memoir*, vol. 1, pp. 304-5. Some notable studies of *Maud* emphasizing stylistic or poetic qualities, include: E. D. H. Johnson's "The Lily and the Rose: Symbolic Meaning in Tennyson's *Maud*," *PMLA*, LXIV (1949), pp. 1222-27; John Killham's "Tennyson's *Maud*—The Function of the Imagery," *Critical Essays on the Poetry of Tennyson*, ed. John Killham (New York, 1967), pp. 219-38; and A. S. Byatt's "The Lyric Structure of Tennyson's *Maud*," in *The Major Victorian Poets: Reconsiderations*, ed. Isobel Armstrong (Lincoln, 1969), pp. 69-92.

31. Professor Buckley describes the resemblance between Tennyson's narrator in *Maud* and the spasmodic heroes (*The Victorian Temper*, pp. 63-65, and *Tennyson*, p. 141). The spasmodic poem that Tennyson admitted having read with some appreciation was Philip James Bailey's *Festus* (*Memoir*, vol. 1, p. 234). But it is possible that what he admired in it were the moral sentiments. For example, in his copy of *Festus*, Tennyson "marked in the margin the line 'who never doubted never half believed.' " (Ricks, p. 948n) Bailey, like Tennyson, felt that "Faith is a higher faculty than reason" (*Festus: A Poem* (Boston, 1854), p. 9). This edition includes a clarifying "Proem" that was not included in the earlier editions. Bailey also stated that his "highest meaning was / The hope of serving God as poet-priest;" (p. 8) a sentiment that Tennyson shared. He summarized the fundamental idea of his poem as follows:

> Let each man think himself an act of God,
> His mind a thought, his life a breath of God;
> And let each try, by great thoughts and good deeds,
> To show the most of Heaven he hath in him. (p. 11)

For Bailey, as for Tennyson, "Free will is but necessity in play." (p. 13) On the other hand, there are certain superficial resemblances. Bailey's poem includes a passionate young man, sometimes haunted by a wraith of a departed loved one, who acts as a heavenly guide. Unlike the narrator of *Maud*, Festus has more than one earthly love. His movement is from self-contained withdrawal to participation in the world. But, as I have noted in the text and notes, this pattern is not uncommon, and in Bailey's case, was clearly derived from the Faust fable.

32. Dr. Mann's *Maud Vindicated* is a clear-headed contemporary appreciation of the poem's intent with which Tennyson was pleased (see *Memoir*, vol. 1, pp. 394-95 and p. 405). And Gladstone, having rashly judged the poem upon its topical and political details, in his recantation admitted the moral and technical excellence of the poem, going so far as to relate it to an earlier moral pattern. "The design, which seems to resemble that of the Ecclesiastes in another sphere, is arduous; but Mr. Tennyson's power of execution is probably nowhere greater. (*Memoir*, vol. 1, p. 399) For other comments, see *Memoir*, vol. 1, pp. 399ff.

33. *Memoir*, vol. 1, p. 396; italics mine.

34. The device of self-imputation occurs time and again in Tennyson's poetry from such early poems as "Mariana" and "The Two Voices," to *In Memoriam, Maud*, and the *Idylls of the King*, among others. That Tennyson held this to be an important perception is evident in the following passage from Frederick Locker-Lampson's account of his tour in Switzerland with Tennyson.

"*1st July*. To-day at Giessbach he said that if he had been one of the 'Wise Men of Greece,' and had been asked for a *dictum*, he would have given 'Every man imputes himself,' meaning that a man, unless he is very sane indeed, in judging of others, imputes motives, etc. which move himself. 'No man can see further than his moral eyes will allow.' " (*Memoir*, vol. 2, p. 76)

35. See also One. IV. ix. for a statement of the narrator's desire to escape passion by withdrawing from it.

36. A. S. Byatt, "The Lyrical Structure of Tennyson's *Maud*," p. 79.

37. Tennyson's note, quoted by Ricks on p. 1079, reads: " 'The shell undestroyed amid the storm perhaps symbolises to him his own first and highest nature preserved amid the storms of passion.' "

38. It is not long before the narrator discovers the true model of humility in Maud herself.

> I to cry out on pride
> Who have won her favour!
> O Maud were sure of Heaven
> If lowliness could save her. (p. 1061)

39. This passage indicates the narrator's dawning comprehension of what the nature of the battle he engages in should be, though full realization only comes at the conclusion of the poem. Contemporaries were confused by Tennyson's use of the Crimean conflict as the narrator's means to grace, though they did not object to a similar use of battle in the *Idylls of the King*, where combat represents the struggle of good and evil. See, for example, the battle song in "The Coming of Arthur."

40. This selfless act in Part Two corresponds to the first selfless act in Part One (One. XIX. x.). The movement of Part One is from morbid passion to love's ecstasy; of Part Two from morbid passion to insanity. Part Three provides a resolution of and liberation from both restricted passions.

41. *Guesses at Truth by Two Brothers* (London, 1889; orig. 1847), p. 159. There is no need to list here the numerous nineteenth-century works in which madness or illness serves this kind of technical function.

42. Tennyson commented on this passage: " '*Sad astrology*' is modern astronomy, for of old astrology was thought to sympathize with and rule man's fate.' " (*Memoir*, vol. 1, p. 404) Of course, the narrator desires such a sympathetic and ordered superhuman guidance and necessarily laments the modern sad astrology. Through Maud, the stars, symbolically if not actually in the poem, once more become sympathetic guides directed by a divine purpose.

43. There seems little doubt that selflessness is the essential step to virtue in *Maud*, but, in the event that evidence is needed, one might cite Thomas Wilson's recollection, in which he remarks that while discussing *Maud* with Tennyson, he asked him "if unselfishness was the essence of virtue? his reply was 'Certainly.'" (*Memoir*, vol. 1, p. 511)

Two: Idylls of the King: The Design

1. Since the time that I completed this study, new works by William R. Brashear, Lawrence Poston and Clyde de L. Ryals have appeared, which precede me in encouraging the same kind of sympathetic reading of Tennyson's *Idylls*.

2. F. E. L. Priestley, "Tennyson's *Idylls*," *University of Toronto Quarterly*, (vol. xix, no. 1 (1949), pp. 35-49.

S. C. Burchell, in "Tennyson's 'Allegory in the Distance,'" *PMLA*, LXVIII, (1953), pp. 418-24, suggests that a simple reading of the allegory is not possible and that the poem must be read more subtly as a picture of a crumbling society. The *Idylls* become a diagnosis of Tennyson's times. It will become evident that I agree with Mr. Burchell's position; however, I do not feel that this invalidates a simple narrative reading of a general and perhaps vague, allegory.

Condé Benoist Pallen's *The Meaning of The Idylls of the King: An Essay in Interpretation* (New York, 1904), which first appeared in 1885, is one of the allegorical readings of Tennyson's poem that Mr. Burchell objects to. I agree with him that, at times, it tries to read too much in an allegorical way, but I have not hesitated to agree with Pallen when I have found him sound. He himself warned his readers: "We must not look for an allegory in every passage, a symbol in every line, a mystery in every syllable, a hidden meaning in every image." (p. 17) Where I disagree most with Pallen is that I find a great deal more in the syllables and images than he did, though what I find is not symbolism and mystery. See part three of this study, which is concerned with Tennyson's consciousness of language. I also feel that my reading is in sympathy, though differing, sometimes markedly at points, with recent studies by Clyde de L. Ryals and William R. Brashear. The latter says "The poem is essentially vitalistic and the forces embodied in the other persons are vital rather than allegorical." ("Tennyson's Tragic Vitalism: *Idylls of the King*," *Victorian Poetry* (1968), pp. 29-49)

3. *Memoir*, vol. 2, p. 127.

4. *Ibid.*, vol. 1, p. 418.

5. *Ibid.*, vol. 1, p. 414, states that Tennyson worked on the poem in February and March of 1856.

6. See Jerome B. Schneewind's "Moral Problems and Moral Philosophy in the Victorian Period," *Victorian Studies* Supplement to Vol. IX (1965), pp. 29-46.

7. I agree with William R. Brashear in his "Tennyson's Tragic Vitalism," and *The Living Will* (p. 129), when he expresses the belief that Merlin stands

for poetic imagination, not the intellect. Later in this study I shall equate Merlin with the creative imagination, but in this early Idyll, I believe he has a more general association with all of the creative capacities of the mind. Still, he is not so much the *reasoning* intellect, as he is the *intuitive* and *imaginative* intellect.

8. Lawrence Poston, III, in "The Argument of the Geraint-Enid Books in *Idylls of the King*," *Victorian Poetry*, II (1964), pp. 269-75, sees this as a symbolic pilgrimage.

9. There is a light and dark imagery in the *Idylls* as there is in *In Memorian*, and it is exhibited in this quotation.

10. Lawrence Poston, III, sees a pattern in the Geraint-Enid sequences that resembles the design I describe.

"The book thus appears to come full circle. Geraint passes from grace through a form of spiritual madness to redemption. But the development of the *Idylls* is more cyclical than circular." ("Geraint-Enid Books," p. 274)

11. In the Third Chapter of this study, I examine the many aspects of language in the Idylls, but I do so from different approaches. Unfortunately, some repetition will occur between chapter two and chapter three; but it is necessary, since the same materials I often use for different purposes and hence must quote them anew or at least re-examine a particular scene that has been examined before.

12. In Chapter Three, the theme of confinement, constraint, and freedom is developed more fully, demonstrating its implications regarding Tennyson's beliefs.

13. Tennyson said of "The Holy Grail": "Faith declines, religion in many turns from practical goodness to the quest after the supernatural and marvellous and selfish religious excitement. Few are those for whom the quest is a source of spiritual strength." (quoted in Ricks, p. 1661)

14. Clyde de L. Ryals, in "Percivale, Ambrosius, and the Method of Narration in 'The Holy Grail,'" *die neueren sprachen*, vol. xxi, (1963), pp. 533-43, comments on Ambrosius' function as an earthly contrast to Percivale, an inadequate moral figure. He also draws the relationship between Ambrosius and Arthur, calling the former an "Arthur on a smaller scale." (p. 543)

15. *Memoir*, vol. 2, p. 90; variation of this passage in Ricks, p. 1661.

16. J. M. Gray, in *Man and Myth in Victorian England: Tennyson's The Coming of Arthur* (Lincoln, England, 1969), remarks that in this "dream the development from chaos to order is clearly marked," and that "the drift of the dream is similar to Arthur's declaration at the close of the Grail Idyll." (pp. 15-16)

Sir Charles Tennyson, in "The Dream in Tennyson's Poetry," *Virginia Quarterly Review*, XL, pp. 228-48, suggests the importance of the contest between spirit and matter implied in all of Tennyson's uses of dreams.

17. Quoted in Ricks, p. 1687.

18. Matthew Arnold, "Self-Dependence," *The Poems of Matthew Arnold*, ed. Kenneth Allott (London, 1965), pp. 142-43.

19. Ibid., p. 144.

20. This passage, in the original context, has a different meaning, but the idea

is similar in its way. (p. 651) A lovely form deceives because the spirit is lacking and the narrator of the poem laments that he has been duped by the appearance which, in his idealistic way, he identifies with the good.

21. Browning, "A Toccata of Galuppi's," *The Poetical Works*, vol. 1 (London, 1897), p. 267.

22. Arnold, "Immortality," *Poems*, pp. 488-89.

23. Charles Dickens, *The Life and Adventures of Nicholas Nickleby* (London, 1950), p. 122.

24. Thomas Traherne, *Centuries, Poems, and Thanksgivings*, ed. H. M. Margoliouth (Oxford, 1958), p. 3. A similar sentiment, secularized, appears regularly in English literature, of course, and finds expression, for example, in Byron's *Childe Harold* (Canto 3, sec. 79) and *Don Juan* (Canto 2, sec. 211) or in stanza-sonnet 77 of Rossetti's *House of Life*.

25. Boyd Litzinger, in "The Structure of Tennyson's 'The Last Tournament,'" *Victorian Poetry*, Vol. I (1963), sees Dagonet as serving the central function in this idyll; and, regarding the failure of Arthur's ideal, concludes that it "can be laid to human frailty, not to supernatural forces." (p. 59)

R. B. Wilkenfeld has, in "Tennyson's Camelot: The Kingdom of Folly," *University of Toronto Quarterly*, Vol. XXXVII (1968), pp. 281-94, traced the important motif of human folly, particularly in "The Last Tournament," but also throughout the *Idylls*.

26. "The Progress of Spring" appeared in the *Demeter and Other Poems*, in December, 1889, though it was presumably written in Tennyson's youth.

27. *Memoir*, vol. 2, p. 131:
"Throughout the poem runs my father's belief in one strong argument of hope, the marvellously transmuting power of repentance in all men, however great their sin."

28. *Memoir*, vol. 2, p. 319 and p. 121.

29. Lawrence Poston, III, ("Geraint End Books") also sees "Balin and Balan" as the turning point of the *Idylls*. (p. 270)

30. *Memoir*, vol. 2, p. 127.

31. Kathleen Tillotson's "Tennyson's Serial Poem," *Mid-Victorian Studies* (London, 1965) thoroughly illustrates the relationship of Tennyson's poem to a growing interest in Arthurian material during the nineteenth century. At the same time, it demonstrates the elaboration of a clear design in the poem as a whole.

Three: Idylls of the King: Themes

1. Johann Wolfgang von Goethe, *Maximen und Reflexionen über Literatur und Ethik, Goethes Werke*, vol. 42, part 2 (Weimar, 1907), p. 142. The German reads as follows: "In der Idee leben heisst das Unmögliche behandeln, als wenn es möglich wäre."

FOOTNOTES

2. Robert Browning, "Andrea Del Sarto," *The Poetical Works*, vol. 1, p. 524.

3. George Meredith, "The Woods of Westermain," *Poems*, vol. 1 (London, 1909), p. 80.

4. *Memoir*, vol. 2, p. 130.

5. Henry David Thoreau, *Walden* (Boston, 1957), p. 221.

6. George Meredith, *The Ordeal of Richard Feverel* (New York, 1950), p. 123.

7. *Memoir*, vol. 2, p. 129.

8. Ludwig Feuerbach, *The Essence of Christianity*, trans, George Eliot (New York, 1957), p. 12.

9. *Ibid.*, p. 7. It is worth mentioning that, while *The Essence of Christianity* appeared in 1841 in German, the English translation by George Eliot was available in 1854. Nor would it be necessary to turn only to the German theological writing of the times. A unitarian such as Theodore Parker held similar views which William C. DeVane suggests might have had some influence upon Browning's poem about the subjective projection of one's deity, "Caliban upon Setebos." (*A Browning Handbook* (New York, 1955), p. 299.)

10. In Novalis' "Klingsohr's Fairy Tale," which appears in chapter IX of *Heinrich von Ofterdingen*, the character of Fable serves as redeemer of a cosmos threatened by The Scribe, who represents sterile Reason. Novalis obviously shared Tennyson's high regard for the power of Fable. Since Tennyson was aware of Novalis' pithy remark on Spinoza, he might have known a few other interesting Novalis maxims such as: "Nothing is more accessible to the mind than the infinite," or "Language is Delphi."

11. A similar pattern of imagery associating clouds and obscurity with the passions, and clear skies and stars with the calm imagination guided by ideals appears in Arnold's poetry. See my article, "Matthew Arnold and the Soul's Horizon," *Victorian Poetry*, Vol. III, No. 1 (Spring 1970), pp. 19-39.

12. *Memoir*, vol. 1, p. 431.

13. *Ibid.*, vol. 2, p. 128.

14. "God gave man language," Trench writes, "just as He gave him reason, and just because He gave him reason; for what is man's *word* but his *reason* coming forth that it may behold itself?" And Trench discovers man's first notable gift in the story of Adam utilizing the power of *naming*. (p. 14) Another of Trench's remarks illuminates Tennyson's use of Arthur as the embodiment of an ideal. Like Christ, Arthur appeared to men in order that they would have a named thing to fix a vague ideal.

'Names,' as it has been excellently said, 'are impressions of sense, and as such take the strongest hold upon the mind, and of all other impressions can be most easily recalled and retained in view. They therefore serve to give a point of attachment to all the more volatile objects of thought and feeling. Impressions that when past might be dissipated forever, are by their connexion with language always within reach. Thoughts, of themselves are perpetually slipping out of the field of immediate mental vision; but the name abides with us, and the utterance of it restores them in a moment. (pp. 23-24)

Trench later declares that new thoughts like new societies require new symbols. When an idea hitherto inexpressible arises, a new embodiment in language must be found for it. (p. 193) Most significant as an explanation of Trench's approach to language is the passage opening his third lecture, "On the Morality in Words."

Is man of a divine birth and of the stock of heaven? coming from God, and, when he fulfils the law of his being, and the intention of his creation, returning to Him again? We need no more than the words he speaks to prove it; so much is there in them which could never have existed on any other supposition. (p. 73)

Of course, R. C. Trench approached language from a scholar's point of view. His moral assumptions about language thus remained strictly subordinated to his didactic purpose. Nonetheless, a similar conviction regarding the significance of language in the realm of morality, thought, and spirit exists in his book and in Tennyson's poem, though Tennyson sought not to explain or illuminate this significance, but to embody it in his own poetic exploitation of language toward a clearly moral end. (*On The Study of Words* (New York, 1892, 22nd ed.)

15. Carlyle announced that "'Language is called the Garment of Thought: however, it should rather be, Language is the Flesh-Garment, the Body, of Thought. I said that Imagination wove this Flesh-Garment; and does not she?'" (*Sartor Resartus: The Life and Opinions of Herr Teufelsdröckh* (London, 1896), p. 57.)

16. There is a noteworthy parallel in Wordsworth's *The Prelude*, Book V, lines 596-605.

> Visionary power
> Attends the motions of the viewless winds,
> Embodied in the mystery of words:
> There, darkness makes abode, and all the host
> Of shadowy things work endless changes,—there,
> As in a mansion like their proper home,
> Even forms and substances are circumfused
> By that transparent veil with light divine,
> And, through the turnings intricate of verse,
> Present themselves as objects recognised,
> In flashes, and with glory not their own.

17. Arthur Symons, *An Introduction to the Study of Browning* (London, 1886), p. 19.

18. I cannot accept Clyde de L. Ryals' reading of this passage, which states that Tennyson is demonstrating Arthur's extinguishing of individuality in his

FOOTNOTES

followers. Of the knights, Ryals says, "In accepting his will they deny their own; in attempting to take on the personality of the King they annihilate their own personalities." (*From the Great Deep* (Athens, Ohio, 1967), p. 75.)

19. Carlyle said that "The Name is the earliest Garment you wrap round the earth-visiting Me; to which it thenceforth cleaves, more tenaciously (for there are Names that have lasted nigh thirty centuries) than the very skin. . . . Names? Could I unfold the influence of Names, which are the most important of all Clothings, I were a second greater Trismegistus. Not only all common Speech, but Science, Poetry itself is no other, if thou consider it, than a right *Naming*." (*Sartor Resartus*, p. 69.)

20. Tristram and Vivien both sing more than they realize in their songs, while Lynette is conscious of the deeper meaning in her cryptic little song, and we are aware of the irony of Enid's song. Lawrence Poston, III ("The Two Provinces of Tennyson's 'Idylls,'" *Criticism*, Vol. IX (1967), pp. 372-82), explains the manner in which Tennyson uses the songs to illuminate the purpose Tennyson had of discussing poetry itself in the *Idylls*.

21. Clyde de L. Ryals is concerned with illusion, but not in the same way that I am; also his use of disguise is not the same. For Ryals, characters in the *Idylls* suffer a loss of identity by becoming dependent upon others, especially upon Arthur.

22. Many of the themes that I discuss in this study do appear in "Akbar's Dream" and much could be said of such clear statements of Tennyson's phenomenological and metaphysical views as "The silent Alphabet-of-heaven-in-man / Made vocal," but I have felt that suggestion might be more valuable than total explication and consequently have even abjured reference to many passages in the *Idylls*, some of which I use for other purposes, that might verify a theme. I hope that the reader may become aware of the interrelatedness of the several themes I have so artificially isolated out of a kind of scholastic necessity.

23. As Emerson declared, "The world is emblematic. Parts of speech are metaphors because the whole of nature is a metaphor of the human mind," and when man's mind can pierce the veil of things to achieve their imaginative symbolization, "the universe becomes transparent, and the light of higher laws than its own shines through it." (*Nature, Selections from Ralph Waldo Emerson* (Boston, 1957), p. 35.)

24. See Meredith's use of music as order blending sense and spirit in "Melampus," "Woods of Westermain," and "The Sage Enamoured." In these same poems, and others, music is also suggested as a natural metaphor for restraint, as in this passage from "The Sage Enamoured": "The nuptial ring / Of melody clasped motion in restraint." (*Poems*, vol. 1, p. 54.)

25. F. D. Maurice, *Theological Essays* (New York, 1854), p. 319.

26. It is amusing to suppose that the old man that Bedivere envisions telling the worthy tale and guarding Excalibur, is himself. It indicates Tennyson's subtle characterization as well.

27. Those who become aware, as Teufelsdröckh did, that all of substantial

251

existence is no more than Clothes to cover the Spirit, will be in a position to re-tailor their views of that existence, fitting and shaping external forms to the spiritual will. This notion is persistent throughout *Sartor Resartus*. Although Tennyson may have first encountered the idea in Carlyle, whom he respected, there is no doubt that he met with it in other philosophical writers as well.

28.   Gerhard Joseph compares the use of disguise in *The Princess* to the use of disguise in Shakespearean drama. (*Tennysonian Love*, pp. 85-87.)

29.   This is Lynette's exclamation in "Gareth and Lynette."

30.   Maurice, p. 52; italics mine.

31.   William R. Brashear concentrates upon the concept of the will in Tenny-son's poetry. He feels that, throughout Tennyson's career, his poetry demonstrated "a complete failure of confidence in the external, a contempt for knowledge and enlightenment, and a reliance on the "living will" to sustain a world of illusion above the chaos of conscious fact. The underlying subject matter of his serious poetry, for the most part, may be taken to be an embodiment of the dynamics of subjective vitalism with the 'living will' pitted as both a shaping and resisting force against the dark and chaotic forces of the infinite realm of over-conscious-ness—the Dionysiac realm." (*The Living Will*, p. 12) Although I believe Mr. Brashear is correct in emphasizing the importance of the will in Tennyson's thought, I also feel that it is making Tennyson too Shelleyan to assume that the world that the will sustained was an esthetic illusion. My feeling is that Tennyson appreciated the power of the will most when it transcended the world of illusion—the material world—and put itself in the service of the unseen or spiritual world, which he considered the true reality.

32.   There is a similar use of confinement as a means of self-awareness in Dickens' novels. See my article, "Character and Confinement in Dickens' Novels," *Dickens Studies Annual*, 1970.

33.   Byron, in *Childe Harold*, refers to the "clay-cold bonds which round our being cling." (Canto 3, sec 73). But this theme of constraint and freedom is im-portant throughout Victorian literature, finding clear expression in several poets, such as Matthew Arnold and, even more profoundly and intimately, Robert Browning. The following passage from *Paracelsus* contains a metaphor that is a condensation of one of Browning's most important themes.

> But, friends,
> Truth is within ourselves; it takes no rise
> From outward things, whate'er you may believe.
> There is an inmost centre in us all,
> Where truth abides in fulness; and around,
> Wall upon wall, the gross flesh hems it in,
> This perfect, clear perception—which is truth.
> A baffling and perverting carnal mesh
> Binds it, and makes all error: and to KNOW
> Rather consists in opening out a way

FOOTNOTES

Whence the imprisoned splendour may escape,
Then in effecting entry for a light
Supposed to be without. (*The Complete Works of Robert Browning,*
vol. 1, Roma A. King, gen. ed. (Athens,
Ohio, 1969), pp. 102-3.)

34. Wordsworth, *Poetical Works,* sonnet XIV, "Desire we past illusions to recall?" p. 469.

35. An effective recent study of the frequently discussed section xcv may be found in Alan Sinfield's "Matter-Moulded Forms of Speech: Tennyson's Use of Language in *In Memoriam,*" *The Major Victorian Poets: Reconsiderations,* pp. 51-67.

36. Tennyson noted that the two stars were "symbolic of the two Isolts," (Ricks, p. 1723n) but, in view of the star motif throughout the *Idylls,* I believe they are symbolic of more as well.

37. It is clear, from an early poem such as οἱ ῥέοντες, that Tennyson had, throughout his life, been aware of the philosophical tradition that saw all existence as inescapably ambiguous and declared that "Man is the measure of all truth / Unto himself." (p. 257)

38. I do not mean to suggest that Tennyson was the only poet of his time to recognize this relationship of language, heavenly ideal, and obscurity. Similar related themes, including the undependability of language, the confinement of man's soul in the flesh (in the way that an idea is confined in words), and the spiritual service of fable, appear in Browning. I offer here only one quotation, but numberless others might be cited from Browning's poetry. In the second half of "Christmas-Day and Easter-Day" Browning writes:

> He felt his song, in singing, warped;
> Distinguished his and God's part: whence
> A world of spirit as of sense
> Was plain to him, yet not too plain,
> Which he could traverse, not remain
> A guest in:—else were permanent
> Heaven on the earth its gleams were meant
> To sting with hunger for full light,—
> Made visible in verse, despite
> The veiling weakness,—truth by means
> Of fable, showing while it screens,—
> Since highest truth, man e'er supplied,
> Was ever fable on outside. (*The Poetical Works,* vol. 1, p. 506.)

Conclusion

1. *William Allingham's Diary,* intro. Geoffrey Grigson (Carbondale, 1967), p. 335. Hallam Tennyson records a similar statement by his father.

"Matter is a greater mystery than mind. What such a thing as spirit is apart from God and man I have never been able to conceive. Spirit seems to me to be the reality of the world." (*Memoir*, vol. 2, p. 424) James F. Ferrier, in whose works Tennyson was interested (Charles Tennyson, *Alfred Tennyson* (New York, 1949), p. 279) offered as his fourth proposition in *Institutes of Metaphysic: The Theory of Knowing and Being* (London, 1854) the following statement: "Matter *per se*, the whole material universe by itself, is of necessity absolutely unknowable." (p. 117)

2. Hoxie Neale Fairchild remarks that "what Froude admired in [Tennyson] was the attempt to be confused earnestly and hopefully, to regard incertitude not as a source of despair but as a challenge and an inspiration." (*Religious Trends in English Poetry*, vol. IV (New York, 1957), p. 102.

3. *Memoir*, vol. 1, p. 102.

4. Allingham records Tennyson's praise of Hinton's *Life in Nature* (*Diary*, p. 186); the *Memoir* notes that Tennyson was reading *The Mystery of Matter* in October, 1873 (vol. 2, p. 151) : though I find no record of this title in Hinton's writings, and Charles Tennyson implies that Tennyson had read more of Hinton's works. "He had for many years studied eagerly any book that seemed likely to throw light on the subject [the prospects of the human race], such as James Hinton's *Man and His Dwelling Place* and *The Mystery of Pain*, which attracted a good deal of attention at this time [1865-67]." (*Alfred Tennyson*, p. 368)

W. E. H. Lecky noted that Tennyson "had a decided leaning to some kind of metaphysics, and the writings of James Hinton especially came home to him in a way which I could not share, or indeed understand." (*Memoir*, vol. 2, p. 206)

5. Quoted from Hinton's paper, "On Physical Morphology, or the Law of Organic Forms," in *Life and Letters of James Hinton*, ed. Ellice Hopkins (London, 1879), p. 156. Elsewhere, Hinton declared that what proved that the self was a defect of being was that "to it the phenomenal is real. Real to the SELF, unreal to the MAN. Man feels and knows that to be unreal which yet is real to him . . . . The defect, unrecognized to be a defect, clothes all things with mystery; surrounds with ever multiplying doubts." (*Man and His Dwelling Place. An Essay Toward the Interpretation of Nature* (New York, 1872) pp. 152-53. Orig. pub. 1857.)

6. *Ibid.*, p. 123.

7. *Ibid.*, p. 82.

8. *Allingham's Diary*, p. 335.

9. W. David Shaw and Carl W. Gartlein, in "The Aurora: A Spiritual Metaphor in Tennyson," *Victorian Poetry*, Vol. III (1965), pp. 213-22, demonstrate Tennyson's subtlety of art in utilizing the metaphor of the aurora to maintain a balance between material and spiritual awareness. "In such metaphors the aurora's deep-lying terror, though the source of its tragic sublimity, prevents Tennyson from following the spiritual Shelley into a Platonic mist, and helps him preserve a complex allegiance to both fact and value, doubt and faith." (p. 222)

FOOTNOTES

10. Quoted in Kathleen Tillotson's "Rugby 1850: Arnold, Clough, Walrond and *In Memoriam*," *Mid-Victorian Studies*, p. 200.

11. *Ibid.*, p. 201.

12. R. J. Mann, "Tennyson's 'Maud' Vindicated: An Explanatory Essay" in Tennyson: *The Critical Heritage*, ed. John D. Jump (New York, 1967), p. 200.

13. Charles Kingsley, in discussing *In Memoriam*, explained that whereas Tennyson's isolated life had "shut him out" from a certain knowledge of human character, he had been engaged in a more significant experience. "Within the unseen world which underlies and explains this mere time-shadow, which men call Reality and Fact, he had been going down into the depths, and ascending into the heights, led, like Dante of old, by the guiding of a mighty spirit." (quoted in *Tennyson: The Critical Heritage*, p. 184)

14. Although I agree with William R. Brashear that "in a conventional good-and-evil sense the *Idylls of the King* is not the moral tract that some have made it out to be," I do, nonetheless, believe that the poem is overwhelmingly moral and positive in its meaning and do not feel that it is "beyond good and evil in any conventional sense." (*The Living Will*, pp. 152-53)

15. Many people have found many patterns in Tennyson's poetry, but I shall cite only one example with which I disagree. I believe that Arthur J. Carr, in his important essay, "Tennyson as a Modern Poet" (*Critical Essays on the Poetry of Tennyson*, ed. John Killham, pp. 41-64), distorts the whole nature of Tennyson's poetry by declaring that "the pattern [in it] is a transition through death, loss, or dream towards ideal moods that dissolve the edges of thought and appetite." (p. 63) To read the poems in this way, it is necessary to overlook Tennyson's belief in the sustaining power of the spirit.

16. J. M. Gray arrives at a related conclusion. "All values and motivations come from within. It is ultimately man that lends dignity to the world, through the medium of myth. But by showing how each kind of speculative approach is inadequate Tennyson affirms that mystery is necessary to life. Without it there would be no imaginative challenge. Poetry is truer than fact." (*Man and Myth in Victorian England*, p. 18)

17. "Tennyson's Paradoxical King," *Victorian Poetry*, Vol. I (1963), p. 271.

18. Tennyson remarked: "I tried in my 'Idylls' to teach men these things [that waves of heroism and nobility in human history advance and recede], and the need of the Ideal." (*Memoir*, vol. 2, p. 337)

James Hinton expressed a similar view, supporting it, as Tennyson would have liked, by a reference to the ways of Nature. Ellice Hopkins summarizes Hinton as follows:

"Nothing stops short at itself. All nature's ends are larger means. 'I don't know whether it is fanciful, a sort of sublime punning,' he once said, 'but what I see in nature is the power of an *end*-less life.' And man, by erecting himself as an end, dislocates this order, and can only be made one with nature by living in others, and subordinating himself to a whole." (*Life and Letters*, p. 259)

255

19. This line refers to the scroll upon the Siege perilous which, Tennyson noted, stood "for the spiritual imagination." (Ricks, 1666n)

20. *The Complete Works*, vol. 1, pp. 259-60.

There were numerous expressions of hope in the gradual improvement of man, but one at least is worth mentioning here because it was written by Tennyson's Cambridge tutor, William Whewell. In *The Plurality of Worlds* (London, 1855; orig. 1854), a book that Tennyson did not consider satisfactory (*Memoir*, vol. 1, p. 379), Whewell speculated on the future when man would, through his capacity for gathering into societies, become something finer. We might, he said, "look forward to a state of the earth in which it should be inhabited, not indeed by a being exalted above Man, but by Man exalted above himself as he now is." (p. 302) Whewell even entertained the possibility that a second divine interposition might institute a "Divine Society," just as the first had instituted a Human Society. (p. 305) Arthur's Round Table is not so far removed from this notion, though it is a fictional ideal, not a proposed event. And the conclusion of *In Memoriam* suggests the same kind of gradual improvement of man, offering Hallam as "a noble type / Appearing ere the times were ripe." (p. 988)

21. In view of clear statements of this kind by Tennyson, I find it impossible to accept the reading of the *Idylls* which would make it essentially a disenchanted poem. Clyde de L. Ryals is among the more recent critics to restate this view.

> "The *Idylls*, then, denies the progressionism of *In Memoriam* and sets forth a new ontology. In place of the brave new world offered in the elegy, the *Idylls* presents a world of near absurdity, a world perhaps with a plan but whose teleology is undecipherable." (*From The Great Deep*, p. 196)

This is only true insofar as men fail to espouse the Ideal, but Tennyson's faith is fixed on the assumption that men always will arise to renew that dedication to the Ideal.

22. *Memoir*, vol. 1, pp. 304-5.

23. "Patterns of Morbidity: Repetition in Tennyson's Poetry," *The Major Victorian Poets: Reconsiderations*, p. 23.

24. *The Central Self*, p. 177.

25. Although he may not have cared for Bulwer-Lytton's *The New Timon* (see his "The New Timon, and the Poets," Parts I and II in Ricks, pp. 736-39), Tennyson would have been likely to support a familiar conclusion expressed in that work. Bulwer-Lytton advised:

> Have faith in things above,
> The unseen Beautiful of Heavenly Love;
> And from that faith what virtues have their birth,
> What spiritual meanings gird, like air, the Earth!
>
> . . .
>
> No more the outward senses reign alone,
> The Soul of Nature glides into our own.

To reason less is to imagine more;
They most aspire who meekly most adore! (*The New Timon*: *A Romance of London* (London, 1846), pp. 175-76.)

26. From an unsigned review that appeared in *Fraser's Magazine* in 1850, reprinted in *The Critical Heritage*, p. 175.

27. "Aurora Leigh," *Poetical Works of Elizabeth Barrett Browning* (New York, 1891), pp. 134-35. Robert Browning's similar expressions are familiar enough not to require quotation. But poets themselves were not the only persons to hold these views. Once more I refer to James Hinton, who declared that poetry's "destiny is to be *trained* to be *created* in its right use of interpreting nature. That is its fruition, its destiny. Our past and present verse is but a prophecy that poetry is to be a true interpretation of the phenomenal into the actual." (*Life and Letters*, p. 242)

Basil Willey, speaking to this point in his essay on Tennyson says: "For there was, I think, a religious, or at least a pantheistic, assumption beneath all this: Nature was God's handiwork, his vesture, or his symbolic language; to study it, then, was not an aesthetic indulgence but a solemn duty, a discipline and a vocation. The poet's satisfaction in his own successes, therefore, was like that of the natural scientist. It was more than the craftsman's or naturalist's joy in his own skill; it was a sense, also, that he had transmitted to his fellow-men a fragment of God's truth." (*More Nineteenth Century Studies*, pp. 78-79)

28. *The Best Tales of Hoffmann*, ed. E. F. Bleiler (New York, 1967), p. 43. For some reason, Carlyle—whose translation Bleiler uses in this collection—translated "Der Goldne Topf: 'Ein Märchen aus der neuen Zeit,' " as "The Golden Flower Pot." Hoffmann first published the story in 1814; it appeared in revised form in 1819. Carlyle's translation was published in 1826.

29. *Ibid.*, p. 70.

Index

Action, in this world, 99-101; useful, 68. See Deed, Deeds, Labor, Participation, Utility
"Abt Vogler" (Browning), 96
Afterlife, 111ff
Albert, Prince, 97
Alford, Henry (Dean), 146
Allegory, in *Idylls*, 48-49; of Time at war with soul, 126-27
Allingham, William, 226, 254n.4
Allott, Kenneth, 247n.18
Ambiguity, of appearances, 115, 195-96; of dreams, 222ff; of fame, 175ff; of identity, 192ff; of language, 147, 183; of material world, 66, 134, 226, 229-30
Appearances, ambiguity of, 195-97
Arnold, Matthew, 7, 96, 103-4, 111, 125, 228, 240n.12, 247n.18, 248n.22, 249n.11, 252n.33
Armstrong, Isobel, 244n.30
Articulation, powers of, 144. See Language, Utterance

Arthur, as authority, 204; qualities of Christ represented in, 112
Augustine, Saint, 3-4, 238n.2
Authority, 50, 56, 62-63, 69, 98-101ff, 198-204, 231; Arthur as, 204; Christ ultimate model for, 100; of institutions, 198ff; lack of 36ff, 121, 166; love as, 203; misunderstood, 199-200; and obedience, 200-2; representative of, 130, 134-35; and service, 200-2; of Spirit, 145; spiritual, 203; truth as, 202; within the self, 198ff, 203. See Mastery, Self-Control, Self-Mastery

Bailey, Philip James, 244n.31
Ball, Patricia, 234, 240n.2, 242n.18
Baring, Rosa, 31
Beauty, and ideal, 187; manifestation of, 37; moral, 100; Tennyson on, 15; of world, 125, 188-89. See Material Beauty

114; in *Maud*, 33ff; in *The Princess*, 25-29, 34; replaced by humility, 4; as supreme sin, 4; temporarily contained, 136; Tennyson's view of, 13; in "The Two Voices," 114; vacuity of, 214. See Vanity
Priestley, F. E. L., 48, 246n.2
Process, ascent to spirit as, 139-40
Progress, of growth, 128; of man, stages of, 96-97; of mankind, 229, 232-33; stages of, in *Idylls*, 96. See Progression
Progression, all things fulfilled by, 96-7. See Progress
Proportion, 67, 228; in *The Princess*, 25-29; requires that ideals be manifest in deeds, 171
Purity, 81-82; 87-88; 90, 101, 123; corruption of, 88; death of, 88; flight of, 88; loss of, 136; passing of, 101

Quest, selflessness necessary for, 154; significance of in *Idylls*, 90

Rader, Ralph Wilson, 31, 241n.7, 243n.30
Reality, world of, as world of spirit, 218
Reason, imaginative, as means to truth, 148
Rebirth, death as promise of, 129. See Regeneration, Renewal
Redemption, 75; as form of grace, 4; pattern of, 6; Tennyson's view of, 4; through humility, love, and selflessness, 137; through love in "The Two Voices," 24-25; through self-fulfilment, 129. See Design, Conversion, Pattern of Redemption
Regeneration, hope for, 100. See Rebirth, Renewal
Relics, as disguises, 192; unrequired in true faith, 192
Religion, Tennyson's intuitional, 6
Remorse, 88
Renewal, and intuition, 4; and mood, 4; spiritual, 67ff. See Rebirth, Regeneration

Reticence, 65, 79, 83, 87, 169; a function of true courtliness, 64; infected by noise of world, 161. See Silence
Reward, Grail as, 91; spiritual, as result of deeds, 76
Ricks, Christopher, 239n.8, 241n.9, 10, 244n.31, 245n.37, 247n.13, 15, 18, 253n.36, 256n.25
Rossetti, Christina, 5
Rossetti, Dante Gabriel, 5, 248n.24
Rules, freedom as voluntary selection of, 205
Rumor, 78ff, 158; opposed to vows, 79. See Falsehood, Language, Slander
Ryals, Clyde de L., 240n.1, 246n.1, 2, 247n.14, 250-51n. 18, 251n.21, 256n.21

Salvation, through selflessness, 93
Schleiermacher, Friedrich, 8
Schneewind, Jerome B., 246n.6
Self, authority within, 198ff, 203; and confinement, 208; as confinement, 93, 204, 225, 233ff; confrontation with, 59ff, 72; as danger, 233-34; descent into in "The Ancient Sage," 107; descent into, redeeming vision through, 210; division of, 84, 130ff; freedom from, 111, 204; as obscurity, 224; limitation of, 215; poetry as escape from, 234; unwillingness to descend into, 107; well-ordered, 63
Self-control, 126; lack of dooms characters of *Idylls*, 101; leads life to power, 106, 202; as means to faith, 54. See Authority, Mastery, Self-mastery
Self-denial, produces vision, 220-21
"Self-Dependence" (Arnold), 103-4
Self-destruction, 134; no inclination to, 127. See Self-injury
Self-discovery, poetry as means of, 237; through disguise, 88ff, 211
Self-examination, Tennyson's concern for, 9
Self-fulfilment, redemption through, 129; through self-knowledge, 125